THE NEW MIDDLE AGES

BONNIE WHEELER, *Series Edit*

The New Middle Ages is a series dedicated . . . . res, with particular emphasis on recuperating wor . . . . ·ses. This peer-reviewed series includes both scho .

PUBLISHED BY PALGRAVE:

Cultural Diversity in the British Middle Ages: Archipelago, Island, England
edited by Jeffrey Jerome Cohen

Excrement in the Late Middle Ages: Sacred Filth and Chaucer's Fecopoetics
by Susan Signe Morrison

Authority and Subjugation in Writing of Medieval Wales
edited by Ruth Kennedy and Simon Meecham-Jones

The Medieval Poetics of the Reliquary: Enshrinement, Inscription, Performance
by Seeta Chaganti

The Legend of Charlemagne in the Middle Ages: Power, Faith, and Crusade
edited by Matthew Gabriele and Jace Stuckey

The Poems of Oswald von Wolkenstein: An English Translation of the Complete Works (1376/77–1445)
by Albrecht Classen

Women and Experience in Later Medieval Writing: Reading the Book of Life
edited by Anneke B. Mulder-Bakker and Liz Herbert McAvoy

Ethics and Eventfulness in Middle English Literature: Singular Fortunes
by J. Allan Mitchell

Maintenance, Meed, and Marriage in Medieval English Literature
by Kathleen E. Kennedy

The Post-Historical Middle Ages
edited by Elizabeth Scala and Sylvia Federico

Constructing Chaucer: Author and Autofiction in the Critical Tradition
by Geoffrey W. Gust

Queens in Stone and Silver: The Creation of a Visual Imagery of Queenship in Capetian France
by Kathleen Nolan

Finding Saint Francis in Literature and Art
edited by Cynthia Ho, Beth A. Mulvaney, and John K. Downey

Strange Beauty: Ecocritical Approaches to Early Medieval Landscape
by Alfred K. Siewers

Berenguela of Castile (1180–1246) and Political Women in the High Middle Ages
by Miriam Shadis

Julian of Norwich's Legacy: Medieval Mysticism and Post-Medieval Reception
edited by Sarah Salih and Denise N. Baker

Medievalism, Multilingualism, and Chaucer
by Mary Catherine Davidson

The Letters of Heloise and Abelard: A Translation of Their Complete Correspondence and Related Writings
translated and edited by Mary Martin McLaughlin with Bonnie Wheeler

Women and Wealth in Late Medieval Europe
edited by Theresa Earenfight

Visual Power and Fame in René d'Anjou, Geoffrey Chaucer, and the Black Prince
by SunHee Kim Gertz

Geoffrey Chaucer Hath a Blog: Medieval Studies and New Media
by Brantley L. Bryant

Margaret Paston's Piety
by Joel T. Rosenthal

Gender and Power in Medieval Exegesis
by Theresa Tinkle

Antimercantilism in Late Medieval English Literature
by Roger A. Ladd

Magnificence and the Sublime in Medieval Aesthetics: Art, Architecture, Literature, Music
edited by C. Stephen Jaeger

Medieval and Early Modern Devotional Objects in Global Perspective: Translations of the Sacred
edited by Elizabeth Robertson and Jennifer Jahner

THE [EUROPEAN] OTHER IN MEDIEVAL ARABIC LITERATURE AND CULTURE

NINTH-TWELFTH CENTURY AD

Nizar F. Hermes

THE [EUROPEAN] OTHER IN MEDIEVAL ARABIC LITERATURE AND CULTURE

Copyright © Nizar F. Hermes, 2012

Softcover reprint of the hardcover 1st edition 2012 978-0-230-10940-7

First published in 2012 by
PALGRAVE MACMILLAN®
in the United States—a division of St. Martin's Press LLC,
175 Fifth Avenue, New York, NY 10010.

Where this book is distributed in the UK, Europe and the rest of the world,
this is by Palgrave Macmillan, a division of Macmillan Publishers Limited,
registered in England, company number 785998, of Houndmills,
Basingstoke, Hampshire RG21 6XS.

Palgrave Macmillan is the global academic imprint of the above companies
and has companies and representatives throughout the world.

Palgrave® and Macmillan® are registered trademarks in the United States,
the United Kingdom, Europe and other countries.

ISBN 978-1-349-29213-4   ISBN 978-1-137-08165-0 (eBook)
DOI 10.1057/9781137081650

Library of Congress Cataloging-in-Publication Data

Hermes, Nizar F.
    The European other in medieval Arabic literature and culture :
ninth-twelfth century AD / Nizar F. Hermes.
        p. cm.—(New Middle Ages)
    On t.p. the word European is enclosed in brackets.
    Includes bibliographical references.

    1. Arab countries—Relations—Europe—Sources. 2. Europe—Relations—
Arab countries—Sources. 3. Europe—Foreign public opinion, Arab—
History—To 1500—Sources. 4. Europeans—Public opinion—History—To
1500—Sources. 5. Other (Philosophy)—Arab countries—History—To 1500—
Sources. 6. Gaze—Social aspects—Arab countries—History—To 1500—
Sources. 7. Christians—Public opinion—History—To 1500—Sources.
8. Muslims—Arab countries—Attitudes—History—To 1500—Sources.
9. Arabic prose literature—History and criticism. 10. Arabic poetry—History
and criticism. I. Title. II. Title: Other in medieval Arabic literature and culture.

DS63.2.E8H47 2012
892.7′0935840902—dc23   2011039092

A catalogue record of the book is available from the British Library.

Design by Newgen Imaging Systems (P) Ltd., Chennai, India.

First edition: April 2012

To my family, professors, and friends here and there!

CONTENTS

PREFACE AND ACKNOWLEDGMENTS

Some Western scholars of the Middle East such as Bernard Lewis have too often claimed that medieval Arabs/Muslims did not exhibit any significant desire to discover the cultures, literatures, and religions of non-Muslim peoples. No less troubling is their contention that only Europeans are endowed with the gift of studying foreign cultures and traveling into alien lands. However, without intending to add fire to the already fiery polemic over Edward Said's *Orientalism: Western Concepts of the Orient* (1978), very few of Said's critics and defenders alike have discussed the counter, or reverse, tradition of Orientalism, especially as found in the rich corpus of medieval Arabic literature and culture.

Through introducing and exploring a cross-generic selection of non-religious Arabic prose and poetic texts—such as the geo-cosmographical literature, *récits de voyages*, diplomatic memoirs, captivity narratives, and pre-Crusade and Crusade poetry, all of which were written from the ninth to the twelfth century (AD)—this work purports to show that there was no shortage of medieval Muslims who cast curious eyes and minds toward the Other and that more than a handful of them were textually and physically interested in Europe and the Euro-Christians they encountered inside and outside *dar al-islam*. Contrary to the monolithic impression left by postcolonial theories of Orientalism, the book also makes a case that Orientals did not exist solely to be gazed at. Before this came to be so, they too had directed their gaze toward the European Other(s) in a way that mirrored in reverse the subject/object relationship described as Orientalism.

Texts were selected based on my personal assessment of their importance, originality, and relative unfamiliarity in the West. My hope is that more Middle East medievalists and comparatists in particular will further lines of inquiry and argument concerning the various aspects of the largely neglected topic of medieval Arabic, nonreligious alterist writing.

The work is a revised PhD dissertation at the University of Toronto. The project might have never been finished without the insights and guidance of Professors John Fleming and Roland LeHuenen. It has been my good fortune to learn from them, and I am enduringly grateful for their scholarly advice, unflattering trust, and unfailing support. I owe my gratitude as well to the University of Toronto's medievalists Suzanne Conklin Akbari and Jill Ross for their invaluable input and superlative stimulation. I am grateful too for Arabists and Middle East medievalists Professors Thabit Abdullah of York University and Walid Saleh and Andrew Lane of the University of Toronto for their constructive feedback, useful comments, and compelling suggestions. I would like also to offer my profoundest thanks to Professors Ian Richard Netton of the University of Exeter, Muhsin Jassim al-Musawi of Columbia University, and Ahmad Nazmi of the University of Warsaw for their most valuable suggestions, corrections, and references.

Warmest thanks are also due to Professors Anne R. Richards of Kennesaw State University—in particular—Iraj Omidvar of Southern Polytechnic State University, and Mel Solman of Humber College for their wonderful edits and comments. The same is true for the anonymous reviewers and editors of journals and edited volumes in which some of the material in this book has appeared or is appearing in slightly different versions: "The Byzantines in Medieval Arabic Poetry: Abu Firas's *Al-Rumiyyat* and the Poetic Responses of al-Qaffal and Ibn Hazm to Nicephorus Phocas's *Al-Qasida al-Arminiyya al-Mal'una* (The Armenian Cursed Ode)," *Byzantina Symmeikta: Journal of the Institute for Byzantine Studies* 19 (2009): 35–61; and "Mirabilia Urbis Romæ through the Eyes of a Ninth Century Arab Captive: Ibn Yahya's Remarkable Account of Rome," in *Journeys to the West: The Occident as Other in Narratives of Travel*, ed. Anne R. Richards and Iraj Omidvar (Syracuse, NY: Syracuse University Press, forthcoming 2012).

Last but not least, I am deeply grateful to Professor Bonnie Wheeler, series editor of The New Middle Ages, for her faith in this project and her strong recommendation to publish it in the series; to Brigitte Shull, Joanna Roberts, and Kristy Lilas of Palgrave Macmillan for their guidance, patience, and professionalism; and to the anonymous reviewer for the insightful comments and suggestions.

NOTE ON TRANSLITERATION

In order to make the text less burdensome for readers with no back-ground in Middle Eastern studies, I have chosen not to use all the defamiliarizing diacritical marks established by rigid transliteration systems of the Arabic language into English. In short, with the exceptions of the *'ayn* (') and *hamza* (')—when it appears within or at the end of a word—and unless they appear in original titles or direct quotations, macrons and dots are not added. For the renderings of classical Muslim names, I have followed the conventions adopted by the *International Journal of Middle East Studies* ('Abd al-Rahman, for example). As for contemporary names of scholars, I use more common renditions (Abdurrahmane instead of 'Abd al-Rahman).

NOTE ON THE TRANSLATION OF
ARABIC POETRY

*In light of the variety of approaches to the translation of classical Arabic poetry, I think it proper
to clarify my own stance. In the present book, I have aimed not at producing a literal translation,
which at best would serve some instructional purposes, but rather at capturing in the English
literary idiom, the meaning and, above all, the poeticality of the Arabic originals. (xii)*

—Jaroslav Stetkevych, *The Zephyrs of Najd:*
The Poetics of Nostalgia in The Classical Arabic Nasib

Translating the idiosyncratically rhymed and metered classical Arabic
poetry into modern Western languages is notoriously difficult, to
say the least. One spends hours and hours deciding what to keep and what
to sacrifice, especially amid the seemingly never-ending debate between
the "literal," or "word-for-word," translation and the "interpretive," or
"sense-for sense," translation (Peter France, *The Oxford Guide to Literature
in English Translation*, 16). Briefly stated, while I have done my best to
capture "quite literally" a number of the most essential keywords of a
particular poem, I have somehow leaned to the second approach especially
as, of course in my personal view, masterfully laid out and practiced by
Professor Jaroslav Stetkevych and a number of his students, such as Michael
Sells and Emil Homerin. In the present book, I do share the concern that
what we need most in translating classical Arabic poetry are translations
that "stand on their own as poems that can be enjoyed and appreciated,"
to quote Emil Homerin (*'Umar Ibn Al-Faridh: Sufi Verse, Saintly Life*, 2).
In short, I struggled to be faithful not only to *the what* but also to *the how*
poets such as Abu Dulaf, Abu Firas, Ibn Hazm, and Ibn al-Qaysarani
said, but at the same time, I have to acknowledge that I strove, perhaps
more, to translate those poets in enjoyable (I hope) English poems that
stand on their own. For readers of Arabic, the original Arabic poems
appear in the appendix.

INTRODUCTION: BE(YOND)FORE ORIENTALISM; MEDIEVAL MUSLIMS AND THE OTHER

Nearly a decade after the publication of Edward Said's groundbreaking study *Orientalism: Western Concepts of the Orient* (1978), the Indian critic Gayatri Chakravorty Spivak posed her provocative question: "Can the Subaltern Speak?" (1988). Mixing, if not blurring, the interrogative with the rhetorical, her question—as much as it furthered Said's critique of Western colonialism—ultimately brought to the fore a number of theoretical and ideological challenges to the then-nascent postcolonial criticism to which she, perhaps second to Said, would contribute enormously in its later development and global fame. Among the concerns Spivak highlighted was the fact that several of her fellow post-colonial "comrades" (in)directly reinforced some dominant discourses they so enthusiastically sought to dismantle. Without claiming her critical perspicacity or expecting any of her success, I have to acknowledge that my present project, at least at its earliest stage, was somewhat inspired by Spivak's question, albeit in a totally different context and certainly in a much less theoretical orientation. In short, Can the Oriental gaze? was the question that haunted me while I was an avid reader of all things postcolonial. It is needless to add that among the plethora of Said's critical phrases, I felt a particular penchant for his "colonial gaze," which he and other postcolonial critics had masterfully delineated in the context of colonial travel literature and the Western genre of *Voyages en Orient* in particular.

During those years, I was introduced to the works of the influential scholar Bernard Lewis through a graduate course on Orientalism at the University of Tunis, taught by Professor Muhsin Jassim al-Mussawi (now of Columbia University), who nourished in me an ineffable interest in Arabic and comparative literature. Of course, to return to my haunting question, for Professor Lewis and many other Western scholars of the Middle East, casting one's curious eye toward the Other is a

distinctively European virtue, a gift of Europeans to humanity at large.
It is the ultimate result of an "intellectual curiosity that leads to the study
of a language, the decipherment of ancient texts," which is in Lewis's
words "still peculiar to western Europe, and to the inheritors and emu-
lators of the European scholarly tradition in countries such as the United
States and Japan" (*Islam and the West*, 124). For Lewis, it is almost predes-
tined that the world had to wait until the European Renaissance to see
"a human society for the first time [that] developed the sophistication,
the detachment and, above all, the curiosity to study and appreciate
the cultures of alien and even hostile societies" (*The Muslim Discovery of
Europe*, 301). Understandably, contrary to Said's contention, it is this very
"curiosity to study and appreciate the cultures of alien and even hostile
societies," that has been the impetus behind the phenomenal interest of
Europeans in the "Orient." In stark contrast, "Orientals" in general and
Muslims in particular, even during the peak of their power (Lewis finds
no reason to hide it), have lacked the curiosity of Europeans in studying
foreign cultures. As he explains it, "Europeans at one time or another
have studied virtually all the languages and all the histories of Asia. Asia
did not study Europe. *They did not even study each other, unless the way for
such study was prepared by either conquest or conversion or both* [italics mine]"
(*Islam and the West*, 123).

Indeed, time and again, and in a plethora of stimulating books he
has authored on the medieval, early modern, and modern encounters
between Islam and the West—such as *The Muslim Discovery of Europe*,
*Islam and the West, A Middle East Mosaic: Fragments of Life, Letters and
History* (2000), *What Went Wrong? Western Impact and Middle Eastern
Response* (2002), and *From Babel to Dragomans: Interpreting the Middle East*
(2004)—Bernard Lewis, one of the West's most renowned scholars of the
Middle East, has strongly espoused the essentialist view that medieval
and early modern Muslims, contrary to Europeans, were never curious
to know about non-Muslim cultures that flourished outside *dar al-islam*
in general and those of Europeans in particular. As Roxanne L. Euben
points out, "Lewis repeatedly notes the lack of curiosity or desire for
knowledge among Muslims about languages, literatures, religions or
cultures beyond Islamic lands" (*Journeys to the Other Shore: Muslim and
Western Travelers in Search of Knowledge*, 32). In *From Babel to Dragomans*,
for example, Lewis writes,

> Muslim historians were not interested in the outside world, which as
> they understood the value and purpose of history, lacked both value
> and purpose. Muslim theologians were little concerned with Christian
> doctrines—why after all should they be interested in an earlier and

superseded form of God's revelation? And for the few that were interested, better information was more easily accessible among the many
Christian communities living in the lands of Islam. There was no interest in the sciences and arts of Europe. They knew there was nothing of
the one; they assumed there was nothing of the other. Only the geographers show some interest in the West, and even that a limited one. One
geographical writer even apologizes for devoting some attention to these
remote and uninteresting places. (206)

In Lewis's opinion, it is disappointing but ultimately unsurprising
that during the concerned centuries "we have almost no information
about Muslim travelers to Europe" (210). Consequently, as he phrases
it elsewhere, "While European travelers to the East—soldiers, pilgrims,
merchants, captives—had already produced a considerable literature,
there was nothing comparable in the Muslim side" (210). All in all and
until the seventeenth, if not the nineteenth, century, less than a handful of Muslims saw Europe with their own eyes, usually against their
own will. "An Arab prisoner of war in Rome in the ninth century, an
Andalusian diplomatic visitor to France and Germany in the tenth, a
princely Ottoman exile in France and Italy in the fifteenth," Lewis tells
us, "[these] and one or two others have left a few notes and fragments
which constitute almost the whole of the Muslim travel literature in
Europe" (210).[1] This handful of involuntary Muslims who found themselves in European lands "had nothing to say after their ransom and
return, and perhaps no one to listen" (210). "In this," Lewis goes on to
conclude, "they differed markedly from their European counterparts,
whose reports seem to have been in some demand" (210).

Oddly enough, when the very few medieval or early modern Muslims
found themselves obliged to know something about "the Greeks, the
Romans, and other Christians," all that they wrote and said was, as
he puts it, "manifest lies and grotesque fables" (*The Muslim Discovery of
Europe*, 280). "For most Middle Easterners, as one can see very clearly
from the references in historical and geographical writings," he notes in
another place, "western Europe was an outer darkness of barbarism and
unbelief, inhabited by primitive peoples with nasty and dirty habits, who
they saw much as Victorian Englishmen might have seen the inhabitants
of the central African jungles or the tribes beyond the north west frontier
of India" (*A Middle East Mosaic*, 24).

When Europeans offered Middle Easterners a golden chance to
learn about them and their cultures during the Crusades, they (Middle
Easterners) did not seize the chance. The fact of the matter, according to Lewis, is that Muslims were not even aware of the Crusades. As
Hadia Dajani-Shakeel points out in her essay "A Reassessment of Some

Medieval and Modern Perceptions of the Counter-Crusade," Bernard Lewis has been one of the leading Western scholars who undermined "the degree of Muslim awareness of the Crusades" (*The Jihad and Its Times*, 14). Dajani-Shakeel goes on to say that according to Lewis, the presumed disinterest of Muslims in the Crusades in general and the Crusaders in particular is no better proved than in their supposed insularity in relation to the Franks, who for more than 200 years became their closest neighbors. "For two centuries the Muslims of the Middle East," Lewis once asserted in his essay "The Use by Muslim Historians of Non-Muslim Sources" (1962), "were in intimate if hostile contact with groups of the Franks established among them—*yet, at no time do they seem to have developed the least interest in them* [italics mine]" (*The Jihad and Its Times*, 41).

Unfortunately, as Nabil Matar has argued in the introduction to his book *In the Lands of the Christians: Arabic Travel Writing in the Seventeenth Century* (2003), a growing number of scholars has echoed Professor Lewis's aforementioned views (xiv). David Morgan, to cite an example, has contended," For most of the Middle Ages, writers in the Islamic world did not rate western Europe very highly, if indeed they thought about that part of the world at all" ("Persian Perceptions of Mongols and Europeans," 210). There is perhaps no more egregious example than Franco Cardini's statement in *Europa e Islam: Storia di un Malinteso* (1999 that the disinterest in the civilizations of the Other is "una caratteristica della cultura uscita dalla rivoluzione religiosa di Muhammad" (23). Commenting on the Abbasids and the foundation of their capital Baghdad, Cardini, one of Italy's most eminent historians of the Middle Ages, comes to the following conclusion:

> The city was founded in 762 and at first was given the name of *Medinat as-Salam*, City of Peace. Here the seeds of that lack of interest in civilizations other than Islamic that was so much a feature of the culture born of Mohammed's religious revolution may already have taken root; with distant hindsight it could be identified as a possible component of today's crisis. In addition, a close watch was kept on Byzantium, India and China, whilst much less attention (quite justified at the period) was paid to the barbarous inhabitants of the extreme north-west who appeared hardly worthy of consideration at the time. (*Europe and Islam*, 13)

There is no doubt that medieval Muslims did not send a Napoleonic expedition to discover and study medieval Europe, nor did they hire an army of interpreters and scholars to translate and explore, let us say, a number of medieval Frankish or Germanic manuscripts as Napoleon did in 1798. The lack of such an expedition and the absence of such manuscripts, however, do not mean that medieval and, by the same token, early modern Muslim politicians, travelers, and writers were totally unaware of this inhabited continent north and west of *dar al-islam*. Nor should it lead us to believe that Muslims had to wait for the nineteenth century to discover Europe and the Europeans, a "discovery" Bernard Lewis and other scholars have exaggeratedly compared to Europe's discovery of the New World. "Lewis so totally discredited Renaissance Muslims' curiosity," Matar declares, "that when the Ottoman Empire opened up to western institutions in the nineteenth century, he compared that opening to a discovery not unlike Christopher Columbus's of America" (*In the Lands of the Christians*, xiv).

As will become evident in many of the texts presented and explored in this study, the problem lies more in the Western neglect of the medieval corpus of Arabic writings about the Other and about the Euro-Christians in particular. In his article "Arab Views of Europeans 1578–1727: The Western Mediterranean" (2005), although focusing exclusively on the early modern period and the Maghribi (North African) tradition, Matar tells us, "With the exception of Alastair Hamilton and G. A. Weigers, scholars have ignored the corpus of western Arabic writings in the early modern period, specifically those writings that describe the meetings and encounters with the Europeans" (127). In many respects, British historian William Dalrymple was not exaggerating when he noted that "this apparent lacuna was more the result of lack of archival research on the part of Lewis and other scholars than any failing by Muslim writers" ("The Truth about Muslims," 1).

In the same connection, one can hardly deny the fact that in spite of the incontestable erudition of its author, the late Said, and his groundbreaking influence on a number of disciplines, *Orientalism: Western Conceptions of the Orient* has failed to capture some of the most important complexities of the relation between Islam and the West. This is true not only of Said's relegation of the multifaceted relation between Islam and the West to the latter's colonialist ventures in North Africa and the Middle East, but also, and most importantly (at least for the present study), of his neglect of the Orient's own tradition of alterity and the reverse/counter Arabic-Islamic views and perceptions of the Euro-Christian Other.

As Daniel Marin Varisco has shown in *Reading Orientalism: Said and the Unsaid* (2007), far from intending to "add fire" to the already fiery polemic over *Orientalism*, and although acknowledging the legitimacy of several of the concerns highlighted by Said's critics and advocates, I contend that very few of them called into question Said's neglect of those who have been most concerned with this debate (i.e., the Orientals).[2] If Said used some "textual gaps" in speaking of a domestic novel such as

Mansfield Park (1814) in order to question, if not denounce, Jane Austen
for her negligence of the indigenous Others and her discursive silence
over Sir Thomas Bertram's imperialist enterprise, economic exploitation, and sexual dalliances on the sugar plantation he owns in Antigua,
one may legitimately question Said's own negligence and silencing of
the Orientals. Said, with or without intending it, fell into the same
Orientalist discourse he did all he could to debunk. Expressing his surprise at Said's failure to see beyond his own theoretical confines in such
a modern Arabic novel of an East/West encounter as Tayyeb Saleh's
Mawsim al-Hijra ila al-Shamal (Season of Migration of the North)—which,
in the broadest of terms, is fraught with tropes of "reverse Orientalism"
(Varisco, *Reading Orientalism*, 154)—Varisco raises some of the same
questions as those proposed in this book.

Gone is the time when the mere *argumentum ad hominem* of Said or
Lewis would add something constructive to the complex and sensitive
subject of Orientalism. The simple reason, in my view, lies in the unfortunate fact that the majority of critics and defenders of Orientalism were
unreasonably theory-bound and logocentric. As Varisco puts it, "It is
time to move beyond PhD cataloguing of what the West did to the East
and self-unfulfilling political punditry about what real individuals in
the East say they want to do to the West" (xii).[3] No one can dare to
interrogate Lewis's and Said's lifelong interest in the Middle East and
Orientalism. However, it is unfortunate that neither of them, nor their
followers, has ever gone beyond their own theories when it is undeni-
able that the encounter between Islam and the West has always been too
complex to be monopolized by one theory or the other, especially when
we know that every group has its own ideological intentions and political
motivations.

Be that as it may, the two sides of the debate seem to have forgotten
that the encounter between Islam and the West since the Middle Ages
has not only influenced the literatures and cultures of the West, but also
that it has had an enormous impact on the medieval, early modern, and
modern Islamic literatures and cultures it confronted (mainly Arabic,
Persian, and Turkish) and has contributed thereby in shaping their generally anti-Western worldview and in providing Muslim writers with a
rich terrain for religious, cultural, and political propaganda of their own.
Varisco was not exaggerating when he blamed both sides of confining
the debate to "the avowedly Western academic scene" (154). "Yes, the
Orient was imagined by the West. Logically, the West has also imagined
itself in the process," he posits before proceeding to state, "The real
Orient has also created imaginaries subsumed under its discourse on the
West, just as it (rather, many of its many constituent parts) defines itself

against an imperial history of recent commercial conquest and political contest" (xvi).

By directing our gaze toward medieval Arabic literature and culture, the present book's goal is to introduce Western readers to the forgotten corpus of medieval Arabic literature that describes Muslim encounters with the non-Muslim Other and Europeans in particular. In fact, much effort will be devoted to exploring Muslim views of Euro-Christians as portrayed in a cross-generic selection of medieval nonreligious prose and poetic texts such as the geo-cosmographical literature, *récits de voyages*, diplomatic memoirs, captivity narratives, and pre-Crusade and Crusade poetry, all of which were written from the ninth to the twelfth century by a wide range of Muslim scholars east and west of *dar al-islam*.

In the first chapter, "Translation, Travel, and the Other: The Fascination with Greek and Oriental Cultures," I will try to challenge some of the views advocated by Lewis and other scholars in regard to medieval Muslims, specifically ideas concerning their presumed lack of intellectual curiosity, their disinterest in knowing about non-Muslim cultures, religions, and languages, and the absence of a Muslim tradition of travel for study.

In the second and the third chapters—"European Barbarity and Civilization in Some Medieval Arabic Geographical Sources" and "Writing the North: Europe and Europeans in Medieval Arabic Travel Literature"—I will try to show how through a plethora of textual and physical journeys, many medieval Muslims from the Mashriq (Muslim East) and the Maghrib (Muslim West) ventured into different parts of medieval Europe, leaving to posterity some of the most genuine accounts of various European races and nations, such as the Vikings, the Franks, the Galicians, the Lombards, the Bulghars, the Hungarians, and the Slavs. It is my biggest hope to prove that Europe was not as remote and as benighted for medieval Arabs as a number of scholars have claimed.

Muslims were also interested, sometimes to fearful extremes, in knowing about the Euro-Christians who were adjacent to them, as was the case with the Byzantines, or those who conquered some of their lands, such as the Franks during the Crusades. Nowhere is this more conspicuous than in the Arabic poetry known as *Al-Rumiyyat* (for the Byzantines) and the poetry of the counter-Crusades (for the Franks). Arabic poetry, we have to remember, has always been seen as the most genuine *diwan* (archive/register) wherein the Arabs, especially during the period under study, have recorded their "life stories, aspirations, feats, and wars," as al-Musawi phrases it in the introduction to *Arabic Poetry: Trajectories of Modernity and Tradition* (1). This is also true of their Others, as I will try to demonstrate in the fourth chapter, entitled "Poetry, Frontiers, and Alterity: Views and Perceptions of *al-Rum* (Byzantines) and *al-Ifranja* (Franks)."

In the course of these chapters, I will try to prove, contrary to the impression left after reading Said's *Orientalism*, that the Oriental has not existed solely to be "Orientalized." In his/her turn, the Oriental has always been an "Othering" Other. Indeed, one should be left with no doubt that if the West has always had its Orient, the East, in turn, has had its own Occident. In the same vein, it is to be stressed that the variety of European *ajnas* (peoples)—such as the Vikings, the Bulghars, the Slavs, the Prussians, the Franks, the Lombards, and the Galicians, to name but a few—encountered physically and textually by medieval Muslims outside and even inside *dar al-islam* were different in several important respects, not least in their geographical locations, religious practices, linguistic traditions, and political loyalties. Yet, as we shall see, it is striking that the majority, if not all, of those travelers and writers had unanimously highlighted what they conceived as a number of *mathalib* (demerits), which can be seen as common denominators of the overall medieval Muslim views of Europe and the Euro-Christians. This is mainly true of the presumed lack of proper hygiene, sexual freedom of women, and absence of manly jealousy among Euro-Christian men.

Ifranjalism is the term I have coined to describe the forgotten premodern Arabic corpus of writing about the Euro-Christians. I have preferred it to the more familiar term *Occidentalism*, which was coined by the Egyptian scholar Hasan Hanafi in *Muqaddima fi 'Ilm al-Istighrab* (An Introduction to the Science of Occidentalism) to describe the modern interest of Middle Eastern intellectuals in the West.[4] Furthermore, the word *Occidentalism* has been used by a growing number of Western and Eastern scholars to depict global anti-Westernism in general and anti-Americanism in particular,[5] as Jouhki Jukka notes in "Imagining the Other: Orientalism and Occidentalism in Tamil-European Relations in South India":

> Actually, there is a kind of Occidentalism, at least in today's Orient, comparable to some extent to Orientalism in the West. In fact, if one were to apply one of Said's definitions of Orientalism to the definition of Occidentalism, one could easily claim there indeed is Occidentalism in the Orient. Just as Said defines Orientalism as "coming to terms with the Orient that is based on the Orient's special place in European Western experience," one might contrastingly define the Occident's special place in Asian Eastern experience. Thus, in my view, it is safe to say different forms of Occidentalism have existed since there has been any interaction between "the East" and "the West." (49)

Yet the fact that the Arabic word *al-gharb* (Occident) in the medieval and early modern Islamic context means nothing but Muslim Spain and North Africa has convinced me to look for a more historically and culturally relevant term.[6] After all, as we shall see in the fourth chapter, since the Crusades, *al-ifranja* (spelled interchangeably *al-faranja* and *al-firanj*) has become the most common Arabic word with which Muslims and Arabs have described Europeans. As Adrian J. Boas has shown, the word *Frank* in Muslim sources is "a generic term," and "it does not necessarily mean someone originating in France or even in francophone lands. Indeed, and since the Crusades, Arab-Muslims have been using it to refer to European Christians whether they be French, Germans, Spaniards, Italians, or other European nationalities" (*Jerusalem in the Time of the Crusades*, 37).[7] In this context, it should be noted that until the present day, whether one is in Casablanca, Tunis, Cairo, Damascus, Riyadh, or Baghdad, modern Arabic expressions such as *al-libas al-ifranji*, *al-qanun al-firanji*, and *al-tarikh al-ifranji*, to cite some examples, mean respectively European (Western) clothes, law, and calendar.

Last but far from least, since this book is comparative in essence, I shall say from the outset that whenever possible and pertinent, Muslim views and perceptions of the Other will be juxtaposed to those of the much more familiar European views of Islam and Muslims of the Middle Ages and the early modern period. This is the case in the second section of the first chapter, "The Orient's Medieval 'Orient(alism)': The *Rihla* of Sulayman al-Tajir," wherein al-Tajir's remarkable account of India and China will be compared to that of Marco Polo. References will also be made to other works such as *Robinson Crusoe* and *Moby Dick*, to name but a few.

Similarly, in the second chapter, medieval Muslim geo-cosmographical views such as the division of the earth will not only be related to certain ancient Greek theories, but they will also be juxtaposed to European ones. Finally, in the second, third, and fourth chapters, Muslim views of the Euro-Christian Others will be weighed against medieval, early modern, and even dominant modern European views of Muslims (Saracens/ Mohammedans, Moors, Turks/Orientals) as depicted not only in familiar works such as *La Chanson de Roland*, Christopher Marlowe's *Tamburlaine*, Elizabeth Carey's *The Tragedy of Mariam*, and Gustave Flaubert's *Voyage en Orient*, but also in less familiar texts such as the German anti-Turkish pamphlets known as the *Türkenbüchlein*.

This is in addition to the appearance of a plethora of literary *chefs d'oeuvre* that have been h(a)unting me ever since I met Heathcliff and Hester Prynne as an undergraduate student of English language and literature at the University of Tunis in 1991. Indeed, as some titles of my chapters and sections attest, works such as Shakespeare's *Othello*, James Fenimore Cooper's *The Last of the Mohicans*, Joseph Conrad's *Heart of Darkness*, Mark Twain's *An American Yankee in King Arthur's Court*, perhaps more than *Wuthering Heights* and *The Scarlet Letter*, seem to have journeyed with me during the more than 1,001 nights that I have spent thousands of miles away from Tunisian shores.

CHAPTER 1

TRANSLATION, TRAVEL, AND THE OTHER: THE FASCINATION WITH GREEK AND ORIENTAL CULTURES

The Curious Minds and Eyes of Medieval Muslims: Translation and Travel for Study

Traveling in search of knowledge is essential for the acquisition of useful learning and of perfection through meeting authoritative teachers and having contact with scholarly personalities.

—Ibn Khaldun, *Al-Muqaddima*[1]

During the classical age of Islam, described hereafter with reservations as medieval Islam, Muslim politicians and scholars alike were keenly interested in knowing about and learning from the Other. Indeed, as we shall see through arguments and examples, there was no shortage of Muslims who cast curious minds and eyes toward the various *thaqafat* (cultures) that flourished east and west of *dar al-islam*. Through translation into Arabic of a myriad of foreign manuscripts, Muslim scholars studied enthusiastically and appreciated greatly the alien cultures of the Greeks, Persians, and Indians, to cite a few specific examples. In the same vein, one may argue that contrary to the presumptions of many, travel for study played a crucial role in shaping the culture of learning in medieval Islam. Of course, similar to other cultural encounters, medieval Muslims in their contact with the Other were residually informed by many of their own peculiar views and concepts of the world (M. N. Affaya, *Al-Gharb al-Mutakhayyal*, 15), although in general they exhibited an impressive cultural relativism and a spontaneous readiness to acknowledge the Other and several of his/her cultural virtues.[2]

Notwithstanding their fascination with their own Orient, the interest of medieval Muslims in knowing about alien cultures is to be seen nowhere more conspicuously than in the phenomenal *harakat al-tarjama* (translation movement). As it has been argued by a number of researchers, during what was known in medieval Arabic sources as *'asr al-tarjama* (the age of translation), Muslim libraries were filled with thousands of Arabic versions of "the best which has been thought and said" by various non-Muslim peoples, especially the Greeks, the Persians, and the Indians.[3] It was so phenomenal a movement that noted cataloger Ibn al-Nadim (d. 995) devoted several entries of his famous bibliographical dictionary *Al-Fihrist* (*The Index* or *The Catalogue*) not only to listing the multiple books that were translated into Arabic but also to exploring the reasons that led to the phenomenon.[4]

Ibn al-Nadim reports that the early interest in translation from Greek, Coptic, Syriac, Pahlavi, and Sanskrit into Arabic began with the Umayyad prince Khalid ibn Yazid ibn Mu'awiya (d. 704), dubbed *hakim al-marwan* (the sage of the Marwanites/Umayyads) because of his zeal for learning and patronage of scholars. As noted by I. M. N. Al-Jubouri in *History of Islamic Philosophy: With View of Greek Philosophy and Early History of Islam* (2004), Prince Khalid "ordered a Greek philosopher should be brought from Alexandria to translate the *Organon* of Aristotle from Greek into Arabic" (22). Although "limited at first to purely pragmatic or semi-pragmatic disciplines of medicines, alchemy and astrology," to quote Majid Fakhry, Prince Khalid was the decisive early figure in the history of *harakat al-tarjama* (*A History of Islamic Philosophy*, 5).

As Demitri Gutas has amply demonstrated in *Greek Thought, Arab Culture: The Graeco-Arabic Translation Movement in Baghdad and Early Abbasid Society* (1998), the interest of the early Umayyads in Greek was rather a necessity dictated by the fact that many of their subjects were Greek speakers. For reasons of continuity, the early Umayyads were obliged to keep "both the Greek-speaking functionaries and Greek in their imperial administration in Damascus" (23). Owing to this reality, Gutas goes on to explain, cross-translation between Arabic and Greek throughout the Umayyad dynasty (661–750) was "a quotidian reality" in the heavily Greek-speaking regions of Egypt and Syro-Palestine (23).[5] In spite of the fact that Ibn al-Nadim and other medieval historians did not seem to find any dearth of literary, and even scientific, titles that had been translated—mainly from Greek, Syriac, Sanskrit, and Pahlavi into Arabic—the Umayyad interest in translation, according to Gutas, lacked the "deliberate and scholarly interest" that became the distinctive feature of their successors the Abbasids (24). According to Gutas, "Deliberate and planned scholarly interest in the translation of Greek works (and Syriac works inspired by Greek) into Arabic appears not to have been present in Umayyad times" (24). He then proceeds to affirm that "only with the earliest Abbasid caliphs was there set into motion a deliberate translation movement that had profound historical, social, and cultural consequences" (24).

By most accounts, this deliberate translation movement became a salient feature of the Abbasids during the reigns of al-Mansur (754–775), al-Mahdi (775–786), Harun al-Rashid (786–809), al-Amin (809–813), and al-Ma'mun (813–833), who is generally credited with the foundation of the famous *bayt al-hikma* (House of Wisdom) in Baghdad. It is mainly during their reign that "almost all non-literary and non-historical secular Greek books, including such diverse topics as astrology, alchemy, physics, botany and medicine, that were not available throughout the Eastern Byzantine Empire and the Near East were translated into Arabic" (43).[6] Gutas goes on to explain that during the reign of al-Mansur and Harun al-Rashid, there developed a new wave of translations from Greek, Pahlavi, and Sanskrit into Arabic. It dealt mainly with medicine, the natural sciences, and logic. Among the translators/scholars who worked for al-Mansur and al-Rashid was Ibn al-Muqaffa' (d. 757), credited with an excellent translation from Pahlavi into Arabic of the Indian fables *Kalila wa-Dimna*, which has become one of the prose masterpieces of classical Arabic literature (34).

It has been well emphasized that it was mainly during the reign of al-Ma'mun that the Abbasids witnessed an unprecedented interest in non-Muslim sciences and cultures.[7] According to L. E. Goodman, "Al-Ma'mun went far beyond his father in establishing routine support for the translation of Greek works. His famous *bayt al-hikma*, formally instituted at Baghdad in 830, sponsored translation as its main activity and employed a regular staff of scholars" ("The Translation of Greek Materials into Arabic," 484). In fact, as recorded by Ibn al-Nadim and other chroniclers, al-Ma'mun did his best to procure all kinds of manuscripts. Among other things, he is said to have sent official envoys to the emperor Leon the Armenian (813–820) to purchase Greek manuscripts. Al-Ma'mun's envoys were most of the time scholars and translators like Ibn al-Batriq (d. 806), al-Hajjaj ibn Matar (d. 833), Yuhanna ibn Masawayh (d. 857), and the famous Banu Musa brothers (ibid., 485).[8] These scholars were not mere clones of foreign thinkers. Indeed, "far from being mere passive translators," Thabit Abdullah tells us in *A Short History of Iraq: From 636 to the Present*, they "contributed their own commentaries followed by original works" (21).

Dramatically enough, it must be said, not without truth, that the fascination with Greek culture and philosophy in particular had its own backlash. Indeed, by and large, the archives of the medieval Islamic world are teeming with entries that record strong opposition to Greek philosophy by mostly

Sunni *'ulama'* (scholars) such as Malik ibn Anas (d. 795) and Ahmad ibn
Hanbal (d. 855), who, according to Fakhry, both vehemently "repudi-
ated the application of the new dialectical methods in any guise or form
to the sacred texts" (*Philosophy, Dogma*, 3). Ahmad ibn Hanbal's *mihna*
(predicament) is the most illustrative example of this backlash.

Ibn Hanbal was imprisoned and severely tortured by the three Abbasid
caliphs al-Ma'mun, al-Mu'tasim, and al-Wathiq, who all embraced the
theological precepts of *al-mu'tazila* (the Mutazilites). The Mutazilites were
a group of scholastic theologians who, among other things, championed
al-qiyas al-'aqli (rational [Aristotelian] syllogism) in their interpretation of
the Quran and the Sunna (prophetic tradition).[9] This led them, according
to traditionists, to propound ideas that were inherently unacceptable to
Islam (Fakhry, *A History of Islamic Philosophy*, 47).[10] When the Mutazilites
gained strong influence during the reign of al-Ma'mun, the greatest patron
of Greek philosophy in the history of Islam, they established a "court of
inquisition" to prosecute all those who did not profess their creed (Gutas,
Greek Thought, 99).

Briefly stated, one of the most vituperative attacks on philosophy
came from al-Ghazali (d. 1111) in *Tahafut al-Falasifa* (The Rebuttal of
Philosophers) and *Faysal al-Tafriqa bayn al-Islam wa-l-Zandaqa* (The
Difference Between Islam and Hereticism). Ibn Rushd (d. 1198), known
in the West as Averroes, wrote a response to al-Ghazali in *Tahafut al-Taha-
fut* (The Rebuttal of the Rebuttal) (Bello, *The Medieval Islamic Controversy
between Philosophy and Orthodoxy*, 5). Later, it was mainly Ibn Taymiyya
(d. 1328) who perpetuated the attack on Greek philosophy and wrote "one
of the most powerful and ambitious assaults on Aristotelian logic" (Groff
and Leaman, *Islamic Philosophy A-Z*, 99).[11] The same was true, although to
a lesser degree, of his fervent follower Ibn Qayyim al-Jawziyya (d. 1350).
Surprisingly enough, Ibn Khaldun (d. 1406)—called a philosopher by
many—devoted the thirty-first chapter of his renowned *Al-Muqaddima*
(Prolegomena) to a strong attack on philosophy and philosophers.[12] "Ibn
Khaldun (1332–1406), perhaps the greatest intellectual produced by medieval Islam," David Grant writes in *A History of Natural Philosophy: From the
Ancient World to the Nineteenth Century*, "was convinced, as was al-Ghazali
and Ibn al-Salah before, that philosophy and logic were great potential
danger to the Islamic religion" (89).[13]

As far as Lewis's erroneous assertion that Muslims had never traveled
to study is concerned, it is important to remember that *al-rihla al-'ilmiyya*
(scientific travel), alternatively known as *al-rihla fi talab al-'ilm* (travel in
search of knowledge), was "a *leitmotiv* of Islam from its earliest days"
and "a cliché in mediaeval Islamic intellectual life," to quote from Ian
R. Netton's seminal study *Seek Knowledge: Thought and Travel in the House*

of Islam (vii). In fact, and in brief, numerous are the injunctions in the Quran and hadith that urge Muslims to travel over lands and seas, contemplate differences in languages and races, and meet learned men in order to acquire *'ilm* (knowledge).[14] The latter, as Franz Rosenthal once put it in his classic *Knowledge Triumphant: The Concept of Knowledge in Medieval Islam* (1970), "is one of those concepts that have dominated Islam and given Muslim civilization its distinctive shape and complexion" (2).[15]

Needless to add, Muslim mobility was further encouraged under the Umayyad caliphs (661–750) in whose era the territorial expansion of *dar al-islam* was unprecedented. After a number of successful military campaigns east and west, the Umayyads found themselves ruling over a vast empire that expanded west into North Africa and the Iberian Peninsula and east to the borders of China. The Umayyads are credited with establishing a strong navy, developing a postal system, and encouraging scholars to acquire information about remote countries and their inhabitants (N. Ahmad, *Muslim Contribution to Geography*, 5). It is with the Abbasids (750–1258), however, that Muslim mobility reached its zenith. From the beginning of their reign, travel within and outside the extended borders of *dar al-islam* became not only "une des caractéristiques de la société musulmane" (M'Ghirbi, *Les voyageurs de l'occident musulman du XIIe au XIVe siècles*, 13) but also "une nécessité et une dignité" (Miquel, *La géographie humaine du monde musulman jusqu'au milieu du 11e siècle*, 114).

Within *dar al-islam*, Muslims traveled not only to perform the religious duty of hajj (pilgrimage) to Mecca but also for reasons as various as seeking knowledge, amassing fortunes, satisfying personal curiosity, or collecting data for geographical studies, diplomacy, or spying and wars (Muwafi, *Al-Rihla fi-l-Adab al-'Arabi*, 82).[16] As Euben points out, "Some travelers undertook journeys for such mundane and less religiously specific purposes as job-seeking, trade, diplomatic missions for sultans, desire for status, or just plain wanderlust" (*Journeys to the Other Shore*, 17). The particular emphasis given to attaining knowledge in medieval Islam led a considerable number of scholars to embark on long journeys in search of knowledge (Gellens, "The Search for Knowledge in Medieval Muslim Societies: A Comparative Approach," 50). Although the latter "is unquestionably religious," Euben reminds us in *Journeys to the Other Shore*, "a hard and fast distinction between secular and religious knowledge misses the scope of *'ilm*" (35).

In fact, traveling for study was so popular, especially among scholars of hadith, that the prolific and polyvalent al-Khatib al-Baghdadi (d. 1072) wrote an entire book, *Al-Rihla fi Talab al-Hadith* (Travel for Learning Hadith), exploring this genre and the sacrifices many had to endure through their lifetime (52). No wonder, given that prominent Muslim scholars of hadith traveled for decades away from their home countries not only to study the sciences of the Quran and the prophetic tradition but also to acquire knowledge of rhetoric, jurisprudence, history, genealogy, literature, sectology, polemics, mathematics, and so forth. For Lenker, these learned men were not restricted to the collection and criticism of hadith since, for the majority of them, the *rihla* was "a many-sided intellectual endeavour, a true '*Wanderjahre*' spent with the best scholars in various parts of [the] Islamic world" (Lenker, "The Importance of the Rihla for the Islamization of Spain," 129).

It must be stressed in passing that the desire to seek knowledge and travel is universal. History teaches us that civilizations in times of power, irrespective of the driving ideology, have always produced curious travelers who have physically and intellectually ventured into unknown places and foreign lands to discover, meet, and study different Others with different cultures. Most of the time, the result has been a journey back to rediscover, re-meet, and ultimately reconsider the Self (Raphael, "Medieval Muslim Travelers to China," 313). Medieval Islam was no exception, and such curious travelers did certainly exist in considerable numbers. Indeed, driven by the same "intellectual curiosity" that impelled several renowned Western travelers to venture into the "non-West," (Euben, *Journeys to the Other Shore*, 26), many medieval Muslims traveled to alien lands and gave evidence of their curiosity and interest in different worlds. Al-Mas'udi (d. 896) and al-Biruni (d. 1048), as will be briefly shown, stand as two compelling examples.

Al-Mas'udi, hailed by many as the Herodotus of the Arabs and by some as the Pliny of the Muslim world, was not only a great historian, geographer, *faqih* (jurist), *adib* (litterateur), and a polyvalent scientist, but he was also a great traveler for study who embarked at a very young age on a lifelong journey of intellectual quest inside and outside *dar al-islam* (Hmeida, *A'lam al-Jughrafiyyin al-'Arab*, 254). "In his exuberance and love of travel," J. F. P. Hopkins comments, "he resembles his junior contemporary al-Muqaddasi, while in his combining of different disciplines in one work [*Al-Muruj*] he has something of the character of the earlier *adab*-writers, but also of the later encyclopaedists" ("Geographical and Navigational Literature," 315). At the age of 20, al-Mas'udi found himself in Persia around 915. In the following years, he explored India and China. Then he crossed to West Africa and visited Zanzibar, Madagascar, Mozambique, and Sudan. In 926, he appeared in Palestine, from which he traveled to Arabia for hajj, followed by Syria, from which he crossed to the vast Byzantine Empire. From there he embarked on a European itinerary that took him as far as the lands of the Slavs and other eastern and central European countries (Miquel, *La géographie humaine*, 259). Al-Mas'udi then settled in Egypt, where he died in 956 (Hmeida, *A'lam al-Jughrafiyyin al-'Arab*, 252). It was al-Mas'udi's penchant for a life of wandering and travels for study to collect historical, geographical, and ethnographical data about different peoples, Muslim and non-Muslim alike, that made him one of the towering intellectual figures of classical Islam. As Giancarlo Pizzi puts it, al-Mas'udi was one of the paragons of "l'umanesimo arabo" who, as a curious traveler, had benefited a great deal from his extensive mobility (*Al-Mas'udi e I prati d'oro e le miniere di gemme*, 7). In his graceful words, al-Mas'udi was "un uomo indubbiamente colto, ma soprattutto dotato di una granda che lo spingeva a esplorare dirrettamente ogni campo delle umane conoscenze compiendo lunghi viaggi" (7).

In the opening lines of his *Muruj al-Dhahab wa Ma'adin al-Jawhar* (Meadows of Gold and Mines of Precious Stones), al-Mas'udi informs us that he exhausted himself "by long and difficult journeys over land and sea" not to seek political power, as Ibn Khaldun did centuries later, but to learn for himself and see with his own eyes "all the remarkable things which exist among different peoples and to study the particular characteristics of each country" (3). "One of the major motives of his travels," we are told by Paul Lunde and Caroline Stone, "seems to have been to gather as much information as possible about the peoples who lived beyond the borders of Islam, in particular about their religious beliefs, which he recounts with a notable lack of distortion" (*The Meadows of Gold: The Abbasids*, 13). Indeed, in his accounts of non-Muslims, he did his best to be as objective as possible. "In dealing with non-Muslim peoples, their lands, history, religions, and other aspects," Ahmad Shboul observes, "al-Mas'udi is anxious to have recourse to the views of the people concerned" (*Al-Mas'udi and His World*, 303).[17] Camilla Adang's *Muslim Writers on Judaism and the Hebrew Bible: From Ibn Rabban to Ibn Hazm* is worth quoting in this regard:

> Wherever he went, al-Mas'udi sought the company of the representative of different religions and sects. Thus he visited fire temples in Iran and discussed Zoroastrianism with *mobeds* and *herbads*; he consulted Christian priests and laymen in Takrit and Antioch, and met Sabians in Harran. It is therefore not surprising to find him in discussion with eminent Jewish scholars in Raqqa, Tiberias, and Baghdad. Al-Mas'udi may also have talked to the Samaritan community during his sojourn in Nablus. (45)

That al-Mas'udi was fully convinced that "true knowledge can only be acquired through practice and observation" (S. M. Ahmad, *A History of*

Arab-Islamic Geography, 63) is evinced by his severe criticism of "armchair" scholars, no matter how famous they were, who did not travel to verify what they reported in their books.[18] In this respect, one may mention his harsh criticism of the great *adib* al-Jahiz (d. 869), the "Shakespeare" of classical Arabic literature and one of Islam's most talented encyclopedic writers, in spite of his appreciation of his [al-Jahiz's] masterful prose and remarkable knowledge (Shboul, *Al-Mas'udi and His World*, 35). As Tarif Khalidi has maintained in *Islamic Historiography: The Histories of al-Mas'udi*, he censured al-Jahiz "for incorporating in his works much geographical and zoological information which he neither witnessed nor was able to confirm" (12). Indeed, in a section entitled *Ba'dh Awham al-Jahiz* (Some of al-Jahiz's illusions), al-Mas'udi derided al-Jahiz's unfounded statement that the River Sind (in India) springs from the Nile in his book *Kitab al-Amsar wa Tafadhul al-Buldan* (Regions of the World and Marvels of the Lands). Al-Mas'udi had no compunction in writing this unsympathetic evaluation of al-Jahiz and his book:

> Al-Jahiz contended that the Mahran River [the Indus], which is the river of Sind, does originate in the Nile. He justified his claim by highlighting the existence of crocodiles in the river. Indeed, I cannot understand how he came to this unfounded conclusion which he mentioned in his book, *Regions of the World and Marvels of the Lands*. The latter is an extremely inadequate [poor] work because the *author had never taken to the seas, nor was he known for travel, nor was he knowledgeable about roads and regions* [italics mine]. He was, however, a night collector of firewood [careless copier] who copies carelessly from other books! (37, translation mine)

Equally suggestive is al-Mas'udi's severe criticism of al-Jahiz's statement, based on reports from some Indian merchants, that female rhinoceroses have the habit of keeping "their young in their stomachs for a period of seven years during which it came out to graze the grass and went back into it again till it was fully grown, and then finally laid it down" (S. M. Ahmad, *A History of Arab-Islamic Geography*, 65). Certainly, the *tajriba* (experience) of al-Mas'udi confirms that the "un-traveled" al-Jahiz used to mix up many scientific *qadaya* (issues/problems), for the animal that is known for guarding its young in this way is none other than the kangaroo (65). A great and reliable scholar, in al-Mas'udi's eyes, should not deal with any scientific issues if he has not studied them personally through real experiences. Such, it seems, was al-Mas'udi's firm motto. At least, that is what some observers have accurately drawn from the title of his, unfortunately lost, travel account *Kitab al-Qadaya wa-l-Tajarib* (The Book of Problems and Experiences) (65). Again Lunde and

Stone are worth quoting in this respect:

> One has only to think of a European contemporary of Masʿudi—say
> the compiler of the Anglo-Saxon Chronicle—to gauge the immense
> advantages the Muslim historian enjoyed. Not only did he have access to
> books by previous writers—even Greek and Persian translation—but he
> was able to travel freely and even at times gain access to official archives.
> It was not until the Renaissance that European historians were able to
> work under the sort of conditions Masʿudi took for granted. (*The Meadows
> of Gold*, 14)

Besides al-Masʿudi, mention could deservedly be made of Abu Raihan
al-Biruni (d. 1050). As we shall see, al-Biruni's life furnished another
example of a medieval Muslim scholar who exhibited a remarkable curiosity "to study and appreciate," the cultures, religions, and languages of the
non-Muslim Other. Al-Biruni was known for his unquenchable thirst for
knowledge per se. "It is knowledge in general," he writes in the introduction to *Tahdid Nihayat al-Amakin* (Defining the Ends of Regions), "that
is pursued solely by men, and what is pursued for the sake of knowledge
itself because its acquisition is truly delightful and unlike other pleasures
that can be derived from other pursuits" (2). It is perfectly understandable
why the versatile *al-ustadh* (the Master), as dubbed by many, was a highly
prolific scholar who is said to have authored "146 titles, including nearly
100 on mathematical astronomy and related subjects and around fifty on
subjects as varied as history, literature, religion, philosophy and pharma-
cology" ("Al-Biruni," 102), to quote Paul Starkey.

As Bill Scheppler has shown in *Al-Biruni: Master Astronomer and Muslim
Scholar of the Eleventh Century*, al-Biruni's 20-year-long travels in India
influenced him the most (26). Al-Biruni is said to have left for India
somewhat unwillingly with the sultan Mahmud al-Ghaznawi (d. 1030)
in 1017. When he arrived there, he was so fascinated by the indigenous
culture that he learned Sanskrit and engaged in an intensive intellectual
investigation of India's geography, people, culture, religion, philosophy,
and sciences. Commenting on his long sojourn in India, S. M. Ahmad
tells us that al-Biruni "must have considered this a god-sent opportunity
for he was already conversant with some of the Indian sciences through
Arabic translations of the *Brahmasphutasiddhanta*, *Khandakhadyaka*, etc."
(*A History of Arab-Islamic Geography*, 137). The fruit of this scholarly interest and real experience in India was al-Biruni's encyclopedic work entitled
Tahqiq ma li-l-Hind min Maqula Maqbula fi-l-ʿAql aw Marthula (Ascertaining
of Statements to Be Accorded Intellectual Acceptance or to Be Rejected
Regarding India). The latter, more commonly known as *Kitab al-Hind*

(The Book of India), was not only "written with utmost objectivity," but it "forms one of the most authentic surveys of ancient Indian culture, and is a reference book on ancient India used by scholars today" (136). In the opening lines of the book, al-Biruni assures us, "My book is nothing but a simple historic record of facts. I shall place before the reader the theories of the Hindus exactly as they are" (*Tahqiq ma li-l-Hind*, 7).

Kitab al-Hind is indeed unique inasmuch as it explored almost exclusively the religions and cultures of the Indians. Throughout the book, al-Biruni proved an exceptionally objective scholar, constantly restless in his detached curiosity about the Other and deeply preoccupied with "scientifically" recording all that he saw and knew during his long travels in medieval India. No wonder, as Tarif Khalidi has noted, al-Biruni "added a portrait of the Indian culture of his age unique in its accuracy" (*Arabic Historical Thought in the Classical Period*, 176). It is therefore understandable why he has been highly praised for his detached and objective erudition by a number of Western scholars. As shown by Kemal Ataman in *Understanding Other Religions: Al-Biruni's and Gadamer's "Fusion of Horizons,"* the noted German Arabist Anne-Marie Schimmel hailed al-Biruni's *Book of India* as "the first objective book ever written on the history of religion" (56). Ainslee T. Embree, editor of the E. Sachau classic English translation of *Kitab al-Hind*, had a similar opinion. Indeed, as Hopkins said, he considered al-Biruni's *Book of India* as "one the most penetrating accounts we have of Indian society" ("Geographical and Navigational Literature," 417). Mehmet Aydin is also worth quoting in this respect:

> This great man stands as a model of the thinker who was able to harmonize with his own intellectual world various forms of knowledge from the science of nature to religion to philosophy. Al-Biruni has an extremely international outlook and worked to remove the misunderstandings between various religions and bring humanity close in their outlook upon the world. He was a key figure in bringing about real cultural contacts between different races and nations. It is because of his great contributions to many fields, especially to the scientific spirit in general, that George Sarton, the well known historian of sciences, wishes to name the eleventh century "the age of al-Biruni." ("Turkish Contributions to Philosophical Culture," 16)

In a suggestively telling contrast to Lord Macaulay and the Orientalists whom he claimed he consulted on the value of Indian and Arabic literatures, nine centuries earlier al-Biruni had expressed his positive appreciation of the language(s) and the literature(s) of the India he visited in almost the same colonial conditions and role.[19] As pointed out by the Indian historian

N. K. Singh, al-Biruni "studied Indian works like Samkhya of Kapil, book of Pantajali, *Vishnu Dharma*, *Vishnu Purana*, *Matsya Purana*, *Vayu Purana*, etc." (*Encyclopaedic Historiography of the Muslim World*, 42). Indeed, at the end of *Kitab al-Hind*, he reveals to us that he translated into Arabic two Sanskrit books dealing with Indian theology and cosmology entitled *Sakaya* and *Patanja* and that he wrote several critical notes on a number of Sanskrit literary masterpieces, such as the *Yogasutra*, the *Bhagavadgita*, and the *Sankhyakarika*.

The previous short survey of the intellectual achievements of al-Mas'udi and al-Biruni is important to this study for two main reasons. Firstly, and contrary to the aforementioned statements of some scholars of the Middle East, it demonstrates that there was no dearth of medieval Muslims who cast curious eyes and minds toward the non-Muslim Other. Secondly, it proves that medieval Muslims were not neglectful of non-Muslim religions and sects. Indeed, without forgetting to stress from the outset the polemical nature of most of their writings, several Muslim scholars authored numerous books and treatises on what has come to be known as comparative religion and the science of sectology. This will be clear from a brief summary of some of the most important books written in these areas.

In short, here one thinks in particular of al-Nawbakhti (d. 912), who wrote *Al-Ara' wa-l-Adyan* (Religions and Beliefs); al-Ash'ari's (d. 935) *Maqalat al-Islamiyyin* (On Muslim Doctrines) and his lost *Maqalat Ghayr al-Islamiyyin* (On Non-Muslim Doctrines), and al-Misbahi (d. 1030), who authored a huge book entitled *Idrak al-Bughya fi Wasf al-Adyan wa-l-Ibadat* (Achieving the Goals in Describing Religions and Worships).[20] Medieval Arab sources mention that this tome numbers three thousand leaves. The sectologist Abu al-Mansur al-Baghdadi (d. 1037) wrote in this same perspective *Al-Farq bayn al-Firaq* (Differences among Sects). The Andalusian Ibn Hazm also wrote a monumental work, *Al-Fisal fi-l-Milal wa-l-Ahwa' wa-l-Nihal* (On Religions, Beliefs, and Sects) in the same century. The last has been hailed by many Western Arabists and historians of religion as one of the world's pioneering studies of comparative religion. The same is true of another well-known work by al-Shahrastani (d. 1153) entitled *Al-Milal wa-l-Nihal* (Religions and Sects), Abu al-Ma'ali's *Bayn al-Adyan* (Between Religions), Fakhruddine al-Razi's *I'tiqadat al-Muslimin wa-l-Mushrikin* (On Muslim and Polytheist Beliefs). Furthermore, during the Crusades, there was a meteoric surge in polemical writing about Christianity and to a lesser degree Judaism. Of interest are Shihab al-Din al-Qarafi's *Al-Ajwiba al-Fakhira 'ala al-As'ila al-Fajira* (Efficacious Answers to Arrogant Questions), Ibn Taymiyya's *Al-Jawab al-Sahih 'ala man Baddala Din al-Masih* (The Pertinent Reply to the One Who Altered the Faith of Christ), and Ibn al-Qayyim's *Hidayat al-Hayara fi Ajwibat al-Yahud wa-l-Nasara* (Enlightening the Perplexed to the Answers of the Jews and Christians).[21]

In the light of all this, it is fitting to say that the great movement of translation especially from Greek, Sanskrit, and Persian into Arabic, the paramount importance of *al-rihla fi talab al-'ilm*, the humanistic intellectualism and detached curiosity of several scholars of the classical age of Islam, and the proliferation of writings about the religions and cultures of non-Muslims constitute abundant and compelling evidence that should leave us with no doubt that medieval Muslims were not disinterested in the Other. Although most of the time painfully aware of the unbridgeable religious *ikhtilaf* (difference), a good many medieval Muslims were particularly keen to study and appreciate foreign and alien cultures, even, as we shall see in the following section, in comparison with their own Orient.

As for the interest in the Euro-Christians, the main focus of this book, one can argue that through the aforementioned translation of almost the entire corpus of the classical heritage of the Greeks, medieval Muslims appear to have been more or less conversant with one of the most basic aspects of the Euro-Christian Other. The European Renaissance has always been defined as a rediscovery of its Greek heritage and a touchstone of Western civilization and European culture lost during the intellectual vacuum of the so-called European Dark Ages. The fact that this rediscovery was made possible much of the time through the medium of Arabic translations and Muslim commentators, especially during the Great Debate of the twelfth and thirteenth centuries, cannot be ignored. As the French historian Jean-Baptiste Duroselle puts it in *Europe: A History of Its Peoples*, "But this new Renaissance, the precursor of that which ended the Middle Ages also arose from the fact that Europeans were now discovering lost Greek texts, and above all further fragments from Aristotle. These came to Europe not from the Byzantines, but from the Arabs" (153). This is in addition to Muslim contacts with medieval Euro-Christendom, knowledge of Christianity, their particular interest in Byzantium, and their encounter with the Crusaders.

The Orient's Medieval "Orient(alism)": The *Rihla* of Sulayman al-Tajir

And whoever sees himself really free.
Let him experience the meaning of the word!
Away from home, I spent most of my life,
Witnessing wonders of ancient times.
My adventurous soul finds peace in alien things.

Not in the comfort of the known world.
For indeed we are people of lands and seas,
Amassing poll taxes from Egyptians and Chinese.
In Tangiers, indeed in all corners, our horses race.
If bored in a space, we leave it for another place.
Muslim and non-Muslim lands are at our hands,
In summers we resort to snow.
In winters the oasis we enjoy!

> —Abu Dulaf (d.1012), quoted in Hassan,
> *Al-Rahala al-Muslimun fi-l-ʿUsur al-Wusta,*
> 3 (translation mine)

Nabil Matar is not totally wrong when he deplores the fact that Anthony Pagden's voluminous collection of articles published under the title *Facing Each Other: The World's Perception of Europe and Europe's Perception of the World* (2000) fails to include "a single entry about the perception of or by any of the civilizations of Islam" (*In the Lands of the Christians*, xv). He has, however, overlooked a "single" exception: it is Jacques Le Goff's reference to the medieval Arabs' perception of the Indian Ocean in his seminal article "The Medieval West and the Indian Ocean: An Oneiric Horizon."[22] For the erudite Le Goff, medieval Westerners' ignorance of the Indian Ocean and India in particular was in part the result of a negative Arabic influence. To the medieval Arabs, Le Goff states, "it is possible that the Indian Ocean was a forbidden and unknown world" (3). This lack of information about the Indian Ocean on the part of medieval Arabs, Le Goff goes on to observe, did nothing but reinforce the "illusions" of medieval Western writers and merchants who "sometimes turned to them for information" (3). Fortunately, Le Goff's statement does not represent the scholarly attitude of the vast majority of Western Arabists, many who have made efforts that have been instrumental in both introducing and safeguarding the rich heritage of medieval Arab-Islamic geo-cosmographical, historiographical, and travel literature.[23]

It would hardly be an overstatement to say that during their own age of discovery and expansion, poetically captured by the aforementioned lines of the poet/traveler Abu Dulaf (d. 1012), medieval Muslims showed an enormous interest in their own "Orient" especially after the conquest of the region of *al-sind* (modern Pakistan) in 711 by Muhammad ibn Qasim.[24] "By the 8th Century," Peter Boxhall notes, "Arabian seafarers were traveling frequently, in the wake of the great Islamic incursion by land into the Sind Province, and by sea along the Malabar Coast, to far-distant 'As-Sin' [China]" ("Arabian Seafarers in the Indian Ocean," 291).[25] In a general sense, outside the borders of *dar al-islam*, it was mainly *al-hind* (India) and *al-sin* (China) that drew the closest attention of Muslim politicians, geographers, merchants, and travelers alike (Khan, "Al-Biruni, the Pioneer Indologist", 34). Although this "Orient" was predominantly conceived as "an actual space," to use Iain Macleod Higgins's phrase, some elements of "the imaginary and the conceptual" were unquestionably present, without, however, attaining the imaginary and the conceptual Orient "envisioned, elaborated, and encountered in the corpus of western writing about the East" (*Writing East*, 6). Indeed, in addition to the economic, political, and religious motives behind the interest in *al-sharq* (East), the Indo-Chinese inspiration of *al-ʿajib/al-gharib* (the marvelous/the unfamiliar) made the Indian Ocean "a desirable destination" and not a "taboo," as Le Goff has assumed (Wink, *Al-Hind, The Making of the Indo-Islamic World*, 17).

The interest of Muslims in the East dates back to the early days of Islam wherein "the caliphs, were probably for political reasons, interested in acquiring information about different countries, their inhabitants and special features of their lands" (S. M. Ahmad, *A History of Arab-Islamic Geography*, 38). It was with the Abbasids, however, that this interest reached its historical climax through the expedition sent to India by Yahya ibn Khalid al-Barmaki (d. 805), the competent *wazir* of Harun al-Rashid. According to Zaki Muhammad Hassan, the expedition was the direct result of the "intellectual awakening and frequent religious debates encouraged by the Abbasid caliphs," which, in his own words, "stimulated an urge in the hearts of the Arabs to make enquiries and researches into the religion of the Hindus" (*Al-Rahala al-Muslimun fi-l-ʿUsur al-Wusta*, 6). Seen in this light, this expedition to study the East's own East, in spite of the almost ten centuries that separate them, conjures up to some extent the French expedition to Egypt in 1789. The outcome of this older nonmilitary expedition was an intriguing report "that covered various arts, skills and scientific achievements of the Indians and a detailed account of the castes and religious practices" (S. M. Ahmad, *A History of Arab-Islamic Geography*, 38).

In this same period, an independent traveler by the name of ʿAbd Allah Muhammad ibn Ishaq made his way as far as Khmer (Cambodia), where he lived for two years. Although Ishaq's report is mostly lost, he is credited with leaving a number of valuable comments not only on the ancient kings of India but also on Ceylon and Khmer that were used by later historians and geographers (38). Years later, the Abbasid polyglot/translator Sallam al-Turjuman is reported to have reached the Great Wall of China (Malallah, *Adab al-Rahalat ʿInda al-ʿArab*, 31).[26]

In his geographical encyclopedia *Kitab al-Masalik wa-l-Mamalik*, Ibn Khordadbeh reported on the authority of al-Turjuman himself that the latter left for China at the request of the caliph al-Wathiq (d. 847), who was terrified by a nightmare in which he saw a hole in *al-sudd* (the dam) that the Quranic character *dhu al-qarnayn* is said to have built to prevent the apocalyptic nations of *ya'juj wa ma'juj* (the biblical Gog and Magog) from invading and ravaging the adjacent territories (Hassan, *Al-Rahala al-Muslimun fi-l-'Usur al-Wusta*, 15).[27] Although one cannot totally exclude the story of the nightmare, Malallah has argued convincingly that this nightmare was rather used by al-Wathiq as a pretext to expose his political and military power by showing that he could reach any corner he wished to reach (*Adab al-Rahalat 'Inda al-'Arab*, 31).

In defense of the historical accuracy of the trip against the doubt leveled by some Western Arabists—such as Sprenver, Grigorev, and mainly Minorski, who described al-Turjuman's trip as "a wondertale interspersed with three or four geographical names"—Zaki Muhammad Hassan has argued that what people should doubt is rather some of the mythical descriptions found in certain reports on the trip and whether Sallam reached the Great Wall of China or just stopped in modern Dagestan (*Al-Rahala al-Muslimun fi-l-'Usur al-Wusta*, 18). As pointed out by Hassan, this is the position espoused by the French Arabist Carde Vaux, who although he defended ardently the authenticity of the trip used to argue that al-Turjuman did not see the Great Wall of China, his prime objective. Referring to Arabists such as De Goje, Tomashek, and Vasmev, who confirmed the authenticity of the trip, Malallah has asserted that the very fact that Ibn Khordadbeh (who was one of the closest advisers of al-Wathiq) mentioned that he heard directly much of the report from his friend al-Turjuman appears to prove that the latter had indeed embarked on such a trip (*Adab al-Rahalat 'Inda al-'Arab*, 31).

This fascination with India and China manifested itself in the publication in 916 of *Silsilat al-Tawarikh* (Chain of Histories), the first "anthology" of Arabic accounts of India and China, by Abu Zayd al-Hasan al-Sirafi (d. 950), who most likely traveled to both countries (Hassan, *Al-Rahala al-Muslimun fi-l-'Usur al-Wusta*, 9).[28] Because he was also "an ardent collector of information from travelers visiting in India and China and other parts of the East," al-Sirafi (after exhaustive editing and correcting) incorporated in *Silsilat al-Tawarikh* a number of accounts and reports of Muslim travelers, sailors, and merchants who had visited India and China (S. M. Ahmad, *A History of Arab-Islamic Geography*, 42).[29] The most interesting of these accounts is *Akhbar al-Sin w-a-l-Hind* (Account of China and India), still attributed by the majority of Middle Eastern scholars to Sulayman al-Tajir. Al-Tajir's account of China and India, according to Hassan, is not only one of the world's most interesting and authentic texts concerning medieval India and China but "the earliest known travel diary of an Arab that has come to us" (*Al-Rahala al-Muslimun fi-l-'Usur al-Wusta*, 8).[30]

Little is known about Sulayman al-Tajir other than his own text and
the fact that he was, as the second part of his name confirms, a *tajir*, that
is to say a merchant. Indeed, what strikes the reader most on reading the
opening pages of *Akhbar al-Sin wa-l-Hind* is the remarkable reticence of
the author on the subject of his own life and career during his journey
in the East. Most probably, however, like his editor Abu Zayd al-Sirafi,
he was from the coast city of Siraf. From there, as mentioned by some
reports, he sailed across the Indian Ocean before reaching India and jour-
neying into China. Al-Tajir's account is a mine of sociocultural, religious,
political, and economic information about India and China in the ninth
century. In fact, from the beginning of his journey, the merchant seems to
abandon his initial trade and become a keen observer and a preoccupied
explorer who finds himself captivated not only by the spectacle of the
Oriental Other he will soon meet but also by the authentic *'aja'ib/ghara'ib*
(marvels/wonders) of the Indian Ocean.

The opening pages of the account are full of rich maritime information about "this sea," as he calls it. It is the detailed and fascinating
description of the sperm whale that proved the most valuable in his
entire account of the Indian Ocean. "In this sea is found a fish that
appears occasionally," he tells us in his opening paragraph. "It has herbs
and shells growing on it back. The captains of boats, sometimes, lay
anchor against it thinking it to be an island, but when they realize their
mistake they set sail from it" (S. M. Ahmad, *Arabic Classical Accounts of
India and China*, 33). Without the necessity of calling (him) Ishmael, for
certainly he was, *Moby Dick* must have loomed large in the oceans of
our memory, conjuring up the harpoons of Queequeq, the destructive
revenge of Captain Ahab, and more importantly *le plaisir* of navigating
through foreign texts.

Perhaps it is not going too far to state that the remainder of the description of al-Tajir's factual Moby Dick, however, appears too classical to fit
in the novelistic structure, if not the colonialist discourse of Herman
Melville, for it is Longinian in essence. Capturing the Muslim sailors'
feelings of the "sublime," whenever they encounter the sublime sperm
whale, al-Tajir writes,

> Sometimes, when this fish spreads out one of its two wings on its back,
> it appears like the sail of a ship. When it raises its head above water, you
> can see it as an enormous object. Sometimes it blows out water from its
> "mouth," which resembles a lofty tower. Whenever the sea is calm and
> the fish gather together, it collects them round with the help of its tail.
> Then it opens its mouth and the fish dive into its belly as if diving into a
> well. The boats sailing on this sea are scared of it, so during the nightfall

they blow the trumpets resembling those of the Christians, for they are afraid that it might lean heavily against their boat and cause it to be drowned. (33)

The "un-Ahabian" al-Tajir was fully aware of the tragic doom of chasing the sperm whale. Hence, he opted for a comic Sindbadian adventure that uses the sea as a means and never an end per se. Apart from the rhapsodic reference to the cannibalistic Andaman, to which we will return later, the awkward opening of *Akhbar al-Sin wa-l-Hind* resembles closely the medieval and Renaissance Western *isolari* (catalog of islands), especially when al-Tajir consumes many pages to list clumsily the numerous islands of the Indian Ocean. Fortunately, however, with the approach to the nearest Indian shore, al-Tajir embarks on a rather pleasant Oriental journey wherein he gratifies the curious reader with a mine of information about ninth-century India and China.

Throughout the remaining pages, al-Tajir engages in a comparative description of the religious, social, political, economic, and cultural conditions of the Indians and the Chinese. He has proved particularly keen in exploring and mapping the topos of difference and sameness between these two non-Muslim peoples most of the time, as his comments are without polemical addition or omission. Yet at other times, he is quick in reporting with implied disapproval, but without much moralizing, what he deems to be religious aberrations and social vices that utterly contradict his own religion and his cultural traditions.

It goes almost without saying that al-Tajir, as is the habit of the "religious minded" Arabs (*Al-Rahala al-Muslimun fi-l-'Usur al-Wusta*, 45), to use Hassan's phrase, seems to be particularly interested in Indian religions and sects. Relatively aware of the differences among the major Hindu castes and main sects such as the Brahmans, Samanis, and Buddhists, al-Tajir (unlike more scholarly medieval Muslim writers on Indian religions) does not explain in detail many of the Hindu tenets and beliefs. Nevertheless, he has filled his account with valuable information on common Hindu religious and social practices, rituals of death, marriage, asceticism, women, justice, and politics. In several important respects, the most salient aspect of his commentary is the comparative mode that dominates the entire account. This can be seen in the traveler's thorough analysis of a number of similarities and differences between the Indians and the Chinese. These latter—in spite of their "superiority" in matters of education, culture, and civilization—in general are, religiously speaking, depicted by al-Tajir as "blind" followers of the Indians. This apparently led to the existence of several sociocultural similarities between the two otherwise different peoples.

In Hindu Serendib (Sri Lanka), which he describes as "the last of the islands and...one of the lands of India" (S. M. Ahmad, *Arabic Classical Accounts of India and China*, 53), al-Tajir informs us that when a Hindu king dies and before his cremation, a woman engages in a number of sacramental rituals wherein she pronounces a moving *tadhkira*, a type of a short but very meaningful admonition on the ineluctability of death. After the cremation, she repeats the same admonition for three consecutive days. Significant too is al-Tajir's accurate exposition of the Hindu practice of *sati*, or the burning of wives with the bodies of their dead husbands. Shunning hasty conclusions and easy generalizations, he proves himself objective in emphasizing the fact that Hindu wives have the final decision when it comes to this highly valued Hindu practice. Evidently, he could have easily made us believe that all Hindu wives must be burnt along with their dead husbands.

Centuries later, this same detail is highlighted almost verbatim by Marco Polo (d. 1324) and Ibn Battuta (d. 1369), the world's best-known globe-trotters: "When a man is dead and his body is being cremated," Marco Polo tells us, "his wife flings herself into the same fire and lets herself be burnt with her husband. The ladies who do this are highly praised by all. And I assure you that there are many who do as I have told you" (Clements, *Marco Polo*, 133). Similarly, Ibn Battuta notes, "The burning of the wife after her husband's death is regarded by them [Indians] as a commendable act, but is not compulsory, for when a widow burns herself her family acquires a certain prestige by it and gains a reputation for fidelity" (Mackintosh-Smith, *The Travels of Ibn Battutah*, 158). Soon, however, he emphasizes the enormous social pressure on all women to practice the *sati*, for as he concludes, " a widow who does not burn herself dresses in coarse garments and lives with her own people in misery, despised for her lack of fidelity" (158). It should be mentioned that, at least in this religious cult of burial and self-immolation, the Hindus have not changed much between the time al-Tajir visited India in the ninth century and the time Marco Polo and Ibn Battuta were there. Even more interesting is this rare medieval moment of agreement among two Mashriqi and Maghribi Muslims and a Euro-Christian on the crucial issue of religious Otherness.

Among the several factual wonders that drew the keen eyes of al-Tajir is the life of a number of Hindu gurus (enlightened masters). These mystics, al-Tajir tells us, dedicate their lives to wandering in uninhabited places such as forests and mountains without having any connections or communication with other human beings (S. M. Ahmad, *Arabic Classical Accounts of India and China*, 53). They starve themselves as much as they can, and it is understood that they are strict vegetarians, for they survive by feeding occasionally on herbs and fruits (53). They also abstain from sexual congress with women by covering their penises with iron rings (53). Al-Tajir's testimony can perhaps be seen as evidence for a Hindu influence on the rise of Sufism in medieval Islam. Among other things, this is especially significant when it comes to the cults of *siyaha* (wandering) and *khalwa* (isolation) that bear close similarities to the aforementioned Hindu cults as reported by al-Tajir.

Indeed, in addition to a number of monistic and pantheistic tendencies among some Sufi *shuyukh* (masters) such as al-Hallaj (d. 922), Ibn ʿArabi (d. 1240), Ibn Sabʿin (d. 1269), and Ibn al-Faridh (d. 1353), Sufi *shuyukh* and *murids* (disciples) chose to wander for years, in some cases for life, in the *sahra'* (desert) and *khala'* (uninhabited places) without taking provisions in search of *kashf* (enlightenment), *haqiqa* (inner truth), and other mystical *karamat* (miracles); this practice continues today in some Muslim countries. This is in addition to the spread of ʿuzubiyya (celibacy) and *tabattul* (sexual abstinence) among some of these masters and disciples.[31]

In al-Tajir's view, the religious influence of the Indians over their eastern neighbors the Chinese is uncontested. Acknowledging some small differences in minor practices, he calls them *furuʿ* (Arabic for "minor issues") and observes that the sciences of religion never developed in China, for "their religion originated in India" (53); this is an apparent reference to the fact that the predominant religion of medieval Chinese was Buddhism, which is Sanskrit for "enlightenment," again a concept of fundamental importance in Sufism. Owing to the religious dependence of the Chinese on the Indians, several social customs related to marriage, hygiene, and food are similar in both countries. Marriage, for instance, is enacted in the same way: "When the Indians and the Chinese wish to perform a marriage," al-Tajir remarks, "they felicitate each other, then exchange presents, and then they make the marriage public by playing on cymbals and drums. Their present consists of money, according to their means" (54). In a similar fashion, he informs us that neither of them practices circumcision, nor do they take a bath after *janaba* (sexual intercourse). This is in addition to the fact that the Chinese and the Indians do not slaughter their animals as Muslims do. Instead, they kill them by a blow to the skull. The Indians and Chinese, however, have different views in other issues of hygiene.

All in all, al-Tajir does not hesitate to imply that the Indians are not only clean, but they are unquestionably "cleaner" than the Chinese for a number of reasons that are intrinsically inspired by his own culture, such as Indians' daily bathing and teeth cleaning. Others are quite obvious, despite slight differences with Islamic practice. This recalls his statement that contrary to the Chinese, who have sexual intercourse with menstruating women, the Indians—more similar to the Jews than to Muslims—not only do not cohabit with them, but "they make them leave their homes and keep away from them" (56).[32]

We may say, then, that when it comes to the matters of conjugal and sexual life of the Indians and the Chinese, al-Tajir never seems indifferent. Of significance is his accurate statement that the Hindus, contrary to the Muslims, consider marriage a religious sacrament that joins the Hindu couple not only for life but, as we saw earlier, in the afterlife. Divorce is therefore not allowed, and at the death of husbands, wives who do not practice the *sati* are not allowed to remarry.[33] It is because, in stark contrast to Marco Polo's affirmation that the Indians "do not regard any form of sexual indulgence a sin" (Clements, *Marco Polo*, 131), *zina'* (adultery/fornication) is considered an extremely serious crime that can end with death. Throughout India, as observed by al-Tajir, consensual adultery among married couples is punished with death for both men and women.

Interestingly, al-Tajir mentions that if a married woman is forced to engage in adultery, she is saved and only the man is killed (S. M. Ahmad, *Arabic Classical Accounts of India and China*, 54). The severe punishment of adulterous married couples does not mean that other forms of sexual relations are inexistent in India. Indeed, prostitution among both the Indians and the Chinese is tolerated. As he tells us, in China prostitution as well as *liwat* (sodomy) with young boys is widely practiced in places built for the purpose (55). In India, legal prostitution is common in Hindu temples through the *devadasis* (temple girls) (55). According to Hassan and others, these women were not only "attached with the temple," but they also "traded in flesh and offered their income to the custodians of the temples" (*Al-Rahala al-Muslimun fi-l-'Usur al-Wusta*, 47). Interestingly enough, al-Tajir does not describe the *fitna* (sexual temptation) of the temple *devadasis* as does Marco Polo, who in his account mentions that the Hindu temple girls were "completely naked except for their private parts" (Clements, *Marco Polo*, 132). "Marco was quite taken with the temple girls," Jonathan Clements humorously tells us, "and noted with great interest their pert, firm bosoms and their taut, tight flesh—*for a penny they will allow a man to pinch them as hard as he can*, he [Polo] adds, without daring to suggest that he had the right change" (115).

In general, if the Indians encountered by al-Tajir were, in his eyes, far superior to their Chinese neighbors in matters related to spirituality, wisdom, hygiene, and to some extent morality, the Chinese excelled over their spiritual masters in matters related to culture. This impression was the outcome of al-Tajir's fascination with ninth-century China's "Universal literacy," political justice, social equality, agricultural and

economic abundance, and their unequalled artistic skills in craftsmanship and painting. For obvious reasons, al-Tajir notes with fascination
what he saw of widespread literacy among Chinese men and women.
Whether poor or rich, young or old, he tells us, the Chinese learn cal-
ligraphy and the art of writing (S. M. Ahmad, *Arabic Classical Accounts of
India and China*, 47). This was the outcome of an effective political policy
of decentralized promulgation of education on the part of the Chinese
politicians. "In every town," al-Tajir writes, "there are scribes and teachers who impart education to the poor and their children; they receive
their maintenance from the treasury" (52).

Since everybody knows how to read and to write, all the disputes and
complaints must reach the king not only in documents written by a *katib*
(scribe) licensed by the *hikam* (laws) but—to our surprise and amaze-
ment—in perfect spelling (51). "[And] before the plaintiff (*sahib-al-qiss*)
is presented in the audience of the king," al-Tajir says, "a person who is
stationed at the gate of the house looks into the written [complaint] of
the person. If he finds that there are some mistakes in it he rejects it" (51).
Universal literacy does not seem to be the invention of our modern times,
and "the Literall advantage" is God's gift to all, to the detriment of the
seventeenth-century English traveler Samuel Purchas (d. 1626).

In *Marvelous Possessions: The Wonder of the New World* (1991, critic
Stephen Greenblatt has persuasively argued that according to Purchas,
author of *Hakluytus Posthumus, or Purchas His Pilgrims*, it is writing that
sets the boundaries between civilization and barbarism. "God hath
added herein a further grace, that as Men by the former exceed Beasts,"
Purchas declares, "so hereby one man may excell another; and amongst
Men, some are accounted Civill, and more Sociable and religious, by
the Use of letters and of Writing, which others wanting are esteemed
Brutish, Savage, Barbarous" (Greenblatt, *Marvelous Possessions*, 10). In
addition to "the Christians' conviction that they possessed an absolute
and exclusive religious truth" and the possession of "navigational instruments, ships, warhorses, attack dogs, effective armour, and highly lethal
weapons, including gunpowder," Greenblatt observes that it is this very
"Literall advantage" that provided Europeans, "with a very few exceptions," with a most powerful feeling of superiority toward "virtually all
the people they encountered, even those like the Aztecs who had tech-
nological and organizational skills" (9). For Purchas and other Europeans,
Greenblatt goes on to say, the possession of writing was equated with the
possession of "a past, a history, that those without access to letters necessarily lack" (10). Through the support of some scholars such as Tzvetan
Todorov, Greenblatt reveals that "Purchas's notion of the Literall advantage" has survived with considerable vigor in certain academic circles.

In his seminal book *The Conquest of America*, described by Greenblatt as not only "thoughtful" and "disturbing" but also as the inspiration behind *Marvelous Possessions*, Todorov (Greenblatt believes) has argued that "the crucial cultural difference between European and American peoples was the presence or absence of writing and that this difference virtually determined the outcome of their encounter" (11). During the older cultural encounter between medieval Arabs and Chinese, "the presence or absence of writing" was not a crucial cultural difference between Muslims and Chinese. Nor was it, as attested by al-Tajir and other medieval Muslim travelers, an "important" let alone "*the* most important element" in the medieval situation of the two "lettered" cultures as it was the case with the European-American "situation," at least as delineated by Todorov (*The Conquest of America*, 160).

Along the same lines, despite its brevity, al-Tajir's account of Chinese justice is particularly remarkable. Not only does the Muslim traveler notice with admiration the absence of bureaucracy, but he also speaks with awe of the Chinese *al-dara*: "Every town has a thing called *al-dara*. This is a bell placed near [lit. 'at the head of'] the ruler of the town and is tied to a cord stretching as far as the road for the [benefit] of the common people" (S. M. Ahmad, *Arabic Classical Accounts of India and China*, 49). If a person is wronged by another person, he/she shakes the cord that is linked to *al-dara*. When doing so, al-Tajir observes, "the bell near the ruler starts ringing. So he [the wronged] is allowed to enter [the palace] to relate personally what the matter is and to explain the wrong done to him" (49). The result of this medieval Chinese "wonder" was the amazing accessibility of the public to the political and judicial hierarchy. In medieval China, it seems, injustice was panoptically controlled and justice was impressively disseminated. This conjures up the modern theory of panopticism. Whereas modern states, as understood by Louis Althusser and Michel Foucault, function through this panoptical controlling of their citizens, the medieval Chinese state, to the surprise of all, used panopticism to repress injustice. Not found even in the most democratic of modern societies, the Chinese *al-dara*, it appears, is a more utopian wor(l)d.

Al-Tajir was also very much interested in Chinese political institutions, for he seems to have been convinced that such a successful government, dealing with its subjects with impressive justice and providing them with numerous economic and social services, must have behind it a very effective political system. This can be inferred from the numerous passages he devotes to the political hierarchy, especially that of the emperor and the regional *muluk* (kings). Among the reasons that lay behind the success of the Chinese political system was the age of the regional governors. "Among them," he says, "no one becomes a ruler unless he is forty years of age, for they say that [at this age] a person becomes mature due to his experiences" (48). Even more interesting are discipline, judicial accountability, discretion, financial transparency, and healthy diets. "The king does not sit [in session] to mete out justice," al-Tajir notes, "unless he eats and drinks beforehand, so that he may not commit an error" (48). These excellent governing qualities of the Chinese in addition to other natural qualities made the China visited by al-Tajir, especially when compared to India, not only a thriving but also a pleasant and healthy place to be. "China is more pleasant and beautiful than India. In most parts of India there are no towns, while the Chinese have large fortified cities everywhere. China is healthier, has few diseases and is most pleasant climatically" (57). It is no accident, therefore, that in this (at least in worldly terms) ideal medieval country "one cannot find a blind or one-eyed person there nor anyone suffering from a disease, but these are found in large numbers in India" (57). Perhaps knowing that al-Tajir was describing the China of the Tang dynasty (618–906), hailed by Herbert Gowen in *An Outline History of China* as "the most power-ful, and the most economically and culturally developed empire in the world" (111), justifies al-Tajir's fascination.[34]

In this medieval "Chinatopia," socialism was a royal matter. "Wherever there is a rise in prices," al-Tajir observes, "the king releases food [food grains] from his stores and sells it at a rate cheaper than the current prices in the market" (S. M. Ahmad, *Arabic Classical Accounts of India and China*, 49). Likewise, al-Tajir was impressed by the free health services the Chinese authorities provided to the poor. "If a person is poor," al-Tajir informs us, "he is given the price of the medicine from the treasury" (52). Even more "modern" is the financial assistance enjoyed by aged persons who receive pensions from the treasury. These pensions are provided from the taxes aged people used to pay when they were active in the work-force. Indeed, al-Tajir notes with accuracy that although the government does not impose any taxes on lands and other private properties, from the age of 18 to 80 all working men provide the treasury with a percentage proportional to what they earn. When they reach the age of 80, in turn, the government is obliged to pay them back and provide for their living. Behind this modern social pension lies the government's firm belief in justice and equity; as al-Tajir puts it, "They say: we took from him when he was a youth, and we pay him a salary when he is old" (52).

In addition to these taxes, the rich and equitably managed treasury of the Chinese government relies heavily on the revenues of a wondrous herb the Chinese produce abundantly and transform into China's most popular and most expensive drink. This herb, according al-Tajir, is "leafier than

green trefoil and slightly more perfumed, and has a soury taste." In order
to transform it into drink, the Chinese "boil water and then sprinkle the
leaves over it." This hot drink, which the Chinese take as a cure for many
diseases, "is called *al-sakh*" (56). Such is al-Tajir's description of China's
universally valued tea. This passage about tea not only makes him the
first Muslim traveler to mention tea in his account, but it also proves the
authenticity of his account of China. This is in stark contrast to Marco
Polo, whose omission of tea, among other things, has led many people to
question the veracity of the latter's visit to China.

Finally, al-Tajir's description of the Andaman Islands may be the most
inviting passage in the entire *Akhbar al-Sin wa-l-Hind*. This is especially
true in relation to this book's aspiration to revisit some of the essentialist views of a number of postcolonial theorists and their dismissal of
traditions and discourses of Otherness in medieval Arabic literature and
culture. As we shall see, al-Tajir's description of the island and its inhabitants conjures up *Robinson Crusoe* (1719) and other Western narratives of
encounters with non-Europeans especially during the height of colonialism. The specific passage runs as follows:

> On the other side of these [islands] there are two islands, and between them
> there is the sea. They are called Andaman. Their inhabitants are cannibals.
> They are black with curly hair, and have ugly faces and eyes and long legs.
> Each one had pudenda, that is to say, his penis, nearly a cubit long; and
> they are naked. They have no canoes, and if they had them, they would
> have eaten up anyone passing by them. Sometimes it so happens that the
> boats slow down, and their speed is retarded due to the [strong] wind. The
> drinking water in the boats gets used up; and so they [sailors] approach
> these [islands] and refill the water. Hence, sometimes they [the cannibals]
> capture some of them [the sailors], but most of them escape. (36)

One is stunned not only by al-Tajir's, or probably his editor al-Sirafi's,
"scientific" confirmation of the cannibalistic activities of these *hamaj*
(uncivilized/barbarian) islanders, but also by his implicit equation
between their barbarism/cannibalism, their presumed *qubh* (ugliness),
and their manifest *sawad* (blackness).[35]

Indeed, the islands are there, the "cannibals/Calibans" are there, the
gaze of power and the power of gaze are there, but it is obvious that
al-Tajir's report of this human *mirabilia* ("wonders") is rather from his
"innocent" interest in and fascination with the marvelous and the unfamiliar. Evidently, many postcolonial readers may legitimately see in this
excerpt a textual proof that betrays not only al-Tajir's Orientalist/colo-
nialist discourse but also a medieval Muslim Orientalism/colonialism.
Although none can impose a single interpretation upon literary texts,

it seems that al-Tajir in the quoted passage is too "innocent" to be an Orientalist/colonialist. Perhaps, one should direct some of this textual "innocence" toward the assessment of a number of Westerners who have described the East.

The obvious example is Marco Polo himself. Like al-Tajir and his editor/coauthor al-Sirafi, in his description of the Andamans "as cruel cannibals who liked their strangers raw and highly spiced," Polo—or perhaps Rustichello of Pisa, his own editor/coauthor—was keenly interested in the "grandsimes mervoilles et les grant *diversités*" of the East in "innocently" embracing his own culture's "topography of wonder" (Daston and Park, *Wonders and the Orders of Things*, 34). In contrast to al-Tajir and al-Sirafi's description of the cannibalism of some Eastern/ African races, Polo and Rustichello "were more taken by the monstrosity of the mythical dog-headed Cynocephali that were "among the most widely discussed and variously described of the exotic human races" (31).

It seems evident, therefore, that *Akhbar al-Sin wa-l-Hind* illustrates a cultural relativism that foreshadows, for instance, Montaigne's *Essais*. Apart from his repulsion at what he deemed un-Islamic rituals, lack or rather imperfection in matters of cleanliness, un-halal meat, and widespread and legalized heterosexual and homosexual prostitution, al-Tajir find no reason not to extol many of the cultural, political, economic, and social achievements of those "infidels" he met. In general, al-Tajir does not make any use of suffixed formulae such as *la'anahum allah* (may God curse them) or *dammarahum allah* (may God destroy them), a common practice in Muslim writings about *al-rum* (Byzantines) and *al-ifranj* (Franks) during the hostile times of the pre-Crusades, as we shall see in the last chapter. This makes more ideological sense when one remembers the Quranic injunction to Muslims to favor *ahl al-kitab* (the People of the Book) over the *mushrikīn* (polytheists) of China and India. "On est surpris, du reste," André Miquel writes, "que rien dans ces voyages n'atteste le sentiment d'une dégradation des choses et des êtres à mesure qu'on s'éloigne du centre vivant du monde et de la foi vers les terres mystérieuses de l'infidélité" (*La géographie humaine*, 73). In many other instances, the "Orient of the Orient" served as a space of sociopolitical self-criticism and cultural experimentalism.

As briefly mentioned in the introduction, there is another theory, contrary to the monolithic impression of modern postcolonial theories of Orientalism, which have not only limited the complex relations between East and West to the latter's colonialist ambitions in the lands of the Other but have also forgotten that every Self has its own Other and that every literature has its own alterity. Throughout Islam's classical age of discovery and expansion evocative of Europe in early modern times, the

Orient had its own Orient but not, it seems to me, its own Orientalism in the essentialist Saidian sense. Nowhere is this better exemplified than in the various accounts of India and China especially during the golden age of the Abbasids. Although none can deny the fact that this interest was in many ways instigated, perpetuated, consolidated, and driven by religious propaganda, territorial expansion, economic interest, or political endorsement, not every Muslim in the age of expansion who wrote about the Orient's own Orient was supremacist, colonialist, or racist. The interest is more related, perhaps, to the centrality of the literary and cultural leitmotif of *al-ʿajib/al-gharib* in medieval and early modern Arabic travel literature.

Of course, one could challenge this seemingly innocent Arabic tradition of *al-ʿajib/al-gharib* through applying, for instance, Stephen Greenblatt's deconstructive critique of the poetics and politics of wonder in *Marvelous Possessions*. Greenblatt probes the "cultural poetics" of what has generally perceived as a mere human emotion (i.e., wonder). This is particularly true of his exploration of the cultural and discursive (in the Foucauldian sense) foundations of wonder as illustrated by the European encounter with the New World—especially as exemplified by Cortes's encounter, contact, and military clash with the Aztecs (128). Wonder, Greenblatt argues, was an indispensable stage in the "othering" of the Other, for it subverts and ultimately contains all possible spaces of "sameness" in that very Other. Indeed, it is the discursive response of the "same" that overwhelms the emotions of wonder. By conjuring up his/her "sameness," the intruder, explorer, or traveler sets a boundary between "self" and "Other" (128). Such a "cultural" boundary would certainly construct the possible space for what Mary Louise Pratt has aptly termed in her book *Imperial Eyes: Travel Writing and Transculturation* (1992) as "contact zone" (6).[36] In Greenblatt's view, this "contact zone," however successful in setting a space of cultural exchange, fails in the end to destroy the "red lines" that protect the "self" from the different "Other" (*Marvelous Possessions*, 128). Greenblatt goes on to assert that wonder was crucial in the ultimate "dispossessing" of the natives by a possessive/ing Other. The latter comes to the shores, intrudes into native territory, meets the native, and wonders at his/her appearance, habits, speech, and so forth. Through an "imperialist" consciousness and unconsciousness of the "self," the intruder confers his/her "sameness," intrudes into the difference of the native, differs in a Derridean sense, and infers through "descriptions judgments, and actions" (135) his/her Otherness. Fortunately, Greenblatt has somewhat questioned his own essentialism when he exempts figures such as Herodotus, Jean de Léry, Montaigne, and Mandeville from the artful maneuver of the experience of wonder for colonial appropriation and consolidation. These authors, Greenblatt concludes, found in the experience of wonder a vehicle for cultural relativism and understanding.

Perhaps it is no exaggeration to suggest that had Greenblatt been familiar with the Arab Islamic tradition of wonder in cultural encounters, the list of exemptions would have been longer. Otherwise, one would be likely to concur with Nabil Matar's position, however debatable it may appear to some, on the theoretical ineffectiveness of some Western theorists when applied to the Arabic tradition. "The Arabic travel accounts cannot therefore be approached through the theoretical models," Matar writes, "with which European accounts have been studied by writers as different as Stephen Greenblatt, Edward Said, and Gayatri Spivak. They belong to a tradition that is different not only in its history but epistemology" (*In the Lands of the Christians*, xxxii).

In sum, in addition to showing that medieval Muslims were not uninterested in the non-Muslim Other, my main objective in referring to the "Oriental theme" in medieval Arabic *adab al-rihla* (travel writings) is to question, if not challenge, the postcolonial equation of travel literature and the traveler's gaze with dominant discourses of power such as Orientalism and colonialism. Cultural Othering is one way, among many, of constructing self-definition and self-identification. Cultural encounters between different humans in different contexts, however, are too complex a phenomenon to be "essentialized" in restrictive Western theoretical models, let alone through a set of binary opposites—Self/Other, civilized/barbaric, white/black, West/East, and so forth. Islam's encounter with its own Orient challenge not only such essentialism but also, as I hope to show in the following chapters, its own medieval encounter with Europe and the Euro-Christians, a subject that has been neglected in the ongoing and heated debate about relations between Islam and the West. Medieval Muslims were not interested solely in the Far East; through a number of textual and physical journeys, many medieval Muslim writers, geo-cosmographers, travelers, envoys, and captives from the Mashriq and the Maghrib with their curious pens and inquiring eyes ventured into different parts of medieval Europe as well and left us with extraordinary accounts of what they saw and experienced.

CHAPTER 2

EUROPEAN BARBARITY AND CIVILIZATION
IN SOME MEDIEVAL ARABIC GEOGRAPHICAL
SOURCES: AL-MAS'UDI AND AL-BAKRI
AS TWO CASE STUDIES

Earliest References to *Urufa* (Europe) in
Medieval Arabic Sources: Brief Survey

It has been widely accepted that medieval Muslims produced a massive corpus of geographical literature, much of which has not yet been comprehensively explored (Heinen, "Geographical Investigations under the Guidance of Islam," 459). In addition to the purely religious factors that contributed to the early growth and subsequent flourishing of medieval Islamic geography, there were unquestionably several other worldly incentives.[1] As previously noted, the vigorous policy of the caliphs of mapping their dominions and extending their territories east and west of *dar al-islam* had important ramifications, as evidenced by the production mainly by the Balkhi school of geographers of the *Atlas Islamicus*. This designates the body of geographical scholarship dealing with *al-masalik* (routes) and *al-mamalik* (kingdoms) and that, in many ways, culminated in numerous works entitled *Kitab al-Masalik wa-l-Mamalik* (Book of Routes and Kingdoms) and *Kitab al-Buldan* (Book of Countries). Although focused primarily on the world of Islam, these works "introduced the concept of a country as a geographical unit and enlarged the scope of their science with elements of 'human geography,' discussing the languages and races of peoples, their occupations, customs, and religions" (Tolmacheva, "Geography," 286).[2]

What is perhaps of more interest to the present study is the development of Islamic cartography and the ensuing promulgation of conceptions and descriptions of the earth, with certainly strong Greek—and to a lesser extent Roman, Phoenician, Persian, Indian, and even pre-Islamic Arabian and Mesopotamian—influences (Karamustafa, "Introduction to Islamic Maps," 4). Of significant value are multiple works that bear the title of *Surat al-Ardh* (Picture or Description of the Earth) or, as was more common with some, *Suwar al-Aqalim* (Picture or Description of the Climes) or *Sifat al-Dunya* (The Form of the World).[3] Ibn Hawqal's and al-Khwarizmi's influential pioneering works have been singled out in this context. "In general, the term *surat al-ardh*," Nazmi explains, "refers to an approach in which data dealing with cosmography and geography together is being gathered" (*Muslim Geographical Image*, 88). As demonstrated by Karen Pinto, these works usually begin "with a brief description of the world, and theories about it—such as the inhabited versus the uninhabited parts, the reasons why people are darker in the south than in the north, and so on" ("Cartography," 139).[4] On this significant era in the history of medieval Muslim geography, Emmanuelle Tixier du Mesnil's "Panorama de la Géographie Arabe médiévale" (2010) is indeed worth quoting in French:

> Les descriptions du seul *dâr-al-islâm*, caractéristiques du genre *masâlik wa-l-mamâlik* du Xe siècle, laissent alors place à des fresques plus vastes encore, renouant avec la description de l'ensemble du monde habité. La géographie califale, qui ne s'intéressait qu'au monde musulman, principalement en sa partie orientale, et qui ravalait les autres contrées au rang de simples marges, disparaît. (26)

It is primarily through the aforementioned works that several Greek concepts, such as *al-qism al-ma'mur* (the inhabited part) versus *al-qism al-ghayr ma'mur* (the uninhabited part) and the ensuing popular theory of *al-aqalim al-sab'a* (the seven zones or climes), entered into the broader medieval Arabic-Islamic conceptions of the world. Related to this is the fact that many of the concerned geo-cosmographers in their exploration of *taqsim al-ardh* (the division of the world) and *tasnif al-umam* (classification of nations), and owing to their fascination with human and cultural geography, began to exhibit an enormous interest in non-Muslim peoples who lived outside their own geographical zones. This was suggestive not only of their interest in the "Orient" or, say, *bilad al-zinj* (black Africa) but also, as we will see, of their efforts to know about and study non-Muslim peoples who lived west and north of *dar al-islam* in what was called *urufa*, *arufa*, or *urufi* especially as found in the less commonly used, but unquestionably familiar, division of the inhabited part of the world into three and perhaps more frequently four parts or continents (al-Kilani, *Surat Uruba Inda al-'Arab fi-l-'Asr al-Wasit*, 96).

Generally speaking, the first reference to *urufa*, *arufa*, or *urufi* (Europe) in medieval Arabic writing dates back to the ninth century (Miquel, *La géographie humaine*, 257). Indeed, the term passed into Arabic, along with many other Greek geo-cosmographical concepts and vocabulary—including the word *jughrafiya* itself. As aptly demonstrated by a growing number of scholars, geo-cosmographers such as al-Khwarizmi (d. 847), Ibn Khordadbeh (d. 885), Ibn al-Faqih (d. 903), al-Yaʿqubi (d. 905), Ibn Rusta (d. 912), and the anonymous Persian author of *Hudud al-ʿAlam* (The Regions of the World) inherited from the Greeks the idea that Europe represented one of the habitable continents of the world (ibid., 275). This is true of both their tripartite and quadripartite division of the world—into three continents (i.e., Asia, Europe, and Libya) or into four continents (i.e., Europe, Libya, Ethiopia, and Scythia), remarkably changed to *urufa* (Europe), *lubiya* (Libya), *atiufia* (Eastern Asia), and finally *asqutia* (Asia Minor).[5] For the former, Europe is always pictured as sharing with Asia nearly half the inhabited space, whereas Libya (i.e., Africa) is represented as occupying the entire remaining half. For the latter, especially as initiated by Ibn Khordadbeh and later best explained in *Nuzhat al-Qulub* by al-Mustawfi (d. 1340), the habitable part of the earth was divided into two longitudinal sections beginning from Egypt. The western section is in turn divided by the Mediterranean Sea into south and north. The northern part represents Europe, and the southern part makes up Libya (Africa). The eastern section forms Asia, which is also "halved into Asia minor and Asia Major by a line going from the northeast down to halfway along the southern side" (Nazmi, *Muslim Geographical Image*, 141).

It must be said that in both divisions, Europe is often conceived as including not only al-Andalus (Muslim Spain), the adjacent lands of the Galicians and the Basques, the Franks, and *al-rum* (Romans and Byzantines) but also the lands of the Slavs, the Bulghars, the Rus, and many other eastern European regions (al-Kilani, *Surat Uruba Inda al-ʿArab fi-l-ʿAsr al-Wasit*, 96).[6] According to Nazmi and others, Europe in both divisions "has in its east the Straits of Constantinople, in its south the Sea of Rum, in its west the western ocean, and in its north the limit of the cultivated world" (*Muslim Geographical Image*, 142). In support of the overall thesis of this study, Nazmi states,

> Bernard Lewis maintains that Muslim writers of history and geography knew nothing of the names that Europeans (including of course the Greeks) had given the continents as a system of division of the world. To the contrary, the Muslim view of the world during the first centuries of the Islamic era was influenced by many different cultural trends. The notion of dividing the world into mainlands or continents was also known to most Muslim writers of geography. (141–142)

It is all remarkable, therefore, that in the earliest descriptions of Europe, medieval Muslim geographers were largely satisfied with their reliance on Ptolemy's *Geography*, especially as adapted by al-Khwarizmi.[7] As Hanna E. Kassis explained, this was in part the result of the fact that these scholars were writing before the availability of the Arabic translation of Paulus Orosius's *Historiarum adversus paganos libri septem* ("The Depiction of Europe in Medieval Arabic Sources," 10).[8] Indeed, as strongly argued by Hussein Munis in his classic *Tarikh al-Jughrafiya wa-l-Jughrafiyyin fi-l-Andalus* (The History of Geography and Geographers in Muslim Spain), medieval Muslim cosmo-geographers, especially those of al-Andalus, in their early accounts of Europe owed no less to Hurushiyush (that is, Orosius) than they did to Btalimus (Arabic for Ptolemy).

In Munis's view, the translation of Paulus Orosius into Arabic in al-Andalus was one of most important events in the history of medieval Muslim perceptions of Europe. This event, as Munis explains, was the outcome of a diplomatic exchange of presents between the caliph of Cordoba 'Abd al-Rahman III (d. 961) and the Byzantine emperor Romanus II (d. 963) (40). Based mainly on the account of the noted Andalusian physician and medical historian Ibn Juljul (d. 994),[9] chroniclers such as Ibn Abi Usaybi'a and Ibn Khaldun confirm that among the gifts received by caliph 'Abd al-Rahman were a copy of Dioscorides's *Materia Medica* and, more important for our purposes, a copy of Orosius's Latin magnum opus (Penelas, "A Possible Author of the Arabic Translation of Orosius' Historiae," 2). As indicated by Munis, the book had to await the succession of al-Hakam II (961–976) to be translated into Arabic as *Tarikh al-'Alam*—that is, *History of the World* (Kassis, "The Depiction of Europe," 21) or *Kitab Hurushiyush* (The Book of Orosius). Although scholars have differed on the first translator(s) of this book, most agree that Qasim ibn Isbagh must have contributed enormously by directing the translation process and editing the Arabic translation (Munis, *Tarikh al-Jughrafiya wa-l-Jughrafiyyin fi-l-Andalus*, 40).[10]

With the completion of the translation of the *Historiarum*, medieval Muslims, according to Munis, began to know more and more about Europe and the Europeans. This is not surprising since, as pointed out by Irmeli Valtonen—albeit in the context of its translation into Old English during the reign of King Alfred the Great (871–899)—the *Historiarum* "is preceded by a geographical introduction to the known world, which became popular material for later authors to copy or adapt throughout the Middle Ages" (*The North in the "Old English Orosius*," 2). Coincidentally enough, Valtonen's statement is equally suggestive of many medieval Muslim scholars. Indeed, as advocated by Kassis, his translation of Orosius's *Historiarum* into Arabic nearly a century after it was translated into Old English led succeeding Muslim geographers and historians "to echo the same type of information about Europe" ("The Depiction of Europe," 10). Yet as Munis has acknowledged, several Andalusian geographers had exceeded the scope of Orosius just as their colleagues of the Muslim East had in several respects exceeded the scope of Ptolemy (*Tarikh al-Jughrafiya wa-l-Jughrafiyyin fi-l-Andalus*, 42).[11] This is particularly conspicuous in their exploration of "the unknown aspects of human geography of medieval Europe especially by studying medieval Europe's customs, peoples, geographical features, languages, industries, and trade" (42).

To support his view, Munis cites the example of the Andalusian cosmographer al-Razi (d. 973) by comparing his depiction of Spain to that of Orosius. Whereas the latter, in the eyes of Munis, stops at mentioning the borders of Spain and its towns, al-Razi includes a very long introduction on the general geography of the peninsula and engages in a detailed description of its towns, its rivers, and its mountains.[12] Al-Razi, Munis notes, went so far as to speak about the different religious denominations that characterized each town. Another Andalusian scholar by the name of al-ʿUdhri (d. 1085) expands on al-Razi and focuses on aspects of life as varied as agriculture, irrigation systems, taxing, trade, and a number of sociocultural practices of al-Andalus. These two scholars ushered in the rise of medieval Andalusian human geography, which reached its zenith mainly with al-Bakri (d. 1094) and al-Idrissi (d. 1154).

On another note, as explained by A. Samarrai, the earliest interest by Muslims in medieval Europe was largely political. In his opinion, this interest began with their particular references to certain eastern European kings. Ibn Khordadbeh, for instance—who is among the earliest Arabic authors to refer in his writings to western European nations in "On the Kings of the World" in *Al-Masalik wa-l-Mamalik*—while speaking quite accurately of the Khaqan of the Khazars, the Basileus of the Romans, the Kniaz of the Slavs, and the chieftains of the Turks, did not seem to care about either the Franks or the Lombards of Italy. This led Samarrai to argue that for mostly economic reasons, medieval Muslim geographers, at least in the beginning, cared more about eastern Europe. In spite of their military enterprises and diplomatic activities in western Europe during the Umayyad and Abbasid reigns, decades after the conquest of Spain, discussion of the latter was still scarce in comparison to their interest in some eastern European nations ("Some Geographical and Political Information on Western Europe in the Medieval Arabic Sources," 317).

This is best exemplified by the differing nomenclatures for the Mediterranean Sea (317). In early medieval Muslim geographical writing, Samarrai tells us, there was much said about this sea, which medieval Arabs used to describe in different suggestive ways. Although they most commonly and significantly used to call it *bahr al-rum* (the Roman Sea), others named it *bahr al-maghrib* (the Western Sea). Still others, it appears, seemed to "arabize" it and preferred either *al-bahr al-shami* (the Syrian Sea) or *al-bahr al-misri* (the Egyptian Sea). As Nazmi stated,

> Of all the above-mentioned names, the Sea of Rum from an early date was the name most in use to denote the Mediterranean Sea. It has always been regarded by Muslim geographers as one of the main seas in the inhabited quarter…Muslims often pictured the Mediterranean Sea as a large sea with many gulfs branching out of it. Usually they described the Mediterranean Sea from the west to east or from *as-Sus al-Aqsa* (western Morocco) to the Syrian coast. The northern coast was usually named *Bilad ar-Rum* or the countries of the Christians (among them the coast of Asia Minor). (*Muslim Geographical Image*, 222)

In this regard, certain Muslim geographers in their writings used to connect the Mediterranean Sea with *bahr al-dhalam* (the Sea of Darkness), the appellation most suggestive of the Atlantic Ocean. This in turn led some of them to hint at the possibility of navigating westward and northward across the Atlantic Sea (Samarrai, "Some Geographical and Political Information," 317).[13]

This brief historical introduction is important in several respects, above all because it provides an overall summary of the earliest references to Europe in medieval Arabic sources. It also quickly traces back to the Greek, and to a lesser degree Roman, concepts of the cosmos, which proved to be significant in fashioning the medieval Arabic-Islamic nonreligious worldview and in furnishing several of the stereotypes that existed in medieval Arabic writing on some European peoples. Some of these peoples have recently been singled out in a number of studies that have, directly or indirectly, dealt with the complex subject of the views and perceptions of Europe and Europeans in Arabic writing. This is especially true of the Iraqi al-Mas'udi and the Andalusian al-Bakri, to be discussed later, who left to posterity two of the richest accounts of medieval Europe and Europeans in the corpus of Arabic geo-cosmographical literature.

Transcending the Stereotypes: The Barbarian *Ahl al-Shamal* (People of the North) versus the Civilized *Ifranj* (Franks) in al-Mas'udi's Account of Medieval Europe

Not only was al-Mas'udi among the first Arab Muslim geo-cosmographers to cast a curious eye on a wide variety of non-Muslim peoples east and south of *dar al-islam*, but he was unmistakably among the earliest to

venture textually into the lands and minds of ancient and (more importantly for our study) medieval European *ajnas* (peoples), ranging from
the ancient Greeks to the Lombards of medieval Italy. As we have seen,
this should not be surprising given al-Mas'udi's impressive travels and
his lifelong interest in knowing about foreign cultures and distant lands.
As his two most famous surviving geo-cosmographical works—*Muruj
al-Dhahab wa Ma'adin al-Jawhar* (The Meadows of Gold and Mines of
Gems) and *Al-Tanbih wa-l-Ishraf* (Warning and Supervision), hereafter
Al-Muruj and *Al-Tanbih*—clearly reveal, medieval Europe, all its shortcomings aside, appears in a positive light in his overall exploration of
the inhabited world. In fact, in spite of the controversy surrounding his
increasingly misquoted passage on *ahl al-shamal* (people of the North),
al-Mas'udi left behind a remarkably rich record of medieval Europe that
is essential for the overall exploration of the representation of Europeans
in medieval Arabic geo-cosmographical writing.

Alavi and others have shown that although al-Mas'udi in his exploration of human geography acknowledged several purely natural factors,
such as "the availability of water, natural vegetation and topography"
(*Arab Geography in the Ninth and Tenth Centuries*, 53), he ultimately
adopted, and sometimes culturally adapted, a number of classical Greek
deterministic theories that strongly influenced his presentation of the
world and its peoples. This is especially true of his infatuation with what
John Hunwick has termed "the climatization of the known world and the
relationship of climate to intelligence" ("A Region of the Mind," 108).
Indeed, in keeping mostly with Ptolemaic ideas, al-Mas'udi divided
the world into a *qism ma'mur* (inhabited part) and a *qism ghayr ma'mur*
(uninhabited part). Borrowing Greek concepts verbatim, he accordingly
divided the inhabited world into *sab'a aqalim* (seven latitudinal zones
or climes).[14] These seven latitudinal zones "began slightly north of the
equator and ended in the realms of perpetual darkness in the north"
(al-Azmeh, "Barbarians in Arab Eyes," 3). Al-Mas'udi was also interested
in marking differences in *tiba' al-bashar* (human character), *lawn al-bashara*
(skin color), *al-lugha* (language), and *al-din* (religion), as well as *harakat
al-nujum* (movements of the stars), *al-abraj* (zodiacs), and other astral or
planetary influences, the detailed exploration of which goes beyond the
scope of this study.

Perhaps more essential to our purposes is the fact that al-Mas'udi
emphasized the determining role of the climate in shaping the attributes
of humans and in the classification of nations.[15] As Thabit Abdullah has
indicated in "Arab Views of Northern Europeans in Medieval History
and Geography" (1996), al-Mas'udi was one of the medieval Arab geographers who believed that the climate "was the primary determinant of

human characteristics" (74). In keeping with this "widely held belief" (74), al-Mas'udi was of the opinion that *al-hadhara* (civilization) cannot be produced outside *al-aqalim al-mu'tadila*, that is to say outside the temperate zones. Thus, the first and seventh zones, universally described by classical geo-cosmographers as being extreme either in *al-harara* (heat) or *al-buruda* (cold), are not suitable for civilization. Both zones are equally remote from *al-i'tidal* (temperance), the sine qua non not only for the cultivation of decent, if not perfect, human behavior but also for the production of (human) civilization (al-Kilani, *Surat Uruba Inda al-'Arab fi-l-'Asr al-Wasit*, 94).

This *i'tidal* is descriptive of *al-aqalim al-wusta* (the central climes) represented in *al-iqlim al-thalith* (the third clime) and perfectly in *al-iqlim al-raba'* (the fourth clime). These third and fourth climes encompass Greece and other Mediterranean lands, many of which became part and parcel of *dar al-islam*. They also include Persia, parts of China, parts of India, and, by ideological association, the extremely hot Arabia and Iraq—the latter made temperate through the tempering nature of the surrounding seas and great rivers dominant in the natural geography of the Arabian Peninsula and especially Iraq, perhaps more suggestively described as *bilad al-rafidayn*, or the country of the two rivers.

Amid al-Mas'udi's ideological manipulation of Greek climatic and deterministic theories, the politically tempering effect of the Tigris and Euphrates is conceived to be more powerful than the "Islamically" tempering effect of the sacred Arabian seas.[16] Indeed, in the cosmological view of al-Mas'udi, as well as for most Abbasid scholars, it was ultimately caliphal Baghdad, not Mecca or Medina or even Jerusalem, that was viewed as *surrat al-ardh wa qalbuha*, that is, (literally and suggestively) the navel of the earth and its heart (*Al-Muruj*, 36).[17] Thus, it is easy to surmise why al-Mas'udi would consume much time and effort in proudly cataloging the virtues of the fourth clime and, above all, in arguing vigorously in favor of the superiority of his homeland in nearly every single aspect: his people's religion, intellect, manners, and skin color; his homeland's history, culture, waters, rivers, weather, soil, air, fauna, and flora (*Al-Tanbih*, 33–44, and *Al-Muruj*, 36–39).[18] Al-Mas'udi's introductory statement on the fourth clime of *Al-Tanbih* is worth quoting in this regard:

> Now, we shall mention the fourth clime, show its superiority over the remaining climes, and speak of its majestic location and honorable status. Let one remember that it is the place of our birth and our growth and, therefore, it is incumbent upon us to publicize it and demonstrate its merits and qualities—although this is an undeniable truth which does not need too much discussion and the fact is that there is no book that can fully entail its virtues! (33; translation mine)

What is perhaps more pertinent to the main topic of this study is the fact that, in the seven-clime division of the *oecumene*, most of medieval Europe belonged to the fifth and the sixth climes described by al-Mas'udi and others, to include Byzantium, the Land of the Franks, the land of Rome (Italy), Spain, the southern parts of the lands of the Slavs, and other southern and central European regions. As for the seventh clime, it included the remotest northernmost parts of the lands of Slavs and Bulghars, the land of Rus, Scandinavia, and other adjacent regions. For al-Mas'udi and others, the northern borders of the seventh clime represent the end of the inhabited world and accordingly mark the outer border of human civilization. It is called *ardh al-shamal* (the land of the North) and, perhaps more suggestively, *ardh al-dhalam*—that is, the land of darkness, where, apart from *ahl al-shamal* (the people of the North), civilized humans cannot survive.

In this regard, in another short passage of *Al-Tanbih*, while explaining the influence of the climate on human character—based on the less common quadripartite division—al-Mas'udi compared the four quadrants of the earth: East-West and South-North. Briefly speaking about the latter (although quite confoundedly mentioning the lands of the Franks and the Slavs, in addition to other northern regions), he asserted that the extreme cold, the abundance of snow, and especially the scarcity of sunlight affected enormously the people living in this northern quadrant. This, he explains, manifested itself in several physical and linguistic *naqa'is* (defects) such as lack of humor, largeness of bodies, extreme skin whiteness, heaviness of tongue, coarseness of language, and lack of firmness in matters of religious beliefs (33). He ends the passage by concluding that the farther people settled in the extreme north of the northern quadrant—in reference to *ahl al-shamal*—the more stupid, harsh, and barbarian they become (34).

Al-Mas'udi's speculations on the northern quadrant have been the *locus classicus* of a plethora of recent studies by scholars from different academic backgrounds and interests. In addition to Bernard Lewis, one can cite Dinesh D'souza, Mona Naggar, and even Carole Hillenbrand.[19]

While briefly discussing the issue of racism in Arabic-Islamic culture and literature in *The End of Racism: Principles for a Multiracial Society* (1995), D'souza finds no more compelling textual evidence to epitomize classical Islam's racism and xenophobia than al-Mas'udi's aforementioned passage. Predictably enough, D'souza goes on to affirm that Arab-Muslim thinkers, as typified by al-Mas'udi, universally "found the Franks and Slavs of Europe to be the ultimate barbarians" (112). Quoting that very same passage from al-Mas'udi, Mona Naggar echoes D'souza in her article "The Barbarians of the North: Venturing into the Darkness of Europe" (2005) as follows: "Thus describes Arab historian and geographer al-Mas'udi the inhabitants of Europe—more precisely, the Slavs, Francs and their neighbors" (1).

Perhaps most surprising of all is Carole Hillenbrand's decision to cite the passage in the section entitled "Muslim Stereotypes of the Franks: The Formation of an Image before the Crusades" of her otherwise extremely insightful book *The Crusades: Islamic Perspectives* (2000). Hillenbrand included a brief statement made by al-Mas'udi on the origin and courage of the *ifranja* (the Franks), which we will return to later, just to draw to our attention that "al-Mas'udi goes on to describe the land of the Franks as follows" (270). She then directly quoted the entire passage, but to one's utmost surprise without including the concluding statement I mentioned earlier—actually as did D'souza and Naggar. Hillenbrand commented on the (incomplete) quotation by stating,

> The above account emphasizes the excessive cold and dampness of the clime within which the Franks reside: it is the climatic characteristics that render the inhabitants dull of understanding, gross of nature, lumbering in stature and coarse in manners. These negative qualities became rooted in the Muslim mind in relation to the Franks. Indeed, they reappear, for example, in a work on the categories of nations written in 1086 by a Muslim judge in Toledo, Sa'id ibn Ahmad. He describes the barbarians who live in the north (that is, Europe) as more like beasts than men. (270)

The plain fact is neither D'souza, Naggar, nor Hillenbrand have apparently examined or cited in detail the range of observations on Europe and Europeans found in al-Mas'udi's two major surviving works.[20] In neglecting to do so, D'souza, Naggar, and Hillenbrand have not only dramatically failed to show any understanding of the influences and complexities of al-Mas'udi's views on Europe and Europeans, but they have erroneously conveyed to their readers that this is what "haughty" medieval Muslims thought of Europe and Europeans.

It should be emphasized at this point that al-Mas'udi did not in any way relegate, let alone equate, the entire European continent to the realm of barbarism and lack of civilization. A review of his numerous references to the Franks and the Slavs, among other European peoples and nations, confirms this.[21] Samar Attar's "Conflicting Accounts on the Fear of Strangers: Muslim and Arab Perceptions of Europeans in Medieval Geographical Literature" (2005) is worth citing in this regard:

> It is true that some medievalist Arabs and Muslims have described certain Europeans as "beasts," or "*baha'im*," a description that Bernard Lewis likes

to quote whenever he talks about the attitude of Middle Easterners to Europeans...The truth lies somewhere else. One has to understand the context in which this word, "*baha'i*" has been used. The tone is not that of contempt, but rather of pity. The Arab geographers who used the term were faithful to their rationalist belief. Man has reason and is expected to use it, but not everyone does. The implicit distinction between "us" and "them," or the "self and the Other" in a variety of medieval Arabic texts expresses some bewilderment at God's work and the inability of man to explain everything in this universe. (26)

What must be recognized is that the term *al-ifranj* (Franks), especially in al-Mas'udi's writings, is not a stock term for medieval Europeans, and it does not relate in any way to the controversial *ahl al-shamal*. As Ahmad Shboul observes, "Earlier Arabic authors (and also later ones) usually apply the name *Ifranj* or *Ifranja* generally and often vaguely to all western Europeans. Al-Mas'udi, as a rule, clearly singles out the *Ifranja*, the Franks proper, as a nation distinct from other western European nations" (*Al-Mas'udi and His World*, 190). In *Al-Tanbih*, more-over, al-Mas'udi unequivocally places both the Franks and Slavs among the great civilized nations of the world. Indeed, in a rather lengthy section entitled *Dhikr al-Umam al-Sab'a al-Salifa wa-Lughatihim, wa Ara'ihim, wa Mawadhi'i Masakinihim wa-Ghayri Thalika*—which can be roughly, albeit suggestively, translated as "Mentioning the Seven Ancient Nations (Civilizations), Their Languages, Their Beliefs, Their Locations, and Other Characteristics"—he included the Franks and the Slavs in the third group of civilized nations, right after the Persians, the Assyrians, the Hebrews, and the Arabs (83). Perhaps Shboul's summary of the section is worth including:

> The seven nations, or rather groups of nations, are enumerated by al-Mas'udi in the following order: the Persians (al-Furs); the Chaldeans (al-Kaldaniyyun wa-hum al-Siraniyyun), under the heading al-Mas'udi includes also the Hebrews (al-'Ibraniyyun) and the Arabs; *al-Yunaniyyun, al-Rum, al-Saqaliba, al-Ifranja*, and other neighboring countries in the north, and the people of Lubya, including Egypt, and neighboring peoples in the south, and the land of *al-Maghrib* as far as the Atlantic Ocean; the Turkic peoples (*Ajnas al-Turk*); the peoples of India, the Indus valley and their neighbors (*Ajnas al-Hind wa' l-Sind wa ma ittasal bi dhalik*), the people of China, *al-Sila* (Korean peninsula) and other adjacent nations. (126)[22]

Strangely overlooked in the speculations of D'souza, Naggar, and Hillenbrand is the fact that al-Mas'udi, in his description of the terra incognita of *ahl al-shamal*, was essentially echoing Greco-Roman views of the *barbaroi* of the northernmost parts of Europe. Indeed, just preceding his lengthy discussion of the seven climes, al-Mas'udi drew attention to the differences of views regarding the circumference of the climes by referring to the ancient *hukama'*, a word commonly used by classical Arab Muslim cosmographers to refer to Greek and, to a lesser degree, Roman (Latin) and other ancient scholars.[23] Interestingly enough, he cited in name Ptolemy and praised his views, along with those of Marinus of Tyre, as the most convincing (*Al-Tanbih*, 33). Perhaps more telling is his reference to Ptolemy's view that *al-jazira al-ma'rufa bi thula*, that is, the Island of Thule, marks the northernmost limit of the North (35).

Thus, one should be left with no doubt that in the passage in question regarding *ahl al-shamal*, al-Mas'udi had in mind, say, the Hyperboreans and the Rhipaens of Ptolemy of the seventh clime and not the medieval Franks or Slavs, as claimed by the previous scholars. In other words, al-Mas'udi's representation of *ahl al-shamal* should be discussed first and foremost in relation to Europe's own ancient perceptions of the peoples of the North, the investigation of which goes beyond the scope of this book.[24] After all, there is nothing evincingly Islamic about the earlier passage on *ahl al-shamal* itself.

Drawing on all these aspects, it is important that we go beyond the controversial description of *ahl al-shamal* if we really want to arrive at a comprehensive picture of al-Mas'udi's views and perceptions of various medieval European peoples and nations. This is extremely imperative given that al-Mas'udi, as Kassis correctly stated, "had a definite influence on subsequent Arabic writers and on the image of Europe that they portrayed" ("The Depiction of Europe," 13). Such was no doubt true, for example, of his depiction of *al-saqaliba*, *al-ifranj*, *al-jalaliqa*, and *al-nukbard*, referring to the multiethnic Slavs, Franks, northern Spanish, and northern Italians.

Mention should be made from the outset that al-Mas'udi's account of *al-saqaliba* is among the most important of medieval Muslim writings about the Slavs and, understandably, has been highly regarded by Western medievalists and Slavists in particular. As Nazmi explains, "The originality of al-Mas'udi's work makes him the first Arab writer who gives us more information about the Slavic tribes of Central Europe and the Southern Slavs of the Balkans" (*Commercial Relations*, 83). Yet, like most of his contemporaries, he uses the word *al-saqaliba* to refer somewhat confusingly to various Slavic peoples.[25] This is clear from the title of his section on the Slavs in *Al-Muruj*, which appears as *Dhikr al-Saqaliba wa Masakiniha wa Akhbar Mulukiha wa Tafarruqi Ajnasiha*, that is, "On the Slavs, their lands, their kings, and their divisions into many races [nations]."

Al-Mas'udi, without explicitly proving or disproving the matter, begins his section on of the Slavs by briefly mentioning that that all Slavic peoples trace their genealogical ancestry back to Noah's son Japheth through the latter's son Mar (*Al-Muruj*, 4). He then added that this seems to be the view of many of *ahl al-diraya* (people of extreme knowledge), an expression that essentially refers to the scholars of Islam. In this particular context, however, since the information fits perfectly into what is known as *al-riwayat al-isra'iliyya* (Judeo-Christian narratives), he may likely be alluding to the religious scholars of Judaism and Christianity.[26] Despite their interest in relating races and nations to the three sons of Noah in conformity with dominant religious narratives, the majority of medieval Muslim cosmographers were not that excited about what Suzanne Conklin Akbari has described as the "standard distribution of the three continents among the sons of Noah" ("From Due East to True North: Orientalism and Orientation," 22).

Al-Mas'udi's second important insight into the Slavs was their geographical location. Although spare on details, he writes that the Slavs lived in the North, certainly referring to the northern quadrant. Given al-Mas'udi's division of the inhabited world into seven climes, it is for us to discern that most of the Slav lands are situated in the fifth and the sixth climes. This is clearly true with regard to southern and central Slavs, who, as al-Mas'udi affirms in a passage in *Al-Tanbih*, lived in great numbers in wide areas extending from the basin of the Danube to the banks of Dnieper and to "the other great rivers which spring from sources located in the north and flow into the Black Sea" (Nazmi, *Commercial Relations*, 83).

Al-Mas'udi gives us as well a brief account of a number of Slavic achievements. Speaking of their powerful kings, he tells us that many of them are strong and popular, priding themselves on possessing cultivated provinces and several bustling towns. In another section entitled *Muluk al-Saqaliba* ("kings of the Slavs"), he cites two of their most powerful kings: the first is called *malik al-dir*, that is, king of the Dir; the second is *malik al-awanj* or in some copies *malik al-ifraj*, that is, king of the Avandj or Ifraj (*Al-Muruj*, 4). Describing both kings, al-Mas'udi writes,

The first of the kings of the Slavs is that of the Dir, who has several large towns and rules over numerous dominions. Muslim merchants are used to travel to his capital town to engage in all kinds of trades. In addition to him, there is the king of the Avandj, who also has large towns and dominions and possess numerous military troops. He is always at war with the Byzantines, the Franks, the Lombards, and other neighboring nations. (4; translation mine)

Scholars have different views regarding the identity of the first powerful Slavic kingdom, identifying it either with the kingdom of White
Croatia and its capital Cracow or the kingdom of Askold around Kiev
(Nazmi, *Commercial Relations*, 84). Other scholars, such as Shboul, have
maintained that it is nearly impossible to identify it.[27] As for the second
kingdom, Shboul has argued that it could well be the Czech kingdom of
Bohemia (*Al-Mas'udi and His World*, 84).

It should be noted, however, that al-Mas'udi portrays medieval Slavs as
multiracial and multinational, despite their apparent shared genealogical
origin through the predominance of (Jacobite) Christianity and the unifying nomenclature (that is, the all-embracing term *Slav*). Having observed
that the Slavs "are made up of different tribes and nations," al-Mas'udi
quickly adds that it is beyond the scope of his book to probe into the
multifarious reasons that led to their numerous divisions (*Al-Muruj*, 5). In
passages shortly afterward, he points out that the Volonian king Majek
was once the king of all the Slavs, but only after a long period of political
unity and economic prosperity

> divisions overtook their diverse groups and resulted in the destruction of
> their unity and the emergence of various factions. Every faction decided
> to have its own dominion and ruler. This was the outcome of several rea-
> sons too many to mention here, especially that we have already explained
> several of them in our account of their kings in our book *The News of the
> Time*. (5; translation mine)

In fact, al-Mas'udi mentions with accuracy the names and achievements of
several influential Slavic tribes and nations, such as the *walyana*, *istibrana*,
namdjin, *manabin*, *sarbin*, and *khorwatin*, which scholars have respectively
identified as the Volinians, the Stodorans, Germans, Bohemians, Serbs,
and Croats. In Miquel's view, the general picture given by al-Mas'udi
of medieval Slavs, although in many ways confusing, did not lack in
accuracy. "Malgré les incertitudes fréquentes de graphie," he notes, "le
panorama esquissé par Mas'udi n'est pas exempt de logique. Il va du
nord au sud, depuis les pays de Brandebourg et Mecklembourg jusqu'aux
Croates des plaines danubiennes, en passant par le bloc central composé
de la plaines-Moravie ainsi que de la Serbie et la Croatie Blanches" (*La
géographie humaine*, 314).

After his account of the Slavs, al-Mas'udi proceeds to describe the
Franks, their lands, and their kings. As stated earlier, in *Al-Tanbih* he
included the Franks in the fourth group of those nations that have contributed to human civilization past and present, but he offered no explanation. Fortunately, there are convincing details in *Al-Muruj* wherein

al-Mas'udi provides important information on the Franks—their origins, lands, cities, military power, and political unity, in addition to a history of their kings.

Al-Mas'udi begins his account by mentioning that similar to several European peoples such as Slavs, *al-lunkbard* (Lombards), *al-ishban* (Spaniards), *al-alan* (the Alans), and *al-jalaliqa* (the Galicians), Franks are descendants of Japheth, son of Noah. As he did with the Slavs, he corroborates his view by referring to the consensus of religious scholars, whom he describes this time as *ahl al-bahth wa-l-nadhar min al-shar'iyyin* (people of research and insight from the religious authority) (*Al-Muruj*, 5). Significantly, he states that compared with all the previously mentioned European peoples who are descendants of Japheth, the Franks excel not merely in courage and military strength but also in political stability, social order, prosperity, and other aspects of civilized achievement (5). Commenting on their military power, organization, wealth, and political unity, all of which Al-Mas'udi considers to be markers of national merit and pride, he states that the Franks are "the most invincible and the most equipped" of all the tribes, are the ones who possess the largest of territories and the biggest number of cities, and pride themselves on being "the most disciplined, the most acquiescent and obedient to their kings" (5–6). In contrast to the Slavs, according to al-Mas'udi, the Franks are unified under one king, display no internal dispute among themselves, and know no *tahazzub*, that is, partisanship.[28]

Interestingly enough, on their kings al-Mas'udi has many things to say. Indeed, in his account of the Franks, al-Mas'udi devotes a special section to the "Kings of the Franks," containing a full exploration that goes beyond the scope of this study. Introducing this section, al-Mas'udi mentions that he based it on an Arabic translation of a Latin source attributed to Gotmar, bishop of Gerona (Spain), which he came across while he lived in Egypt (7). Briefly stated, in this much-praised section, al-Mas'udi provides a full list of Frankish kings from the fifth century to his own time. The list starts with what he describes as *awwal muluk al-ifranja* (the first of the kings of the Franks), and he calls him in Arabic *qludiwi*, whom scholars tend to identify as Clovis I (466–511). The list ends with *ludhwiq*, whom he describes as the contemporaneous Frankish king Louis IV (Shboul, *Al-Mas'udi and His World*, 190). In support of the importance and accuracy of the information provided by al-Mas'udi is his statement that Clovis I was the first of the kings of the Franks and his assertion that Clovis I was initially pagan before his wife, whom he called *ghrotla* (Clotlide), converted him to Christianity (*Al-Muruj*, 7). Fascinatingly, this is how Steven Fanning introduces Clovis I in the highly regarded *Medieval France: An Encyclopedia*:

> The most important of the Merovingian kings, Clovis I was the unifier
> of the Franks, the conqueror of most of Gaul, and the real founder of the
> kingdom of the Franks under Merovingian rule. He was also the first
> Christian king of the Franks…In the course of one of his battles against
> the Alemmani, at Zulpich (Tolbiac) in the mid-490s Clovis converted to
> Orthodox Christianity. This was not a sudden move, however. Like his
> father Childeric, Clovis had been careful to maintain good relations with
> Christian authorities in his lands, and he had also married an Orthodox
> Christian, the Burgundian princess Clotlide. (239)

In regard to Frankish lands, al-Masʿudi reports that the Franks had approximately 150 cities, in addition to what he describes as country towns and
villages. Most significant is his allusion to *buwayra* (Paris) as the actual
capital city of the Franks, which he hails as "a great city" (*Al-Muruj*, 6).
According to Shboul, al-Masʿudi must be credited with being among the
earliest, if not the first, medieval Muslim writers to refer with accuracy to
Paris as the capital city of the Franks (*Al-Masʿudi and His World*, 190).

Perhaps it is worthwhile to divert here by stating that Paris was to
become legendary and would later captivate the imagination of generations of modern, and even premodern, Arab Muslim visitors to Europe.
An everlastingly ambivalent love/hate reaction in visitors to Paris has
for centuries been the favored locus of many of the precolonial, colonial, and postcolonial Arab-European encounters described in modern
Arabic literature and the Arabic *riwaya* (novel) in particular.[29] Given this
perception, one may conclude that al-Masʿudi, as the earlier passage on
ahl al-shaman suggests, represents a premodern anticipation of the positive impression with which several (early) modern Arab Muslim travelers/
writers approached French civilization and *tout ce qui est français*. Important
figures such as the Moroccan ʿAbd Allah bin ʿAʾisha (d. 1700), the Egyptian
Rifaʿa Rafiʿ al-Tahtawi (d. 1873), the Syrian Francis Marrash (d. 1873),
and the Tunisian Khayruddine al-Tunisi (d. 1881) are among the most
well-known examples.[30] Al-Tahtawi, for instance, in *Takhlis al-Ibriz fi
Talkhis Baris* (The Refinement of the Gold in a Comprehensive Depiction
of Paris), in spite of the dissimilar times and contexts, seems to quote
al-Masʿudi verbatim:

> The power of the Franks multiplied on account of their skills, organiza-
> tion, their knowledge of an adaptability and inventiveness of warfare. If
> Islam had not been protected by the might of God—praise be to Him the
> Almighty—it would be nothing compared to their [the Franks] prowess,
> population, wealth, [and] skills. (9)[31]

In the same context of al-Mas'udi's praise of the Franks' political stability, lack of factions, social harmony, and especially their loyalty to a single leader, perhaps it is legitimate to add that by doing so, he seems to deplore, if not implicitly to criticize, the volatility that characterized Abbasid politics throughout much of his life. Indeed, in spite of their numerous military successes, robust economic policies, cultural and scientific achievements (especially during the Abbasid golden age), and most importantly their endeavors in publicly marketing their piety, the Abbasid caliphs had suffered from continuous *fitan* (schisms) and witnessed numerous *thawrat* (revolts) fomented by religious-political and socio-ethnic groups and minorities.[32]

In brief, one might say that al-Mas'udi's account of Frankish kings from Clovis I to Louis IV, his early reference to Paris as the capital of the Franks, along with his accurate reports of Frankish achievements have convinced some to credit al-Mas'udi as the author "of the single most important Arabic source for the history of the *Ifranj* (and indeed other foreign peoples), their rulers and kingdoms," to use D.L. Newman's words ("Arab Travelers to Europe until the End of the 18th Century and Their Accounts," 15). Al-Mas'udi's positive view of these Europeans, however, is in stark contrast to his view of their neighbors, *al-jalaliqa*, the Spanish Galicians, who represent for him one of the epitomes of the Other in medieval Arabic literature.

Indeed, while speaking of the courage of the Franks, al-Mas'udi somewhat hyperbolically considers the Galicians to be not only stronger but by far more atrocious and ferocious than the Franks (*Al-Muruj*, 6). The atrociousness and ferocity of the Galicians are later explained in more detail in a separate section he entitles "'Abd al-Rahman and the Galicians." In it, al-Mas'udi refers to past historical events that illustrate, according to him, the evil nature of the Galicians, whose utmost goal is the destruction of the Muslims of al-Andalus, not only by engaging them in continuous wars but also by spreading *fitan* (plural of *fitna*)—that is, internal seditions— among them. The example al-Mas'udi cites is the story of the military support offered by the Galicians to Umayya ibn Ishaq during the reign of 'Abd al-Rahman III (912–961). Briefly summarized, the latter put to death his *wazir* Ahmad ibn Ishaq as a just penalty for a major crime he had committed. In order to avenge the blood of his brother, Umayya ibn Ishaq defected to the Galicians and sought help from their king, Ramiro II (932–950). The Galicians offered assistance wholeheartedly and won several battles before they were crushed in 940 (*Al-Muruj*, 8–10).

Contrary to what we saw of the Slavs and the Franks, and as we shall see of the Lombards, there is hardly any information on the Galicians except their atrociousness and their constant wars against Muslims. Indeed, al-Mas'udi fails to provide details on their geographical location, towns, capital city, or ethnic affiliation. He does state in the closing sentence of the section that, similar to the Franks, Galicians are *Melkite* Christians, or Catholics (10). Thus, for al-Mas'udi, the main characteristic of the Galicians is their enmity toward the Muslims of al-Andalus. They are not only depicted as the Other of the Muslims of al-Andalus but also in several respects serve as opposites to the more civilized Franks and even the Lombards of medieval Italy, to whom al-Mas'udi devotes a section entitled *Dhikr al-Nunkbard wa Mulukiha* ("Mentioning the Lombards and their kings").

Although he does not provide as detailed an account here as he does of medieval France, al-Mas'udi does furnish valuable information on medieval Italy.[33] Indeed, as he does in his accounts of the Slavs and the Franks, he opens his section by tracing the Lombards back to Japheth, son of Noah, before highlighting that their lands were situated in the North (that is, Europe) and were adjacent to the Maghrib, which is North Africa and al-Andalus (10). He adds that the Lombards possess many lands on which various tribes and peoples have settled (10). Like the neighboring Franks, the Lombards are politically unified under the rule of one king and depicted as having many towns (10). Al-Mas'udi seems to relate the Lombards' political unity to the strong leadership of their kings, whom he called *adankibs*, an allusion to the famous dukes and duchies of medieval Italy.

Al-Mas'udi furthermore indicates that the Lombards, not unlike Franks, have many great towns, with the greatest of these being their capital. As confirmed by Charles Pellat and others, this city, referred to as *banabant*, is doubtlessly Benevento (Pellat, *Al-Muruj*, 347).[34] This is textually corroborated by his following statement that Lombard's capital city is known for its great river, which he calls in Arabic *saybat*, a distorted Arabic form for the famous Sabato River. The river, he explains, crosses their capital city and divides it into *janaban*, that is, two sides (*Al-Muruj*, 10). Add to this the historical fact that Benevento had been the capital city of a major Lombard duchy that had ruled much of southern Italy from the late sixth century until the eleventh century. During the Lombard rule of the city, as noted by John W. Barker and Christopher Kleinhenz and in confirmation of al-Mas'udi's assertion, Benevento "flourished as a center of commercial and cultural activities, with extensive patronage of architecture and letter" ("Benevento," 107).

Al-Mas'udi closes his account by stating that the Lombards had successfully regained several important cities such as *bari* (Bari), *tarniyyu* (Taranto), and *shabrama* (Sardinya) from the Muslims of North Africa and al-Andalus. He deplores that fact that these cities and many others are *fi-aydi al-nukbrad*, that is, in the hands of the Lombards (*Al-Muruj*, 10).

In his account of medieval Italy, al-Mas'udi provides useful if somewhat incomplete information on the expulsion of Muslims from central and southern Italy; however, it is surprising how little interest he exhibits in discussing the then extremely important relations between Muslims and Lombards.[35] In short, unlike his attitude toward the Spanish Galicians, al-Mas'udi does not vilify or single out the Lombards as the enemy despite their constant wars with Muslims.

In sum, it is safe to say that in addition to al-Mas'udi's keen interest in ancient European civilizations of the Greeks and Romans and his lifelong appetite for knowing about the cultures and religions of India, China, and Africa, various medieval European *ajnas* (peoples) and *buldan* (countries) appear relatively often in his overall commentary about non-Muslims. This is typical not only of his examination of many eastern, central, and (most importantly for us) western European peoples such as the Slavs, Franks, Galicians, and Lombards, but also of his controversial references to European barbarism through his stereotypical depiction of some northern Europeans.[36] One must not stop at al-Mas'udi's controversial *locus classicus* if one really wants to establish a comprehensive idea of his views and perceptions of medieval Europe especially, and to quote Kassis, al-Mas'udi "had a definite influence on subsequent Arabic writers, and on the image of Europe that they portrayed" ("The Depiction of Europe," 13). In fact, al-Mas'udi's influence was not confined to the Muslim East. As we shall see with al-Bakri, al-Mas'udi's representation of Europe also found a strong echo in the Muslim Occident (i.e., al-Andalus), of course, in spite of the calls of many Andalucentric scholars to resist what they saw as the cultural hegemony of eastern Baghdad and Damascus over western Cordoba and Granada.

The Wrongs of the Galicians and the Tongues of the Prussians: European Barbarity and Civilization through al-Bakri's Andalucentric Eyes

Judged as the greatest geographer of al-Andalus, polyvalent scholar Abu 'Ubayd 'Abd Allah al-Bakri belonged to the powerful Arab tribe of Bakr ibn Wa'il. Medieval Andalusian chronicles cite that he was born in Saltés, a town west of Seville around 1014. He came from a prominent family that established an independent principality around Saltés and Huelva several years prior to the fall of the Umayyad caliphate in 1031 (Gilliot, "Bakri, Al-, Geographer," 96).[37] His own father was the emir of the short-lived Bakri Principality (1012–1051), known in Arabic as *imarat al-bakriyyin*. Little is known of his early years, but it is evident that his schooling comprised several branches of the traditional Islamic knowledge. His subsequent life bears ample evidence that, unlike his father, he showed little interest in politics, which he likely found constricted his intellectual quest. The observation of noted Andalusian historian Ibn Bashkuwal (d. 1182) that he was having a love affair with books captures well al-Bakri's great expectations in life (al-Bakri, *Jughrafiyat al-Andalus wa Uruba*, 29). Al-Bakri spent most of his youth visiting different Andalusian cities in search of learning and met several famous scholars of his time, including the historian Ibn Hayyan al-Qurtubi (d. 1076) in Cordoba and the geographer al-'Udhri (d. 1085) in Almería. Al-Bakri is thought to have died either in Seville or Cordoba in 1094 at the age of 80 (29).

Although al-Bakri was himself a prolific writer, unfortunately most of the books attributed to him are not extant, and even his monumental work *Al-Masalik wa-l-Mamalik* (Routes and Kingdoms) seems not to have survived the centuries intact (34). Nowadays, al-Bakri is remembered primarily for his remarkable account of medieval West Africa contained in this work.[38] It is judged by N. Levtzion and J. F. Hopkins as being "by far the most important source for West African history until the fourteenth-century" (*Corpus of Early Arabic Sources for West African History*, 9). Apart from this West African account, no other section has been completely translated into English.[39] The unjustified scholarly neglect of his fascinating accounts of the Iberian Peninsula and his native al-Andalus, as well as his observations on medieval France, Bohemia, Poland, Prussia, and Italy, is most regrettable.

It is fair to suggest from the outset that al-Bakri has bequeathed to posterity the richest Arabic account of medieval Iberia. In the lengthy section entitled *Dhikr Jazirat al-Andalus wa-Jumalin min Akhbariha* (*Mentioning the Andalusian Peninsula and Several of Its News*), he cites Iberia, Baetica, Hispania, and Hesperias as the pre-Islamic appellations for the Iberian Peninsula, noting that Iberia took its name from the Ebro River (*wadi ibro*) (*Jughrafiyat al-Andalus wa Uruba*, 57). Its name became more widely known as *batika*, from the Baetis River (*wadi bayti*), which, he explains, is Cordoba's principal river (57). Medieval Arabs more commonly called it *al-wad al-kabir* (the big/great river). It now goes by its Arabic name, the Guadalquivir River, Spain's second longest river.

Ishbaniya (Hispania), continues al-Bakri, was derived from Ishban, the man who conquered and ruled over the peninsula at one time (57). No doubt al-Bakri is here referring to Hispan, the Celtic king who conquered the northwest parts of the peninsula during the pre-Roman rule.[40] He also cites the suggestion made by others that the peninsula's actual ancient name was *ishbaria* after *ashbarush*, which he defines as *al-kawkab al-ma'ruf bi-l-ahmar*, that is, the planet that is known as the red one (57). This is unquestionably a reference to Hesperus (Greek Ἕσπερος), the famous evening star or the planet Venus in Greek mythology. John Armstrong Crow in *Spain: The Root and the Flower: An Interpretation of Spain and the Spanish* (2005) observes in this regard that "when the Greeks arrived on Spanish soil around 600 B.C., they referred to the peninsula as Hesperia, which means 'lands of the setting sun'" (7).

Despite some differences in views and interpretations, it can be stated with certainty that most of al-Bakri's statements on the history of the ancient appellations of the Iberian Peninsula are strongly supported by modern historians, including Crow. Most of said historians concur that the Greeks were the first to use the name Iberia after the Iberus River (now the Ebro) and that for long periods afterward it, or parts of it, were called Baetica. This was before the Romans conquered it around 218 BC during the Punic Wars and renamed the peninsula Hispania.[41]

Al-Bakri proves very informative on the ancient and contemporary geographical and administrative divisions of the peninsula.[42] In his account of al-Andalus, he devotes long sections to its geography, mountains, and most importantly its geographical and administrative districts past and present, the full discussion of which goes beyond the scope this study. Also of value is his mention of several major European and Andalusian towns and their iconic monuments. While discussing what he describes as Constantine's six districts of the peninsula, he cites, in the first district—which he notes is situated at the borders of *galiosh*, that is, Gallos (Gaul)—Narbonne (now in southern France), along with Baziers, Tolosa, Maguelonne, and Nemauso. He writes principally of Carcassonne and describes *al-kanissa al-'udhma*, literally the great church, adding that it is called *shanta mariyya grathiya*, certainly a distortion of Santa Maria de la Grasse (*Jughrafiyat al-Andalus wa Uruba*, 60).[43] Writing of the second district, he mentions Braga, Porto (now in Portugal) and singles out what he calls *shant yago* (Santiago). Of the latter, he adds that it is *madinat kanisat al-thahab*—that is, the city of the golden church—to which people flock every year from *ifranja* (the lands of the Franks), *ruma* (Rome), and elsewhere (61). In this passage, al-Bakri is undoubtedly referring to the yearly pilgrimage to the shrine of St. James in the Cathedral of Santiago de Compostela.

In other lengthy sections, he singles out towns such as Toledo, Talavera de la Reina, Tudela, Barabstro, and Barcelona, writes of their histories, and relates anecdotes of their famous rulers, some of which have proved most valuable. He observes that Barcelona's Jewish inhabitants equal in number the Christians who lived there (96). Although this suggested number is definitely far-fetched, al-Bakri's interesting information on the prominence of eleventh-century Barcelona Jewry is generally confirmed by a score of modern studies. These include

Yitzhak Baer's classic *A History of the Jews in Christian Spain: From the Age of Reconquest to the Fourteenth Century* (1961) and, more recently, Elka Klein's *Jews, Christian Society, and Royal Power in Medieval Barcelona* (2006) and Robert Chazan's *The Jews of Medieval Western Christendom, 1000–1500* (2007).[44]

Perhaps more important for our purposes here is al-Bakri's anecdote about Ramón Berenguer I (1035–1076), whom he calls *al-qomes* (count) and describes as *sahib barchalona al-yawm*, that is, the then ruler or governor of Barcelona (96). Al-Bakri writes that around 446 AH (that is, 1053–1054), Ramón left Barcelona for a pilgrimage to Jerusalem. On his way, he stopped in Narbonne, where he was hosted with honor by one of its *kubar'i ahliha* (luminaries or leaders). There, al-Bakri continues, Ramón fell in love with the wife of his host, who reciprocated his love and agreed to elope and join him later in Barcelona. After his return home from his pilgrimage, presumably to Jerusalem, Ramón sent a delegation of Jews from Barcelona to try to help in the endeavor, another indication of the importance of the Jews in eleventh-century Barcelona. After many attempts, the Narbonian woman made it finally to Barcelona, and this led Ramon to divorce his wife to marry her. Ramón's divorced wife decided to travel to Rome with some of her family members to take up this matter with the pope. Al-Bakri refers to him as *al-baba* and describes him as ʿ*adhimuha wa sahib al-dini biha*, which means Rome's greatest man and the one who has the authority over the (Christian) religion.[45] The pope took the side of Ramón's divorced wife and ordered Ramón's excommunication because, as stressed by al-Bakri, divorce is not allowed in their religion (98). Ramón did everything he could to overturn the pope's decision by bribing those whom al-Bakri describes as *mashahir al-asaqifa wal-qississin*, that is, high priests and bishops. The latter intervened in Ramón's favor by falsely attesting that he divorced his first wife only after discovering that she was one of his blood relatives. A similar tactic was used on behalf of his new Narbonian wife, who (it was alleged) had discovered her former royal husband was also a blood relation to her. Al-Bakri ends his anecdote by confirming that the pope revoked his decision against Ramón (99).

One may wonder here how Scheherazade of *Al-Layla wa-Layla* could have missed such a wonderful Barcelonian night! But the fascinating fact is that, although one should acknowledge al-Bakri's Arabian flavor, the core of the story is a historical reality. Indeed, as indicated by Martin Aurell in his intriguing book *Les Noces du Comte: Mariage et pouvoir en Catalogne (785–1213)* (1995), in addition to an official document, al-Bakri is credited with leaving one of the most valuable external records of the marriage between Ramón Berenguer I and the divorcee of Pons II de

Toulouse (1037–1060), Almodis de la Marche (d. 1071), the Narbonian woman in al-Bakri's account. To quote Aurell,

> Abu 'Ubaid al-Bakri (+1094) est le témoin privilégié du troisième mariage de Ramon Berenguer Ier, comte de Barcelone et ravisseur d'Almodis de la Marche, la Narbonnaise de son récit, femme légitime de Pons II de Toulouse. Le géographe andalou jette un regard étranger, extérieur, sur les pratiques matrimoniales des comtes catalans; sa plus vive attention est attirée par le triomphe de la morale des prêtres sur celle des guerriers.[46] La fréquentation assidue des mozarabes, qu'al-Bakri côtoie à Cordoue, n'est guère parvenue à effacer les traits énigmatiques que revêt pour lui le mariage chrétien. Qui plus est, les victoires grégoriennes accroissent le fossé culturel qui sépare, sur le sol de la péninsule ibérique, Occidentaux et Orientaux en matière matrimoniale. L'étonnement d'al-Bakri provient, en premier lieu, de l'interdiction du divorce, relativement facile à obtenir dans l'Islam. (262)

Al-Bakri's "étonnement" at the prohibition of divorce in Christianity, as Aurell has phrased it, underscores the fact that matrimonial practices of medieval Europeans are among the preferred themes upon which al-Bakri and most medieval Arab writers routinely constructed and consolidated their topoi of differences between the Arab Muslim Self and the Euro-Christian Other.

Although they are not as interesting and rich as his account of Barcelona, al-Bakri also mentions other major Euro-Iberian cities such as Bordeaux, Gerona, and Lisbon. Al-Bakri, however, does turn his attention to numerous towns associated with the Golden Age of al-Andalus, such as Toledo, Cordoba, Seville, Algeciras, Almería, and others. Indeed, the otherwise prosaic al-Bakri, when "narrating" his own nation, does not only seem at his poetic best, but he proves "impossibly romantic and exceedingly metaphorical" (*Nation and Narration*, 1), although Homi Bhabha may sound too anachronistic here. Representing the best of East and West, al-Andalus has ended up in al-Bakri's text as the ultimate metaphor of excellence and superiority. Thus, it becomes in his own words

> Levantine in its fragrance and air, Yemenite in its moderation and temperance, Indian in its scent and fragrance, Chinese in the preciousness of its metals, Adanese in the abundance of its coasts.[47] In it, one finds great monuments of the Greeks, the masters of wisdom and the bearers of philosophy. (*Jughrafiyat al-Andalus wa Uruba*, 80; translation mine)

The previous passage is interesting in several respects, not the least because it strongly evokes the overriding nationalism/patriotism of al-Bakri and perfectly conjures up what one may call the Andalucentric rhetoric that was dominant in the corpus of the medieval literature of al-Andalus. In a pure Andalusian context, these metaphors are remarkable in their poetic articulation of the *fadha'il al-Andalus* (superiority of the al-Andalus genre). In broader terms, the latter refers to the plethora of literary texts in which Andalusian writers not only narrated romantically what they saw as the virtues of their homeland, but also unwaveringly to the point of chauvinism advocated its superiority over the Maghribi (North African) and, mainly, Mashriqi (Eastern) Muslim countries.[48]

Towering above all writers of the genre is a contemporary of al-Bakri, the polymath Ibn Hazm (d. 1064). As noted by Peter Heath, Ibn Hazm "composed the first of the series of essays on the virtues of al-Andalus praising Andalusian accomplishments in all fields of learning" ("Knowledge," 114). This refers to his *Risala fi Fadhl al-Andalus* (Epistle on the Excellence/Superiority of Al-Andalus). It was written to refute the Tunisian scholar Ibn al-Rabib al-Qayrawani, who in a letter to one of Ibn Hazm's cousins had belittled the cultural and scientific achievements of the Andalusians especially in comparison to their Maghribi and Mashriqi coreligionists. Two centuries later, as if echoing Ibn Hazm, al-Shaqundi (d. 1232) wrote a similar epistle in response to the Moroccan Ibn al-Mu'allam al-Tanji.[49]

Andalusian poetry is also no less suffused with such rhetoric. To cite briefly an illustrative example, the famous poet Ibn Khafaja (1058–1138) had this to say:

> Oh inhabitants of Spain, how lucky you are:
> water, shade, river and trees;
> the eternal Paradise is only in your country;
> if I could choose, I would choose it.
> Do not fear to enter Hell, since that is not possible
> after having been in Paradise! (Marín-Guzmán, 48)[50]

In its radical aspect, however, this "Andalucentricism" found its most vocal opposition in the calls of a number of Andalusian scholars to resist what they saw as the literary and cultural domination of the Mashriq and to lash out at several of their compatriots for what they conceived of as their blind imitation of their Mashriqi "masters." The most articulate of these was certainly Ibn Bassam (d. 1147), hailed by J. A. Abu-Haidar as "one of the earliest and foremost anthologists and literary historians of al-Andalus" (*Hispano-Arabic Literature and the Early Provençal Lyrics*, 140).[51] In *Al-Dhakhira fi Mahasin Ahl al-Jazira* (The Treasury in Proclaiming the Merits of the People of Iberia), he voiced his most biting satire when he declared,

> The people of these lands refuse but to follow in the footsteps of the
> Easterners. If a crow should croak in those lands, or flies buzz somewhere
> in Syria or Iraq, they would kneel before the latter as before an idol, and
> treat the crowing of the former as an authoritative text...I was enraged by
> all this, and full of contempt of such an attitude, so I took it upon myself to
> highlight the merits of my own time, and the achievements of the people
> of my own country. Whoever, I wish I knew, restricted learning to a par-
> ticular period of time, and made (literary) excellence an Eastern preserve.
> (quoted in Abu-Haidar, *Hispano-Arabic Literature*, 140)

In short, this passage is an ostentatious display of Ibn Bassam's much celebrated talent in prose and prowess in parody. What is perhaps equally
impressive about the passage, in my view, is the cultural message it powerfully conveys. Ibn Bassam is boldly promoting an independent Andalusian
literary canon to safeguard Andalusians from the cultural hegemony of
the Mashriq, an undertaking that presages in several aspects the modern
debate on literature and nation-building.[52]

To return once more to al-Bakri, one finds for him that the
most ideologically "mortal enemies" ("Mortal Enemies, Invisible
Neighbors," 268), to quote al-Azmeh, come neither from the south nor
from the east. Indeed, they are none other than the Galicians, universally
portrayed in Andalusian sources as the most notorious and feared Other
par excellence—at least before the rise of the Castilians. "Altogether, the
Galicians," al-Azmeh tells us, "are the representative type of northern
barbarity, in whom are conjoined the inversion of reason in foolhardy
bellicosity, the subversion of the proper order of gender relations and
the inversion of the hygienic requirements of refined society" (268). If it
were possible to apply the modern category of historicist to al-Azmeh,
it would be possible to consider his pioneering scholarship regarding
the predominance of the Galicians in Andalusian sources in this light,
notably when he posits, "It is unclear why the Galicians in particular should have acquired a privileged position in accounts of Northern
Spaniards" (268). What is clear to contemporary scholars in retrospect
is that the land of the Galicians was the nucleus of the Reconquista, and
the Galicians were the earliest and fiercest opponents of the very presence of Muslims on the Iberian Peninsula.

Al-Bakri, who was unquestionably better-versed in Iberian affairs than
his "Eastern master," to use Ibn Bassam's ironic expression, devotes two
separate sections to the Galicians: *Dhikr Jilliqiyya* ("Mentioning Galicia")
and *Dhikr al-Jalaliqa* ("Mentioning the Galicians").[53] In these sections, he
manages to confirm Ibrahim ibn Ya'qub's statements on the Galicians by

incorporating them into a general section that includes the Galicians, the Franks, the Slavs, and "other Christian peoples," as he phrased it.

In broader terms, al-Bakri speaks about Galicia's geography and physical locations within the Iberian Peninsula. He also includes information on its counties and towns, which he corresponds to the views of the ancients.[54] In this regard, al-Bakri writes that its first county stands in the western part of Galicia and describes Braga as one of the major towns settled by the Romans in Galicia; he adds that it is known for its great buildings and forts (*Jughrafiyat al-Andalus wa Uruba*, 71). Perhaps the most important information in the first section is his reference to the southwest region of Galicia inhabited by a people called *al-burtuqalish*, that is, the Portuguese (72).

In the second section, far lengthier than the first and reminiscent in content of the accounts of al-Mas'udi, al-Bakri focuses squarely on the revolt of Umayya ibn Ishaq. The telos of this historical incident is the perpetuation of the "demonic" and "barbaric" picture of the Galicians. This is aside from al-Bakri's praise for the emir's goodness, righteousness, and *rahma* (mercy) in his acceptance of the *tawba* (repentance) of Umayya. In al-Bakri's own words, the foremost manifestation of the Otherness of the Galicians is that "they are people of distrust and misdemeanour" (81). As shown in the *fitna* of Umayya, al-Bakri makes sure to remind his readers that the Galicians represented a constant threat not only to the political, social, and cultural stability of al-Andalus but also to the very existence of Muslims in the Iberian Peninsula.[55] The physical prowess and invincibility in battle of the Galicians, in al-Azmeh's own words, must not be seen as proof of bravery and strength exclusive to them alone, for bravery and courage are attributes of civilized humanity at large. Certainly the bravery of the Franks, as mentioned earlier, was universally acknowledged by medieval Muslim writers. Even at the time of the Crusades, this bravery served as a kind of affidavit of their humanity and civilization, although none of these writers ever dared to extend to a non-Muslim Other what they deemed the highest level of human bravery, that is, the Muslim concept of *al-furusiyya* (chivalry).

Al-Bakri's final judgment on the Galicians, in which he harks back to their utter *tawahhush* (bestiality) and *takhalluf* (backwardness), should be understood as accurate, at least by the discerning "civilized" reader, given the historical record and the established tendencies of the Galicians. In the end, there is nothing more repugnant for the refined Andalusian than to discover that there are some people who are unashamedly unclean and blatantly rude. Most appalling for Muslims was the fact that Galicians did not have any prohibition about exposing *'awrat* (private parts) and displaying *al-ta'arri* (nakedness). Quoting

Ibrahim ibn Yaʿqub, al-Bakri writes,

> They lack hygiene since they wash themselves only once or twice a year
> with cold water. As for their clothes, they do not wash them until they
> are torn in the wearing and they are so tight and so open that their private
> parts are often exposed. They claim that their bodies get healthier because
> of their sweat. (81; translation mine)

One may see in this passage an ethnopolitical transposition of the dominant rhetoric of *al-tawahhush* in "Muslim" climatic ethnography. The
threat posed by the Galicians made them, in spite of their geographical
and religious proximity, not only among the remotest and most unfamiliar Others but, by ideological association, the ultimate personification of
ahl al-shamal of the seventh zone.

Whereas it was the Galicians who epitomized fear bordering on para-
noia of the Other in medieval Andalusian culture and literature, it was
the Franks who received al-Masʿudi's highest regard for their attributes
of civilization. Al-Bakri, in contrast, was unequivocal in his categorical
denial of any positive attributes of the Galatians of northern Iberia.

Although al-Bakri does not seem to be as conversant with the ancient
and contemporary history of the Franks as al-Masʿudi, he equaled in many
ways the Eastern encyclopedist in the geo-cosmographical information
he included in the introductory passage of his lengthy section on the
bilad al-ifranj (The Country of the Franks) (143). It should be noted here
that al-Masʿudi's designation of *bilad* in reference to the Franks suggests a
dramatic transformation from the language of extremity and barbarism
to that of relative temperance because only the civilized can have a *bilad*,
that is, a country. To make this point further, al-Bakri emphasizes in the
introductory sentence of the section that the country of the Franks lies in
the middle of the fifth clime. Thus, despite its coldness, the country of
the Franks is still far from the extreme north of the seventh clime. The
sign of temperance is indicated by al-Bakri's statement that its summer is
moderate—*masifuha muʿtadil* (143).

Al-Bakri speaks with admiration as well of the fruits, rivers, and especially the numerous towns spread across the country of the Franks. All in
all, in his own words,

> It is a country land abundant in fruits and has many rivers which spring
> from the melting snow. Also, it has excellent forts and extremely well-
> built towns. Its [southern] limits extend as far as the Mediterranean Sea.
> Whereas, from the North it is the Atlantic. From the southeast, it is also
> bordered by the land of Rome (Italy) and the country of the Slavs. From
> which they are separated by a thick forest which requires many days to

cross and separates them. From the East, it is also the land of the Slavs that
borders it, while from the West, it is the land of the Basques. (143–144;
translation mine)

In another passage, al-Bakri extols the superiority of Frankish craftsmanship
as unmatched in the Muslim East, citing the superior Frankish sword over
that of India. In lauding the Frankish sword to this extent, al-Bakri is telling
us much about the great value of the sword in medieval Arabic culture, surpassed only perhaps by the horse and the pen. It seems appropriate to stress
here the significance of medieval trade and how open medieval Andalusian
society was at least to non-Muslim economies, as illustrated in the *mufadhala*
(comparison) between Frankish and Indian swords. In this East-West competition, one may see a glimpse of the modern world being born.

Thus, we not need be overly surprised by al-Bakri's subsequent statement that the civilized Franks, like the civilized Andalusians confronted
by the barbarian Galicians, were constantly threatened by their own
"northern" enemies. If the Galicians were the foremost threat to the civilization of the Andalusians, the no less barbarian *bartaniyyun*—that is, the
Bretons—were the primary danger to their far more civilized neighbors
the Franks. In his commentary presumably based on Ibn Ya'qub and perhaps echoing Frankish (Roman) views of the Bretons rather than purely
Arab Muslim ones, al-Bakri asserts that the Bretons "have a language that
offends the ears, ugly faces, and bad manners" (82). He goes on to affirm
that "among them, there are thieves who raid the Franks and rob them."
Seemingly very understanding of the violent response to the Bretons,
if not supportive of their actions, he observes that the "Franks, in turn,
crucify any one they could capture" (83). In somehow justifying the cruel
behavior of the Franks toward the Bretons in the war between civilization
and barbarism, al-Bakri may be justifying a wished-for extermination of
the Galicians by the Andalusians.

Al-Bakri may be quite revealing in the manner in which he closes his
short section on the Bretons with a perhaps unwarranted reference to the
siege of Jerusalem in the year 70 AD. He states that the Britons, along
with the Galicians and *al-bashakisa* (the Basques), were among the fervent
soldiers who joined *titish*, a term that conflates this assault with the assault
of the Roman general Titus against Jerusalem (83). In so doing, al-Bakri
is portraying the Galicians and their cohorts as not only inherently violent
and prone to war but also as historical enemies of the East, no different
than Romans who attacked one of the birthplaces of Islam and the spiritual home of the Andalusians.

To a considerable extent, al-Bakri seems to employ several modern
discourses of representation, notably in his demonization of the medieval

European peoples known for their fierce resistance to the Muslim conquest of Spain. At least in his depiction of the Galicians, it appears that al-Bakri is practicing a kind of double standard. His conclusion that a single Galician on the battlefield is worth several Franks, though seemingly complimentary, is in fact quite derogatory. Here he is applauding not Frankish courage but Galician ferocity, in other words, lauding northern *tawahhush* (barbarity) rather than Frankish *tamaddun* (civilization). As shown in other Arabic sources, the Franks had opted for diplomacy and political subtlety, especially during the reign of Charlemagne, a marked contrast to their initial responses to the conquering Arabs.

Inasmuch as Galician resistance is juxtaposed with Frankish diplomacy and Galicians bravery and martial prowess become cruelty and bestiality, contrary to the civilized Frank, medieval Muslim writers seem to have been more impressed with the "passive" Charlemagne than the "militant" Charles Martel (d. 741). The silent functioning of the horologe presumably presented by Harun al-Rashid to the submissive delegation of Charlemagne (d. 814) seems to find a much stronger echo in al-Bakri's account of medieval western Europe, as was undeniably the case in the Abbasid *diwan* (court), than the resisting hammer of Charles and his Frankish armies during the Battle of Tours in 732.

Irrespective of the era in question or its politics, culture, race, gender, or religion, dominant nations who are the protectors of civilized values have always invented barbarian Others deserving of annihilation. From the vantage point of post-9/11 international politics, it is not too far-fetched to argue that al-Bakri is both tapping into "a plethora of tropes and narratives" related to the civilization/barbarism dichotomy and conjuring up modern discourses on international wars and the present war on terrorism. In this he appears to be anticipating Richard Jackson's outlook in his 2005 *Writing the War on Terrorism: Language, Politics and Counter-Terrorism* (154).

Al-Bakri also incorporates a brief but intriguing passage on Old Prussians, which he has gleaned from the account of Ibrahim ibn Ya'qub. In fact, in his lengthy account of the Slavs,[56] which includes a description of the realm of Polish king Mieszko I, al-Bakri writes that the northern neighbors are the *brus* who dwell nearby *al-bahr al-muhit*, identified as the Baltic Sea in this context, not as the Atlantic Ocean (Spekke, "Arabian Geographers and the Early Baltic People," 157). Even though al-Bakri does not say much about the identity of these Baltic tribes of pre-Teutonic Prussians or their lands, apart from his statement that that they are under constant sea assaults from *al-rus* (Rus), he does note that they use *marakib*, that is, ships, and come from *al-maghrib* (the West). As will be discussed with Ibn Fadlan, the *rus* here refers to the Northmen (Vikings), who assaulted the pre-Teutonic Prussians by sea from the west (157). Under attack, al-Bakri states, the pre-Teutonic Prussians proved particularly courageous and valiant, and as soon as an assault was imminent, the individual pre-Teutonic Prussian would not wait for his fellows, or any command, before engaging in battle to the last drop of his blood (*Jughrafiyat al-Andalus wa Uruba*, 168). Significantly, these warriors' near-invincible swords are contrasted with their near-unintelligible words. Al-Bakri describes their language as *'ala hidda* (harsh) and claims the pre-Teutonic Prussians were seemingly incapable of understanding their neighbors' languages (168).

It should be noted here that in medieval Arabic sources, the accustomed phrase in describing harsh or unintelligible speech is *al-'ujma* rather than *'ala hidda*. In the context of inter-Muslim cross-perceptions, all non-Arab Muslims are accordingly called *al-a'ajim*. Although the highly complex issue of *al-'ujma* and *al-a'ajim* goes beyond the scope of this work, we should mention briefly that the central topos of differences in medieval Arabic literature and culture is the linguistic one. Especially during the height of the anti-Arab and predominantly Persian movement known as *al-shu'ubiyya*, now standardized in Western sources as Shu'ubism, certain Arab scholars responded to anti-Arab literature in various ways including by highlighting the presumed purity and superiority of the Arabic tongue.[57] Thus, the word *al-a'ajim* was employed initially to designate the Persians, but later it included all non-Arabs. The term is reminiscent in several respects of the Greek concept of the *barbaroi* (barbarian); an *a'jami* (plural *a'ajim*) is a person whose native language is not Arabic.

Mention should also be made here even in passing of the Arabian cult of *al-furusiyya*—chivalry—in both pre-Islamic and Islamic forms. The willingness to fight the enemy and the eagerness to die in battle are placed among the most praised qualities of a *faris* (knight).[58] This being the case, what should be noted is the particular interest of medieval Arabs in acknowledging the courage of the Other, even in times of rivalries and wars. In brief, this was intrinsically related in several aspects to their own cultural horizons of expectation.

Directly after his account of the Slavs and their kingdoms, al-Bakri devotes three lengthy consecutive sections to the affairs of the Romans and their majestic capital Rome: *Bilad al-Rum wa Akhbarihim* (The Country of the Romans and Some of Their News), *Ruma* (Rome), and finally *Dhikru Shyain min Siyar al-Rum wa Akhbarihim wa Mathahbihim* (Mentioning Some of the Histories of the Romans and Their Religious Beliefs). The chapter that follows will offer a more detailed treatment of this subject.

Al-Bakri tells us in his account that Rome is one of the most fortified cities in the world and includes a passage on *kanissat shant bater*, the Basilica of St. Peter (203).[59] As for *ahlu ruma*, that is, the inhabitants of Rome—hereafter the Romans—he confirms the dominant medieval Arab view about their physical beauty by stating that their faces are the most beautiful of God's creatures (202). He then goes on to state that they are ruled by *al-baba* (the pope), who is not only respected by his people but also venerated by the kings themselves (202). Al-Bakri disapprovingly points out that the Romans bow down and kiss the pope's foot. None, he continues, would raise his head until the pope has given him the order to do so (202). He discusses at length certain Christian precepts and rituals without polemical comments. He tells us that Christians have the habit of shaving their beards (205) and of venerating Sunday because they believe Jesus rose up to heaven from his tomb on a Sunday after meeting his apostles (206).

Reminiscent of the previously discussed comment of al-Tajir on the Chinese and the Hindus, Al-Bakri states that the Romans do not respect the obligation of cleansing oneself after intercourse and do not practice ablution before their prayers (206). They only accept sacrifice after saying *hatha lahmuk hatha damuk* ("This is your body, this is your blood") in reference to Jesus (206). Al-Bakri is describing with precision here the Catholic rite of transubstantiation during celebration of the Eucharist. He also remarks with admiration that Christians, like Muslims, disallow drunkenness. However, contrary to the polygamous Muslims, they allow only one wife. *Zina'* (adultery) is prohibited, and if a husband finds out that his wife is unfaithful, he will punish her by selling her as a slave (207).

As mentioned earlier in reference to Ramón Berenguer I of Barcelona, al-Bakri accurately points out that divorce is not permitted among the Christians of Rome (206). He mentions as well that Christians have their own ritual of fasting. Contrary to the challenging month of fasting during Ramadan, Christian Lent, he observes, is extremely easy (207). Although it is 40 days in duration and technically longer than Ramadan, al-Bakri notes that Christians fast neither the whole day nor the whole night but rather they fast no more than half a day (208). Christians, unlike Muslims, al-Bakri remarks, are not obliged to attend religious services, and no one would ever reprimand them for not doing so. According to al-Bakri, the Bible has 557 subject elements, many of which are mistaken and apocryphal since they are not part of authentic revelations (208).

It can be plainly stated that we have at our disposal one of the richest reports of medieval Europe thanks to the Andalusian al-Bakri's monumental work, *Al-Masalik wa-l-Mamalik*. It is no exaggeration to claim that al-Bakri clearly surpasses his Eastern predecessor al-Mas'udi in many aspects, not only in the breadth of his geo-historical information but especially through his incorporation of rich anecdotes about some of the most important European towns and *gents*. This is not only the case for the Iberian Peninsula and his native al-Andalus but also in the sections he devoted to western and central European towns and lands, such as medieval (Iberian) Galicia, France, and Italy.[60] In his descriptions of the latter, he may have relied in part on the eyewitness account of the ninth-century captive Harun ibn Yahya, whose intriguing journey to Europe and his description of Rome and its marvels we focus on in the following chapter.

CHAPTER 3

WRITING THE NORTH: EUROPE AND EUROPEANS IN MEDIEVAL ARABIC TRAVEL LITERATURE

Captives and Emissaries from the Mashriq

Mirabilia Urbis Romæ *through the Eyes of a Ninth-Century Arab Captive*

When it was the Eight Hundred and Ninety-third Night:

She [Scheherazade] pursued, It hath reached me, O auspicious King, that the King of France wrote to the Caliph and Prince of True Believers, Harun al-Rashid, a writ humbling himself by asking for his daughter Miriam and begging of his favour that he write to all the Moslems, enjoining her seizure and sending back to him by a trusty messenger of the servants of his Highness the Commander of the Faithful; adding, "And in requital of your help and aidance in this matter, we will appoint to you half of the city of Rome the Great, that thou mayst build therein mosques for the Moslems, and the tribute thereof shall be forwarded to you."

—*Arabian Nights* (12)

Almost three centuries before the publication—most likely by a canon of St. Peter's named Benedict[1]—of *Mirabilia Urbis Romæ* (*The Marvels of Rome*), the Abbasid postmaster and chief of intelligence (*sahib al-barid wa-l-khabar*) Ibn Khordadbeh had devoted an entire section of his previously mentioned *Kitab al-Masalik wa-l-Mamalik* (*The Book of Roads and Kingdoms*) to the European city that held pride of place in medieval Arabic-Islamic imaginings of the West, as attested by the introductory quotation from *The Arabian Nights*.[2] Serendipitously, *Sifat Rumiyya wa ma Fiha min al-'Aja'ib* (*The Description of Rome and Its Marvels*), the title Ibn Khordadbeh chose for his description of Rome, presages the title of Benedict's much later text. Again in several respects anticipating Benedict, Ibn Khordadbeh strove to "embellish and exaggerate" the city he described (Miedema, "Mirabilia Urbis Romae," 723), for instance, in dazzling reports of the extent of Rome's monuments and riches.[3]

We may therefore appropriately begin our exploration of the topic by looking very briefly at Ibn Khordadbeh's description of Rome. Beginning his section with plausible topographical information about its location, Ibn Khordadbeh stunned his readers with far-fetched claims about the extent of the city's mainly Christian monuments. For instance, he wrote of 1,200 churches and a colossal wall made up of 1,200 pillars, atop each of which stood a statue of a monk (*Kitab al-Masalik wa-l-Mamalik*, 115). These and other marvels such as the 4,100 public baths, the copper-covered river that he described with the enigmatic word *qastitlis*, and the strange *shajara min nuhas* (copper tree) made Rome one of the four wonders of the world (*'aja'ib al-dunya al-arba'a*).[4] Setting an example for subsequent Muslim travel writers, Ibn Khordadbeh did not fail to end his entry on Rome with the prophetic sayings that singled out the conquest of Rome by Muslims as one of the major portents not only of the ultimate triumph of that religion but of the end of the world, as will be discussed in more detail later in this chapter (al-Kilani, *Surat Uruba Inda al-'Arab fi-l-'Asr al-Wasit*, 134).

Quite recently, in his article "Italy in Arabic Travel Literature until the End of the 19th Century: Cultural Encounters and Perceptions of the Other," D. L. Newman characterized Ibn Khordadbeh's description of Rome as "mythical" but nonetheless "the very first description" of the city proper by a Muslim and "the first of any Western European town" (198). He added that "Ibn Khordadbeh's description of Rome would serve as a template for subsequent travelers and geographers, with very little of substance being added, except more *mirabilia*" (199).[5] Newman's statement regarding Ibn Khordadbeh's position as the first and, mainly, foremost Muslim chronicler of Rome is not incontestable.[6] In fact, it is Harun ibn Yahya who should be credited with leaving to posterity the foremost medieval eyewitness account of *la città eterna*.[7]

Almost nothing is known about Harun ibn Yahya beyond his Levantine heritage. To some extent, since the famous Italian Arabist Ignazio Guidi published his groundbreaking article "La descrizione di Roma nei geographi arabi" in 1878, Harun ibn Yahya's name has become somewhat recognizable in the West.[8] This is so in large part because he is thought to be the first medieval Arab to see with his own eyes several of Rome's *mirabilia*. "Among all the Arab geographers who spoke about Rome," Francesco Gabrieli wrote, "there is perhaps only one who saw with his own eyes the banks of the Tiber and drew from his own observation the numbers which he provided on the palaces, monuments, and inhabitants of Rome" ("Rome au IX siècle chez un voyageur arabe," 43). Failing, however, to mention that the Andalusian Ibrahim ibn Ya'qub (d. 999), who will be discussed later, is also said to have visited Rome a number of decades after his Mashriqi predecessor, Gabrieli added, "There is however one exception, or at least a case, which presents itself as such: it is that of the enigmatic Harun ibn Yahya, a ninth-century Arab from Syria" (43).

Most likely, a little before 886, Harun ibn Yahya was captured by *rumi* (Byzantine) pirates in the seaport town of Ascalon (al-Kilani, *Surat Uruba Inda al-'Arab*, 177). After his capture, he was taken to Constantinople and held as a prisoner of war for an unknown period. After his ransom in 886, he did not return home but chose instead to embark on a long European journey. Harun ibn Yahya, as we are told by M. 'Izzidin, "left Constantinople for Slaukiya (Thessalonica), from where he traveled to Venice and later Rome, of which [too] he left a description" ("Harun b. Yahya," 232). Fortunately, fragments of Harun ibn Yahya's account of Rome were preserved by geographer Ibn Rusta (d. 903) in *Al-A'laq al-Nafisa* (*The Precious Things*) before later geographers such as al-Bakri and al-Qazwini began to incorporate several of its passages sometimes verbatim without acknowledging Harun ibn Yahya as the original source.

As demonstrated by Gabrieli, Harun ibn Yahya's adventure in Byzantium, the Balkans, and Italy is valuable in several important respects, not the least because modern scholarship is indebted to him for, among other things, the eyewitness description of two non-Muslim metropolises of his age: Constantinople and Rome (44). In the erudite Gabrieli's words,

> Ce texte reste précieux à plusieurs égards, pour sa haute antiquité (dernières décennies du IX siècle), et pour son contenu, qui se présente, répétons-le, l'expérience directe de son auteur. Nous lui sommes en effet redevables, entre d'autres données, de la description des deux métropoles de son temps en dehors du monde musulman, Constantinople et Rome. (44)

Harun ibn Yahya's account of Rome has been not only eclipsed by but even confused with that of his undoubtedly better known description of Constantinople, hailed by a growing number of scholars as "one of the most—if not the most—important accounts left by visitors to the Byzantine capital in the Middle Ages" ('Izzidin, "Harun b. Yahya," 232).[9]

Ibn Yahya's Account of Rome

Harun ibn Yahya began his account of Rome by providing some general information on its geography and location. He stated that the city was huge, with a length equaling its width (40 miles). In the western part of Rome, he wrote, there was a river (the Tiber) that divided the city into two parts. Along this river were many *jusur* (bridges), and on the outskirts of the city were beautiful *basatin* (gardens) and numerous *zayatin* (olive trees). Ibn Yahya did not forget to remind his fellow Muslims from the outset that Muslim Berbers from the Maghreb and Andalusia had attempted to conquer the city not only from the sea but also along its western borders (Ibn Rusta, *Kitab Al-A'laq al-Nafisa*, 128–130).[10]

Contrary to most medieval Muslim views of non-Muslim cleanliness and hygiene, Ibn Yahya was impressed by the cleanliness of the city and its people.[11] He cited the existence of numerous *hammamat* (public baths) and an abundance of running water thanks to the city's great *qanawat* (canals). He added that Rome was surrounded by two stone walls and had many majestic *abwab* (doors). He seems especially impressed by two gates—*bab al-dhahab* (the golden gate) and *bab al-malik* (the king's gate)—both of which he described in detail. Between these two gates, he informed the reader, was a huge *suq* (marketplace), which he claimed was 12 miles in length (131). It is needless to emphasize here that Ibn Yahya was greatly impressed with the rich economic and social life of Rome. He was particularly taken by Rome's markets, evoking the later Western fascination with Oriental *aswaq* (markets). After stating that the city housed markets in 92 different locations, he observed that all 92 were closed on Sunday because on that day *yansarif ahluha fihi li-l-salat*, that is, its residents devote themselves to prayer (131).

As for the cultural life of the city, Ibn Yahya characterized Rome as *mdinat 'ilm* (a town of knowledge). With admiration, he stated that the city housed more than 120 *majma' 'ilmi* (scientific institutions), as a result of which Rome was a mecca for anyone who possessed the desire to master all branches of knowledge and wisdom (128). No doubt a comparison to Baghdad first and then to Muslim cities of learning such as Damascus, Kairouan, and Cordoba entered the mind of Ibn Yahya.

Perhaps mention should be made here that other non-Christian medieval travelers were also fascinated with many of the buildings and institutions referred to by Ibn Yahya. To cite just one example, the Jewish traveler Benjamin of Tudela (d. 1173),[12] a visitor to Rome in the twelfth century, had the following to say concerning the "the metropolis of all Christendom":

> The city contains numerous buildings and structures entirely different from all other buildings upon the face of the earth. The extent of

ground covered by ruined and inhabited parts of Rome amounts to four and twenty miles…Rome contains many other remarkable buildings and works, the whole of which nobody can enumerate. (Sandra Benjamin, *The World of Benjamin of Tudela*, 87–88)

It is surprising to discover that, in spite of their authors' fascination with the architectural marvels of the city, the records left by non-Christian medieval travelers (unlike those left by earlier and later Muslim travelers) rarely addressed the riches and treasures said to be hidden in many of Rome's remarkable buildings. In his "Letter from Rome" for example, Benjamin of Tudela, who was known for his curiosity, seemed unaware of the riches and marvels Harun ibn Yahya claimed to have seen with his own eyes in some of the city's famous churches.

As with his account of Constantinople, Ibn Yahya, in spite of religious and historical sensitivities, found reason to devote the largest part of his otherwise short account of Rome to its churches, whose "number and majesty," according to al-Kilani, "drew Harun ibn Yahya's utmost attention" (*Surat Uruba Inda al-'Arab fi-l-'Asr al-Wasit*, 185). However, he singled out what he called in Arabic *al-kanisa al-'udhma* (the great church) in reference to St. Peter's Basilica, which, although not the building recognized today by that name, was then as now one of the historical icons of Rome and one of the largest churches, if not the largest church, in the world. Ibn Yahya spoke with wonder about the church's size and grandeur, claiming that it was two Persian *farsakh* in length (the equivalent of 12 to 14 kilometers) and had 360 doors. He reported that in the middle of the church was a high tower rising almost 100 arms in the air. Atop this tower was a huge dome made of lead. Most of the church's interior walls and doors, he wrote, were covered with gold, whereas its exterior walls and doors were made of Chinese copper. According to Harun ibn Yahya, in every corner of the church stood high structures atop which rested silver domes in which monks rang bells.

Ibn Yahya also spoke with awe about many of the strange and beautiful drawings, statues, and altars residing in the church and then cataloged specific riches and treasures of its interior: 1,000 golden fans encrusted with pearls and rubies, 600 golden crosses, 1,200 pearl-encrusted cups. He finished this passage by stating that approximately 3,200 priests and monks lived in this great church (Ibn Rusta, *Kitab Al-A'laq al-Nafisa*, 132).

Ibn Yahya is cited as claiming that in Rome there were, altogether, 24 churches, 23,000 monasteries, and even more monks and priests, of whom he is said to have counted no fewer than 48,000 (132). These exaggerated numbers as well as other *mirabilia* appear to be the addition of Ibn Rusta and taken principally from Ibn Khordadbeh. "The exaggerated figures suggested by the traveler," Gabrieli points out, "should not cast doubt on the overall authenticity of Harun ibn Yahya's account or on the information that his report provides especially when it is commonplace that the fascination with the marvelous was typical of the medieval man" (45).

Among the real *mirabilia* that drew the attention of Harun ibn Yahya, however, was the appearance of the people of Rome. He reported with evident confusion that Roman men, young and old, shaved their beards and heads and did not leave a single hair remaining (Ibn Rusta, *Kitab al-A'laq al-Nafisa*, 130). He was not satisfied with recounting this Roman oddity but was curious to know the reason for it. He wrote that he asked certain Romans in person about this custom, for in his understanding as a Muslim "the beauty of men lies in their beards" (130). "The importance of this question," Gabrieli wrote, "does not lie in the question itself or in the received answer, but rather in the quest itself, triggered in the first place by the foreign traveler, a compelling evidence of his contact with the environment he is describing for us" (45).

Intriguingly, Harun ibn Yahya transmitted the Romans' own point of view about their shaven heads, leaving the reader to judge whether the explanation was convincing or not. The Romans, he informed readers, considered the shaved head a symbol of contrition. He reported that he had been told by the Romans that when Simon and his poor companions came to Rome to propagate Christianity, the then-pagan Romans tortured and humiliated them by shaving their beards and heads. At their conversion to Christianity, the Romans decided to shave their own beards in expiation for shaving the beards of the saints (Ibn Rusta, *Kitab al-A'laq al-Nafisa*, 130).

Notwithstanding the fact that the beard was, and in many ways still is, one of "the strongest and most nuanced markers of adherence to the Islamic community" (Bromberger, "Hair: From the West to the Middle East through the Mediterranean," 358), to a medieval Muslim (Arab), the fact that a man shaved his beard not only would have been shocking on the face of it but might have been regarded as a source of homosexual *fitna* (sexual temptation).[13] Regardless of the Islamic ruling on shaving beards, which ranged from *muharram* (prohibited) to *makruh* (reproachable), Harun ibn Yahya must have thought of the beardless male Romans as *mirdan* (singular *amrad*; a beardless young man).[14] For many medieval Muslims, an *amrad* could be a source of sexual *fitna* like that which women were generally thought to provoke, or more so. Briefly stated, during the ninth century, despite Islamic law's strict prohibition, the homosexual *fitna* spread among some classes of Abbasid society—especially those of the military and literary elites—leading to the rise of homoerotic literature and to the poetry of *al-mudhakkarat* (love of males) and especially *al-ghilmaniyyat* (love of boys).[15]

It is understandable then why Harun ibn Yahya, like many Muslim writers after him in their accounts of the Romans and the Byzantines alike, appeared tireless in recounting the *fitna* of Roman/Byzantine men and women. As demonstrated by el-Cheikh, classical Muslim authors often believed that "the king of the *Rūm* is called the king of human beings because his subjects, among all human beings are those who have the most beautiful faces, the best built bodies and the most robust constitution" (*Byzantium Viewed by the Arabs*, 132). Although this statement conveys a positive view and general appreciation of the Romans/Byzantines, it might also be said to hide a rather negative connotation that could, in my view, be related not only to a possible *takhnith* (effemization) of Roman/Byzantine males but also to a consolidation of some dominant Arab views on female slavery and sexuality. As shown by the Syrian Christian physician Ibn Butlan (d. 1066) in his bizarre *Risala Jami'a li Funun Nafi'a fi Shira' al-Raqiq* (*Epistle on the Arts of Purchasing Slaves*), Roman (Byzantine) slave girls were among the most preferred by Abbasids for both their physical appeal and domestic prowess (el-Cheikh, *Byzantium Viewed by the Arabs*, 239).

After reading Harun ibn Yahya's account of Rome, one may indeed wonder why that traveler, and before him Ibn Khordadbeh, became obsessed with enumerating the marvels and cataloging the riches of Rome, although Rome, like any other great city, had more than marvels and riches to offer for its visitors. In addition to its economic importance as one of the greatest cities of the time, the answer should be sought within Muslim apocalyptic beliefs and relates to what is known in classical Muslim sources as *fiqh al-sa'a* (jurisprudence of the end of the world), in which an ultimate Muslim conquest of Rome is believed to be one of the major signs and portents of the end of the world.[16] As Miquel explained in his article "Rome chez les géographes arabes," the Muslim "fabulation," "exaltation," and "heroisation" of Rome—to use his own words—found their inspirations in what he describes as Muslim mythical and eschatological perspectives (291).

Indeed, as mentioned in the Quran and the Sunna (prophetic tradition), *al-sa'a* (the hour), which refers to the end of the world, is preceded by minor as well as major signs and portents. The first refers to a number of events that have already taken place and others that are ongoing and will continue for the coming centuries. Chief among the events of the past that Muslim scholars cited, based on a number of Quranic verses and hadiths (prophetic sayings), were the coming and death of the Prophet, early triumphs of Islam, the conquest of Jerusalem, the appearance of *fitan* (tribulations/trials/dissensions) among Muslim sects, the emergence of claimants to prophethood, and the conquest of Constantinople.

As for ongoing signs and portents, the Muslim exegetes mention the *ghurba* (estrangement) of Islam, the dominance of ignorance, the spread of all types of vice, the spread of promiscuity, a lack of modesty among men and women, women's dominance over men, the drinking of alcohol, the spread of the practice of usury, the deterioration of morals and manners, loss of trust, spread of music, and attachment to the world. These minor signs and portents were to continue for centuries until the approach of the major signs.[17]

Apart from a number of important battles, among them the battle and conquest of Rome, one of the most significant of the signs and portents that Muslim scholars mentioned were ten signs based on several sayings attributed to the Prophet, including the appearance of *al-mahdi al-muntadhar* (the guided savior or messiah) and *al-masih al-dajjal* (the antichrist), the descent of Jesus from heaven, the reappearance of Gog and Magog, and the sun rising from the West. As for the conquest of Rome, Muslim sources often referred to the following hadith attributed to the Prophet and narrated by the famous hadith collector al-Hakim (d. 1015): "'Abd Allah ibn 'Amr said: While we were around the Messenger of Allah, the Messenger of Allah (peace be upon him) was asked: 'Which of these two cities will be conquered first, Constantinople or *rumiyya* (Rome)?' He said, 'The city of Heraclius (Constantinople) will first be conquered'" (*Al-Mustadrak*, 508).

This hadith makes it clear why certain medieval Muslim travelers, unlike others, were tireless in their devotion to describing the riches of Rome. Far from being a mere fascination with the great city, such devotion was, it seems, religiously related and ideologically motivated by the belief that after centuries of *fitan* (tribulations) and defeats, there would come the time of *malahim* (major victories and triumphs). One of these would take place in Rome. This battle would end in the conquest of the legendary city, thus ushering in the ultimate triumph of what Muslims considered pure monotheism over what they saw as distorted faith, a direct reference to the Christian belief that the prophet Jesus is a son and partner of God.

Last but not least, although Ibn Yahya is famous today largely for his description of Constantinople and to a lesser degree of Rome, he is thought to be the first medieval Arab traveler to refer in writing to Britain and its capital, London. Without claiming to have visited the British Isles, while speaking of Rome's location he observed the following:

> From this city (c. Rome) you sail the sea and journey for three months, till you reach the land of the king of the Burjan (here Burgundians).

You journey hence through mountains and ravines for a month, till you reach the land of the Franks. From here you go forth and journey for four months, till you reach the city (capital) of Bartiniyah (Britain). It is a great city on the shore of the Western Ocean, ruled by seven kings...They are Christians. They are the last of the lands of the Greeks [Romans/ Europeans], and there is no civilization ['*imran*] beyond them. (Dunlop, "The British Isles According to Medieval Arabic Authors," 12).

Harun ibn Yahya's brief reference to Britain and London and his emphasis on its civilization should be seen as additional compelling evidence that for medieval Muslims the majority of European nations and countries were not synonymous with the barbarian people of the North, as indicated earlier in light of al-Mas'udi's increasingly (mis)quoted passage from *Al-Tanbih*.

To return to Harun ibn Yahya's reference to Britain, it is not an over-statement to indicate the important, yet forgotten, role played by a plethora of medieval Muslim captives in providing Muslim geographers with valuable information on regions outside the Muslim world. Although very few left written accounts, these captives were instrumental in fashioning medieval Muslim views and perceptions of the Other. To give a compelling example, perhaps the most well-known Muslim captive of the Middle Ages was the Syrian scholar Muslim al-Jarmi, who was captured by the Byzantines most likely around 845 before being transferred to Constantinople, where he was held prisoner for several years. After his ransom, paid by the Abbasid caliph al-Wathiq, he was set free in 847. Al-Jarmi is said to have traveled extensively in the Byzantine Empire— which, as explained earlier, was the archrival of the Abbasid caliphat—and several adjacent Euro-Asian lands. After his return to Baghdad, he wrote an account of his travels that became the most valuable firsthand narrative on the Byzantines, Khazars, and Slavs. His account of Byzantium and some fragments of his report on the Khazars and the Slavs were preserved by Ibn Khordadbeh and al-Mas'udi and extensively used by others, such as Ibn Rusta and Ibn al Faqih (al-Kilani, *Surat Uruba Inda al-'Arab fi-l-'Asr al-Wasit*, 162).

In sum, the importance of Harun ibn Yahya's forgotten account of Rome—like his description of Constantinople—must not be undervalued. Despite its brevity and fragmentation, it is one of the most valuable texts of its kind, not least because it captures medieval Muslims' fascination with Rome, which held a special place in Muslim apocalyptic beliefs. In this ninth-century account, Harun ibn Yahya provided a unique firsthand report of Rome from the perspective of a Muslim traveler. Indeed, regardless of some *mirabilia* à la Ibn Khordadbeh and other shortcomings, Harun ibn Yahya's report would turn out to be a *"unicum* of its age," to use Gabrieli's phrase (44). Suffice to say that ever since the rise of Islam, Rome had captivated medieval Muslims and gained a place that evoked, albeit in different ways, a place like Baghdad of *The Arabian Nights* in the Western Orientalist imagination. If Paris has been the most captivating city in modern Arabic secular literature and in Arabic fiction especially, in many ways Rome was the Paris of medieval Arabic-Islamic culture and literature.

Most importantly, and given what we have seen of medieval Muslim descriptions of Rome as a city of worldly riches, marvels, and wonders, one is tempted to suggest that if the Baghdad of Western Orientalism conjured up images of cruel Saracens and lustful Moors, eunuchs, naked harems, idols of the Prophet, crowns of Apollo, carbuncles of Tervagant, exotic flutes and lutes, and mosques inundated by the cacophonous voices of turbaned sheiks,[18] the Rome of medieval Muslim "Ifranjalism," ipso facto, conjured up extravagant *baba* adored by beardless young men and Roman damsels, churches filled with exotic crosses, strange words and drawings, all awash in gold, silver, and pearls and drowned within the tumultuous melodies of a Christian organ.

Utter Alterity or Pure Humanity: Barbarian Turks, Bulghars, and Rus (Vikings) in the Remarkable Risala of Ibn Fadlan

Recently the name of Ibn Fadlan has surfaced as one of the most quoted "Oriental" names in the West. As shown by Tabish Khair, this tenth-century Arab traveler owes much of his current international fame to Michael Crichton's novel *Eaters of the Dead* (1976) and perhaps mostly to its 1993 filmic adaptation *The 13th Warrior* by John McTiernan (*Other Routes: 1500 Years of African and Asian Travel Writing*, 273–274). No doubt both Creighton's novel and McTiernan's film were partly and freely inspired by Ibn Fadlan's *Risala* (Epistle), whose main section had fortunately been preserved by a number of medieval Arabic-Islamic chroniclers before the Turkish scholar Zeki Validi Togan discovered the most complete and reliable manuscript in the library of the Iranian city of Mashhad in 1923.[19] In a broader view, as outlined by Ibn Fadlan himself in the exordium of his *Risala*, this cultured and sophisticated Baghdadi *faqih* and *da'iya* (missionary) was selected by the Abbasid caliph al-Muqtadir (d. 932) to be among the leading members of an important delegation he dispatched to the city of Bulghar, near modern Kazan (central European Russia) in the year 921.[20]

What is known about Ahmad ibn Fadlan is derived chiefly from the scanty autobiographical notes bequeathed to us by a number of chroniclers, such as Yaqut al-Hamawi (Hmeida, *A'lam al-Jughrafiyyin al-'Arab*, 199). With the increasing interest in his account of this journey, more autobiographical information has surfaced. According to Hmeida, Ahmad ibn Fadlan ibn al-'Abbas ibn Rashid ibn Hammad was one of the most trusted clergy of the Abbasid caliph al-Muqtadir and his military chief Muhammad ibn Sulayman. In spite of the paucity of information about Ibn Fadlan, what one can glean from his text is that he was a man of integrity and piety, who was endowed with a respectable amount of religious knowledge and an exquisite literary style. This is in addition to a great willingness to advance the cause of Islam (al-Dahhan, ed., *Risalat Ibn Fadlan*, 28).

Hailed by several scholars as one of the world's earliest classics of ethnography and anthropology, Ibn Fadlan's *Risala* proved particularly valuable in describing some of the customs and manners of the many Eurasian peoples, mainly Turkic, Slavic, and northern (Rus) whom he encountered in the course of his fascinating journey. "Ibn Fadlan is unique in that he has left us virtually the only eyewitness account," J. E. McKeithen notes, "of the composition of peoples and forces in the Eurasian Steppe region between the time of Herodotus and the Dominican and Franciscan missions to the Mongols in the thirteenth century" ("The *Risala* of Ibn Fadlan," 3). Indeed, Ibn Fadlan's *Risala* is one of the richest medieval Arabic-Islamic sources wherein one can explore and examine the topoi and discourses of alterity in medieval Arabic literature and culture.

Ibn Fadlan opens his text with a brief exordium in which he provides the reader with a detailed description of the mission the caliph selected him to be part of in response to a letter that was sent by Almish ibn Yaltwar, the recently converted Muslim *malik* (king) of the Bulghars of the Middle Volga. The latter, Ibn Fadlan explains, had in turn sent an embassy to Baghdad to meet the caliph al-Muqtadir (908–932). It was led by a Muslim Khazar by the name of 'Abd Allah ibn Bashtu al-Khazari. The letter the envoy of Almish handed to the caliph, Ibn Fadlan reveals, contained a number of demands from the king of the Bulghars.

Among these demands, Ibn Fadlan mentions a request for a knowledgeable *faqih*, or a scholar of Muslim law, who will instruct the newly converted Bulghars in the laws of Islam and will help the king in managing the religious affairs of his kingdom. In addition, there is the demand to build a *masjid* (mosque) and erect a *minbar* (pulpit) to ensure the daily prayers and the weekly Friday sermon and prayer. Last but not least, the king asks for help in constructing a strong *hisn* (fortress) that will protect Yaltawar's realm from the growing assaults of the powerful Jewish

Khazars, their southern neighbors (al-Kilani, *Surat Uruba Inda al-'Arab fi-l-'Asr al-Wasit*, 195).

Ibn Fadlan tells us that the embassy left Baghdad on the eleventh of *safar* 309 AH (June 21, 921 AD) and reached the city of Bulghar on the twelfth of *muharram* 310 AH (May 12, 922 AD). Throughout this long Eurasian journey, the embassy had to cross thousands of miles through what are now Iran, Uzbekistan, Kazakhstan, Tataristan, Bashkoritan, Azerbaijan, Russia, Ukraine, and probably Scandinavia.

As pointed out by al-Kilani and others, the embassy was well planned and prepared by Nadir al-Harami (195). Al-Harami, who did not partici-pate in the journey, selected many non-Arabs as essential members for the mission. With the exception of Ibn Fadlan, these men came originally from several regions crossed by the delegation, and they were conversant with many of the languages spoken by different peoples they met en route to Volga Bulgharia. This was the case with Ibn Sawsan al-Rassi, an ex-Russian slave; Tekin al-Turki, a Muslim Turk; and Bares al-Saqlabi, the Slav; in addition to Almish's envoy 'Abd Allah ibn Bashtu al-Khazari (the Khazar), who journeyed back home with the caliph's delegation (al-Dahhan, ed., *Risalat Ibn Fadlan*, 69).

Ibn Fadlan mentions that the caliph in person had appointed him to read the letter he wrote for the Bulghar king, to present the caliphal gifts, and to hand over the requested money to build the mosque and the fortress. He emphasizes as well that he would supervise the *fuqaha'* and *mu'alimin* (the instructors) dispatched by the caliph to instruct the Bulghars in the teachings of Islam as requested by the Bulghar king. We have no reasons to doubt some of these roles or to disbelieve what is said about the many peoples he came across during his journey.

After leaving Baghdad, the hub of tenth-century Muslim civilization and the place that ninth- and tenth-century Iraqi geo-cosmographers made the indisputable omphalos of the civilized world, Ibn Fadlan and his companions took an indirect route that allowed them not only to visit a number of major cities of central Asia such as Hamadan, Ray, Nishapur, Sarakhs, Bukhara, Khwarezm, and Jurjaniyya but also to encounter a number of seminomadic Turkic tribes. After passing various Iranian and Caucasian cities, the group headed to Bukhara, the famous Silk Road city that was also hailed as one of the richest cultural centers of the Abbasid caliphate.

As the long route stretched from Baghdad to Bukhara, the keen eyes of Ibn Fadlan apparently did not discover any significant change in the environment or the customs and manners of the various non-Arab (Muslim) peoples the traveler and his comrades encountered in the doz-ens of cities, towns, and villages they passed by. As soon as the delegation

began to leave the realm of the Abbasids, however, Ibn Fadlan's unprecedented powers came into play, not only observing but also recording
and exploring (most often with an impressive ethnographical talent) the
many changes and numerous differences he encountered. Although this
started in the border regions between *ardh al-islam* and *ardh al-turk* (land
of the Turks), it reached its full power during the embassy's meeting with
three Turkic tribes namely the Oghuz, Pechenegs, and Bashkirs.

After a few days in Bukhara, Ibn Fadlan and his companions headed
toward the city of Jurjaniyya (Urgench). The city, as we are told by Caroline
Stone, is currently located in Uzbekistan, "near modern Kungrad just south
of the Aral Sea" ("Ibn Fadlan and the Midnight Sun," 1). Because of the
freezing of the Jaihun River, whose crossing was necessary for the continu-
ation of the journey, the delegation had to hibernate almost three months
grappling with the extreme cold (al-Dahhan, ed., *Risalat Ibn Fadlan*, 83).

Ibn Fadlan, who could not hide his nostalgia for the warmth of the
East, has movingly captured the hardships endured by the local inhabitants during this cold weather. He speaks sympathetically of frozen cattle,
empty markets and vacant streets, and native beggars who had to find
shelter and sit by the fire before asking for bread. The cold was so extreme
that it was considered a great act of generosity if one man invited another
to sit by his fire (84). Ibn Fadlan's personal experience of the cold of
Jurjaniyya was bitter and unpleasant. He complains that because of the
severe cold he had to thaw his own beard before the fire every time he
had to use the bath, which was outside the main house (85).

This versatile Iraqi scholar, who must have been conversant with the
dominant cosmographical views outlined earlier, does not evoke any theories in his perception of the Jurjanis in spite of the fact that he seems to
acknowledge the enormous influence of cold on the everyday life of the
Jurjani. Nor does he appear to find any *tawahhush* (barbarity) in the local
people's *tiba'* (attributes). Contrary to his description of their climate, Ibn
Fadlan's portrayal of the Jurjanis is unquestionably positive. He mentions
with admiration that throughout the months he lived with them, they
were always kind, compassionate, and hospitable. Perhaps the fact that
the Jurjani were predominately Muslims made them "similar" in his eyes.
During the relatively long period of three months, there seemed nothing *gharib* (strange) or worth recording about Jurjani manners, customs,
beliefs, or women. This is not the case with the Oghuz, the Petchenegs,
and the Bashkirs, the three Turkic tribes the embassy encountered after
leaving the town of Jurjaniyya.

There is little doubt that Ibn Fadlan's firsthand account of the
Oghuz Turks is one of the most detailed of its kind in classical Arabic
writing. In keeping with Arabic sources, he calls them *al-ghuzziyya*.

Commenting on their way of life, he states that they are all nomads who live in tents made of felt and survive by breeding cattle. Although he notes that some of them are extremely rich, possessing thousands of horses and sheep, the majority of the Oghuz are not only poor but living in utter *shaqa'*, a strong Arabic word that denotes complete wretchedness (91).

Even more disturbing for Ibn Fadlan is that instead of turning to God, the poor Oghuz chose to lead a life divorced from religion and reason. In his own harsh words, the Oghuz are like *al-hamir al-dhalla*, that is, strayed asses (91). Given that they lack a monotheistic *din* (religion) and are uncaring about *'aql* (reason), it is no wonder that the Oghuz count their chieftains as gods. After Ibn Fadlan fails to convince one of the powerful Oghuz chieftains to convert to Islam, he denies them any positive attributes in religious affairs. Perhaps the result of this failure pushed him to accuse all Oghuz of religious ignorance. Doubting possible future conversions to Islam, Ibn Fadlan warns his readers that the Oghuz care more about filling their own purses than enlightening their souls and minds. Every time an Oghuz man, he tells us, wants to gain money or gifts from Muslim merchants, he pretends to be Muslim by saying *bir tengrich*, meaning there is only one God (92).

How prescient was Ibn Fadlan in his prediction about a possible and sincere Oghuz future with Islam? Contrary to this traveler's prediction, no more than a century after his journey, the Oghuz turned into some of the most fervent Muslims in the entire history of Islam. As demonstrated by historians, it all started when an Oghuz chieftain by the name of Seljuk "embraced Islam with deep fervour" (Sykes, *A History of Persia*, 8). "The Seljuks with the fervour of recent converts revitalized Islam as the Norsemen revitalized Christendom," Percy Molesworth Sykes tells us, "and when Europe under Norman leaders attacked the East under the impulse of the Crusades it was the light horse of the Seljuks which met the heavy horse of the Crusaders" (28).

Equally unacceptable to Ibn Fadlan are Oghuz hygiene and sanitary customs. Recalling the Chinese (and to a lesser degree the Hindus of al-Tajir's account as well as the Galicians of al-Bakri) and anticipating the Franks of Ibn Munqidh, Ibn Fadlan seems to adopt an extreme view of Oghuz relations with water. In keeping with Muslim opinions of non-Muslim hygiene, he expresses his disgust at what he describes as not merely a lack of cleanliness but rather an inherent (water)phobia dominant among these Turkic nomads. They do not wash themselves after defecation, urination, and sexual intercourse, he observes reproachfully. Without any details, however, he ends his notes on Oghuz hygiene by denying them any relations at all with water: "They have nothing whatsoever to do with water, especially in winter," he comments (Frye, *Ibn Fadlan's Journey to Russia*, 43).

Ibn Fadlan's description of the embassy's meeting with one of the leading Oghuz chieftains convinces us that these are more than preconceived prejudices and hasty stereotypes. While taking off "the coat of brocade, which he wore to don the garment of honour" presented to him by the embassy, the Oghuz luminary gave his sophisticated guest an unsolicited chance to notice with disgust that his underclothes were "fraying apart from dirt" and to assert that "it is their custom that no one shall take off the garment which he wears on his body until it disintegrates" (40). Against Ibn Fadlan's negative representation of Oghuz hygiene and cleanliness, one is forced—yet again—to point out that medieval Arab travelers most often compared themselves favorably, if not haughtily, with the non-Muslim and even Muslim Others they encountered in their journeys, whose presumable lack of proper cleanliness they met with varying degrees of superciliousness and sometimes, as we will see later with Ibn Fadlan's views of the Bashkirs', (Muslim) Bulghars', and Vikings' hygiene, with utter revulsion and disgust.

Yet the most horrifying thing that Ibn Fadlan noticed about the Oghuz was their permissiveness and shamelessness. These are no more brutally represented than in the unprecedented *takashshuf* (exposedness/nudity) of their women and the unmatched *dayatha* (lack of jealousy) of their men. In one shocking passage, the conservative Baghdadi *faqih* describes himself in a situation that perhaps no other premodern or even modern Muslim traveler ever witnessed in a non-Muslim land. This took place when he accepted an invitation from an Oghuz family. The outcome of this invitation turned dramatic:

> Their women do not veil themselves before their men nor before others, and in the same way, does a woman not conceal any part of her body from any man whatsoever. When we happened to be staying with a man of them as guests, we came and sat down. The man's wife was with us, and while she was talking to us, she uncovered her pudendum and scratched it, while we were looking at her. We covered our faces saying "I seek forgiveness of God (astaghfir Allah)." Her husband laughed and said to the interpreter: "Tell them, she uncovers it in your presence and you see it, but she safeguards it, and it is not attainable. This is better than if she were to cover it, while making it accessible." (McKeithen, "The *Risala* of Ibn Fadlan," 54–55)

Perhaps even more illustrative than al-Tajir's encounter with the Orient, this passage conjures up the cultural poetics of wonder as we saw earlier.

Indeed, Ibn Fadlan, especially after describing this first encounter with Oghuz women, quickly gave his own cultural judgment of the (scandalous) behavior he had just seen.

The question that one may raise here is why Ibn Fadlan has asked for repentance especially if we know that according to Islamic law *al-nadhra al-ula* (that is, the first inadvertent sight of a foreign woman) is *mubah* (permissible). Hence, it does not necessitate *istighfar*, which is asking for repentance. What is certain is that he has not just seen but rather gazed at the Oghuz woman's private parts, a thing that is *haram* (forbidden), thus it necessitates an act of repentance. If it is, Islamically speaking, illicit to look at unveiled women out of fear of *fitna* (sexual attraction), it is a graver *ma'siya* (disobedience) to gaze at the most sexual of (foreign) women's parts.

What tells us more when it comes to the character of Ibn Fadlan is the fact that he is not inclined toward unfounded generalization and stereotyping about Oghuz women. Contrary to our expectations, he soon informs us that the excessive bodily display of Oghuz women and the shamelessness of Oghuz men should not be interpreted as sexual promiscuity or tolerance of *zina'* (adultery). Against all odds, Ibn Fadlan gives full authorial voice to the Oghuz themselves to explain the underlying philosophy behind letting their women freely and shamelessly expose their bodies. As articulated by the Oghuz husband himself, Oghuz women are as chaste as Ibn Fadlan would think veiled Muslim women are: "Tell them, she uncovers it in your presence so that you see it and be abashed, but it is not to be attained," the Oghuz man complacently asserts. "This, however, is better than when you cover it up and yet it is reachable" (Frye, *Ibn Fadlan's Journey to Russia*, 43).

This strong statement not only betrays an Oghuz philosophy of body exposure that is ultimately congruous with the Muslim philosophy of body covering; at the same time it implicitly hides a strong Oghuz critique of the veil that brings to mind the mostly Western critique of female Muslim attire. If Muslim men cover the bodies of their women to prevent them from engaging in any illegal sexual relations, Oghuz men expose the most private parts of their women to attain the same objective. Contrary to our expectations, soon Ibn Fadlan will confirm this Oghuz philosophy when he writes that, like Muslims, the Oghuz are extremely intolerant of *zina'*. As a matter of fact, all Oghuz men and women found guilty of *zina'* are sentenced to death by tearing their bodies into two halves after being tied between two trees (al-Dahhan, ed., *Risalat Ibn Fadlan*, 93).

Ibn Fadlan's perception of the Petchenegs and the Bashkirs does not differ greatly from that of the Oghuz. All in all, their manners and customs are as barbaric as the latter. For obvious reasons, however, Ibn Fadlan chooses to single out the Bashkirs as the most savage of all the tribes the embassy met in its journey. With all possible disgust, he pictures them as beardless, dirty, and bloodthirsty. With horror, he writes that eating *qaml* (lice) is considered a delicacy: "One of them will examine the seam of his tunic and grind the lice with his teeth" (Frye, *Ibn Fadlan's Journey to Russia*, 42). Another found "a louse in his clothing. He crushed it between his fingernails and licked it, and he said when he saw me: 'Good.'" (42). In a possible reference to their cannibalism, although perhaps exaggeratedly, he writes that it is common among the Bashkirs that one will cut off another's head and take it home (al-Dahhan, ed., *Risalat Ibn Fadlan*, 108).

Throughout his negative account of the Bashkirs, Ibn Fadlan does everything to convince us that their savagery is intrinsically related to their paganism. Far worse than the Oghuz, the Bashkirs are depicted by Ibn Fadlan as the most religiously confounded and confounding of all Turkic tribes. He writes with disgust that he saw with his own eyes Bashkirs who claimed that for every thing in the world there is a *rabb* (god) and others who worshipped snakes, fish, cranes, and so forth (109). Nevertheless, there is nothing quite so unimaginable in the mind of Ibn Fadlan as the suggestion that there exist some humans who worship what he calls in Arabic *al-ihlil*, that is, the phallus:

> Each of them sculpts a piece of wood the size of a phallus and hangs it on himself. If he is to undertake a trip or to meet an enemy, he kisses it and prostrates himself before it saying: "Oh my Lord do unto me such and such." I said to the interpreter: "Ask one of them as to their justification to this, and why he believes it to be his lord." He said: "I came out of something similar to it, and I do not know any creator of myself other than it." (Frye, *Ibn Fadlan's Journey to Russia*, 43)

In addition to a number of Muslim travelers to India who recorded with shock the existence of this phallus worship or phallism in medieval India, Ibn Fadlan is among the earliest Muslim travelers to mention the existence of this same ancient cult outside India.[21] Along with the accuracy of the information he provided about phallus worship, Ibn Fadlan's keenness and curiosity are also remarkable. In fact, his strict belief in monotheistic Islam does not appear to interfere with his pursuit of questions about many aspects of what he undoubtedly saw as ultimate *dhalal* (misguidance). No wonder the concluding and formulaic statement *ta'ala allahu 'amma yaqulu al-dhalimin 'uluwwan kabiran*

(May God be greatly exalted above what the iniquitous say) expresses his reaction (al-Dahhan, ed., *Risalat Ibn Fadlan*, 109).

After another long journey during which they crossed many rivers, such as the Jaramshan, Uran, Uram, Watigh, Niyasnah, and Jaushir, Ibn Fadlan and his companions reached their final destination in the city of Bulghar. The embassy seems to have been eagerly awaited by Almish, the king of the Bulghars. As mentioned by Ibn Fadlan, the impatient Almish commissioned four of his top officers, his brothers and his own sons, to meet the embassy before its arrival in the city. Initially impressed by Bulghar hospitality, Ibn Fadlan marks with a sense of appreciation Almish's move to meet the caliph's honorable envoys at the outskirts of his capital and to supervise the setting up of tents for them. Ibn Fadlan's first impressions did not linger long (113).

After resting for four days, Ibn Fadlan and his companions were summoned by Almish to read the caliph's letter in the presence of his wife, family, top officers, and a throng of the common people. After displaying the caliphal presents to the Bulghar king and his wife, Ibn Fadlan read the letter, which was well written and full of religious and political rhetoric. Not much interested in the caliph's words, Almish seemed to have cared more about the huge amount of money mentioned in the letter, which for some reason Ibn Fadlan did not hand to him (114–115).

The day after the reading of the letter, which coincided with the first Friday the embassy spent in the city, Ibn Fadlan after attending the *jumu'a* prayer demanded that the Bulghar king Almish ask his *khutaba'* (preachers) to stop calling him *malik* (King): "Verily God is the king, and no one but He, majesty and might be His, should be called by this name from the pulpit" (Frye, *Ibn Fadlan's Journey to Russia*, 46). Citing the supreme example of the then caliph as well as previous Abbasid—not Umayyad—caliphs and referring to a hadith by the Prophet Muhammad, Ibn Fadlan suggested to Almish that he take rather the title of 'Abd Allah, that is, the slave of God. Almish accepted the suggestion and changed his name to Ja'far in imitation of the caliph himself (al-Dahhan, ed., *Risalat Ibn Fadlan*, 117). No doubt Ibn Fadlan proved to be sincere in instructing the Bulghars concerning the teaching of Islam in accordance with the stated *raison d'être* of the embassy.

The newly named Ja'far ibn 'Abd Allah, emir of the Bulghars, "Servant of Allah," and client of amir *al-mu'minin* (the commander of the faithful)—that is, the Abbasid caliph—soon grew impatient with the mission. Wary about the money, he summoned Ibn Fadlan for another meeting, which turned dramatic. It ended in the unfortunate detention of Ibn Fadlan by Almish, but it represented a good opportunity for the keen Abbasid observer to note some bizarre Bulghar customs:

> He called for a table and it was brought, and on it was roast meat only. He
> himself began, took a knife, cut off a bite-size morsel and ate it. Then he
> cut off a piece and gave it to Sawsan the ambassador. As the latter took it, a
> small table was brought and placed in front of him. Such is the custom, no
> one extends his hand to the food until the king gives him a bite, and as soon
> as he takes it a table is brought to him...We ate, each one from his own
> table, no one sharing it with him, and no one taking anything from a table
> other than his own. (McKeithen, "The *Risala* of Ibn Fadlan," 87–88)

Obviously one expects that in the lands of the Muslim Bulghars, Ibn
Fadlan will feel more culturally relaxed than he proved to be during
his journey into the land of the pagan Turks. Although it is clear that
the almost Manichaean rhetoric of Muslim civilization versus pagan
savagery that colored Ibn Fadlan's perception of the Turks had dramatically diminished, the Abbasid traveler never ceased to depict the
Bulghars as "scarcely civilized, barbarians but for their embrace of
Islam," to use James E. Montgomery's conclusion ("Ibn Fadlan and the
Rusiyyah," 17). All through his Bulghar narrative, Ibn Fadlan pictures
the Muslim Bulghars as culturally non-Muslim. As the earlier passage
illustrates, Bulghar customs and manners are too utterly un-Abbasid to
pass unnoticed by the culturally inquisitive Ibn Fadlan.

Not eating a bite of the food that was blessed by the Bulghar king's
saliva foretold the cultural unease that characterized Ibn Fadlan during
his encounter with his royal brother. Nor did it seem to be a good omen
for the fortune of Ibn Fadlan and his companions. Indeed, as soon as Ibn
Fadlan revealed to Almish that for a number of reasons the embassy had
not brought the money, the Bulghar king dropped all signs of brotherly
akhlaq (manners):

> He [Almish] threw the letter of the Commander of the Faithful and said:
> "Who brought this letter?" I replied: "I did." He then threw the letter of
> the wazīr and said: "And this one too?" I replied: "I did." He [then] said:
> "And the money that has been mentioned in both of them, what has been
> done with it?" I said "it was impossible to collect it. Time was short, and
> we feared lest we fail to gain entry [into the lands of the Turks on time].
> We left the money behind to catch up with us later." He said: "You came,
> the whole lot of you, and my master spent on you, only in order that this
> money be brought to me, so that I might build a *fortress which would protect
> me from the Jews who have enslaved me. As for the gifts, gulam* [servant] *would
> have been able to bring them* [italics mine]. (McKeithen, "The *Risala* of Ibn
> Fadlan," 89–90)

This passage is remarkable, not least because it leaves us with no doubt that what was ultimately sought by Almish had more to do with politics and money than with spirituality and religion.

As a growing number of scholars have observed, there seemed to be a political agreement between the Bulghar king and the Abbasid caliph. With this arrangement, the former would receive financial and military help in exchange for paying religious-political homage to the Abbasids. The Russian Arabist A. P. Kovalevsky, as we are told by historian Mirfatykh Zakiev, alluded to the political connotations of a number of idiosyncratic religio-cultural complexes, such as *al-minbar* (pulpit), *khutba* (sermon), and *du'a' li-l-sultan* (invocation of allegiance), which are all related to the importance of *salat al-jumu'a* (Friday prayer) (*Tatars: Problems of History and Language*, 82).[22]

Kovalevsky refers to two Friday sermons mentioned by Ibn Fadlan in his account. The first was prepared by Ibn Fadlan before his arrival in the realm of the Bulghars, apparently to serve as his first *khutba*. In the latter, he incorporated a *du'a'* (invocation) in which he invokes the name of the Bulghar emir. The second refers to a *khutba* presumably given at a later time by the Bulghar emir, now called Ja'far. In this sermon, the Bulghar king declares himself to be "the vassal of the emir of faithful," as we saw earlier (85). Others have alluded to strategic and economic objectives behind the Bulghar request and the quick response of the Abbasid caliph. For instance, without questioning the initial religious motivation for the embassy, Montgomery has suggested that caliph al-Muqtadir must have thought of strengthening the northern borders of his caliphate and reducing "the influence of the Samanids by diverting northern trade in slaves, Furs, and silver from Transoxania to Iraq" ("Ibn Fadlan," 579).

The historian Thomas S. Noonan has revealed more thoroughly the sociopolitical and economic motifs behind the "eastern" move of the Bulghar king. Firstly, there was certainly a necessity for internal power consolidation related to his unease with the continuous challenge represented by the powerful "tribal leaders" and "the ruling elite which included 500 prominent families" ("European Russia: c500–1050," 505). Secondly and more vital, there was the external pressure related to the Bulghar king's frustration with the Khazars. As convincingly explained by Noonan, the Bulghars were unfairly exhausted by the excessive yearly tax they had to pay to the Khazars, who had taken the king's own son as a hostage (505). "The Bulghars sought independence in order to control and sell their own pelts," Noonan affirms, "and in part, [as] a means to obtain support from co-religionists against Khazar domination" (505).

Ibn Fadlan's quarrel with Almish ended amicably. After further disputes over certain jurisprudential issues, the tenacious Almish was won over by Ibn Fadlan's knowledge and integrity. "He began to favor me [over others] and to draw me close to his person, while keeping my companions at a distance" (Frye, *Ibn Fadlan's Journey to Russia*, 49), Ibn Fadlan tells us quite conceitedly. Almish had nothing to hide from the one whom he had recently called Abu Bakr al-Siddiq, regarded by many Sunnis as Muhammad's greatest supporter and closest companion. Ibn Fadlan leaves us no doubt as to the pertinence of many of the previous critical speculations in relation to his own status with Almish.

In the concluding paragraphs of the section on the Bulghars, Ibn Fadlan recounts that he knew from Almish that the Bulghars were suffering all types of exploitation and intimidation from the Khazars. In addition to his son held hostage by the Khazar king, Almish told Ibn Fadlan that the Khazar king, knowing of the beauty of his two daughters, had asked for one of them in marriage. At Almish's refusal, the Jewish Khazar king sent his troops and seized her by force. Refusing to marry the Khazar king, Almish's first daughter died in the Khazar court. After the death of the first beautiful daughter, the Khazar king asked for the second. To prevent another tragedy, Almish gave his daughter to the king of the Eskel, who was one of his subjects (al-Dahhan, ed., *Risalat Ibn Fadlan*, 114–115).

To history's delight, Ibn Fadlan was lucky enough to accompany his now close friend Ja'far ibn 'Abd Allah (Almish) in his seasonal journey to the Bulghar heartlands. The inquisitive Ibn Fadlan exploited this opportunity to the full. The outcome has been one of the most fascinating documents about tenth-century Volga Bulghars and Rus (Vikings), then active around the Volga River. Ibn Fadlan has given us a spectacular sketch of many aspects of the socioeconomic and cultural life of the Volga Bulghars at that time as well as a marvelous description of Bulghar fauna and flora. However, it is to be noted that the highly religious Ibn Fadlan had mixed feelings about some of the customs and manners of his Bulghar coreligionists, although he does not seem to doubt their sincere attachment to Islam.

In contrast to the Turks, at least economically speaking, the Volga Bulghars are portrayed as enjoying life. This is the result of their rich agricultural resources. Ibn Fadlan cites with admiration the abundance of hazelnut trees, the delectable berries, the sour apples that made young women plump, and many other trees that he failed to identify. He goes on to notice with a sense of comparative surprise that in spite of the abundance of wheat and barley, the Bulghars feed principally on millet and horse meat (129). This abundance does not mean that the Bulghars had everything. Ibn Fadlan highlights things lacking in comparison to what he was used to. This is shown by his discovery that the Bulghars use fish oil but know "neither olive oil, nor sesame oil, nor cooking oil of any kind" (Frye, *Ibn Fadlan's Journey to Russia*, 54). This statement certainly has more cultural significance if one remembers the place of olive oil in particular in the dietary customs of the Arabs past and present.

Perhaps the most interesting information he records when it comes to the Bulghar diet is its class implications. Knowing beforehand that Islam makes it incumbent on Muslim men and women to feed their slaves and servants from the same food they themselves eat, Ibn Fadlan notices with disapproval that his Bulghar coreligionists, with the confusing exception of goats' heads, do not allow their slaves to eat any type of *lahm* (meat). The Bulghar treatment of their slaves, at least when it comes to food, is inconsistent with Islamic laws, whose promulgation and implementation among the Bulghars was Ibn Fadlan's most urgent business.[23] Surprisingly, he seems to have preferred silence on this specific issue contrary to his obsessive "activism" in matters of gender and sexuality. Inasmuch as this prohibition appears to be related to a Bulghar belief that eating meat decreases the productivity of slaves, it tells us much about the condition of slaves in tenth-century Volga Bulgharia.

Quite priggishly, Ibn Fadlan does not always seem satisfied with Bulghar beliefs and customs even when they are insignificant. He refers to their superstitious appreciation of dogs barking and their lack of fear of snakes (al-Dahhan, ed., *Risalat Ibn Fadlan*, 127). He also expresses his confusion at their strange *qalanis* (head caps) especially when the *'awam* (populace) appeared to him obliged to take them off in the presence of their king: "Whoever sits in the presence of the king seats in a kneeling posture, and does not take out his cap, nor does he make it visible until he leaves the presence of the king" (Frye, *Ibn Fadlan's Journey to Russia*, 55).

Read in light of Ibn Fadlan's aforementioned request that Almish should change his title from the King of the Bulghars to the Servant of Allah, it becomes clear that Ibn Fadlan is wary of the cult of *ta'dim* (human veneration), deemed inconsistent with pure *tawhid* (monotheism) for it can be seen as an act of *shirk* (associationism). This passage recalls al-Bakri's previously mentioned condemnation of the Romans' venera- tion of *al-bab* (the pope).

What is even more repugnant in Ibn Fadlan's eyes is the fact that Bulghar men and women bathe together naked in the river in oppo- sition to Muslim modesty and decency (al-Dahhan, ed., *Risalat Ibn Fadlan*, 134). Perhaps anticipating condemnation of his presence in such a place, Ibn Fadlan soon reminds his readers that he was there so as to order the Bulghar women to cover themselves while swimming. As the religious authority of the embassy, Ibn Fadlan must prove that he has done his duty in *al-amr bi-l-ma'ruf wa-l-nahy 'an al-munkar*, which is enjoining proper behavior and prohibiting inappropriateness. The question that raises itself here is why Ibn Fadlan has singled out the Bulghar women when he knows well that Islamically speaking both men and women must be reminded of their religious obligations in this respect. As with the Oghuz Turks, the exposure of Bulghar women's bodies should not make readers think that the Bulghars are liberal in sexual matters. Similar to the Oghuz attitudes concerning adultery, Ibn Fadlan tells us that the Bulghars abhor adultery, and they sentence those who commit it to a death more horrifying than the one practiced by the Oghuz. As described by Ibn Fadlan, the adulterer and the adulteress are cleft with an axe from the scruff of their necks to their thighs. Then the pieces of their bodies are hung on trees (134).

As demonstrated by J. E. Montgomery, in the course of his account of the Bulghars, Ibn Fadlan has shown an insatiable appetite for plausible *'aja'ib* (marvels) presumably seen with his own eyes during his tour with Almish. In his own words, Ibn Fadlan tells his readers that he had seen so many *'aja'ib* that he is unable to enumerate them (al-Dahhan, ed., *Risalat Ibn Fadlan*, 123). In addition to his notes on the strangeness of Bulghar nights and days and unfamiliar Bulghar flora and fauna, his quasi-surrealist description and interpretation of the northern lights and what were likely thunderbolts proved particularly startling: "I beheld a red, fire-like cloud close to me, and the hum and the noises seemed to be issuing from it" (McKeithen, "The *Risala* of Ibn Fadlan," 94).

Against our expectation, the otherwise unsuperstitious Ibn Fadlan stuns us by claiming that "within it there seemed to be something similar to men and horses, and in the hands of these phantoms resembling men there were spears and swords which I could both clearly make out and envision myself" (94). This bizarre interpretation of purely meteorological phenomena, it seems to me, is a rare attempt on the part of the author to flavor his rigid *Risala* with the highly regarded literary and cultural leitmotif of the *'ajib/gharib*. Similarly, the juxtaposition of the "scientific" response of the locals to the superstitious interpretation and the ensuing religious reaction of the foreigners adds more flavor to the *gharaba* (strangeness) of the event: "We were frightened by this phenomenon and turned to supplication and prayer," Ibn Fadlan writes, *"while the people [of the town] laughed at us and expressed their astonishment at our actions* [italics mine]" (94–95). This is similar to his description of a fallen Bulghar tree with a massive trunk. When he got closer to it, to his awe and terror, a giant snake that was nearly as big and tall as the trunk threw itself down and vanished among the trees (al-Dahhan, ed., *Risalat Ibn Fadlan*, 127–128). When it comes to the distant lands of the Bulghars, these are as real and familiar as the sunny days of Baghdad. And one must be an Ibn Fadlan to see with one's own eyes and give credence to such marvels and wonders.

Ibn Fadlan's rare resort to the implausible should not encourage us to associate the *Risala* with the genre of *'ajib/gharib* literature, as a number of medieval Muslim and modern Western scholars such as Yaqut al-Hamawi and Regis Blachere have done and as pointed out by J. E. Montgomery in "Traveling Autopsies: Ibn Fadlan and the Bulghars" (7). Although failing to mention the previous examples, Caroline Stone is correct when she asserts, "Unlike later medieval travelers, whose accounts tend to run riot with implausible detail, Ibn Fadlan mentions only one marvel: the bones of a 'giant'—possibly the remains of a mammoth" ("Ibn Fadlan and the Midnight Sun," 3).

Among the many cultural encounters that fill Ibn Fadlan's *Risala*, it is his "remarkable account," to use Frye's phrase (*Ibn Fadlan's Journey to Russia*, ix), of the people called *al-rusiyya* (Rus) whom he met around the Volga River that has proved of enduring value and has recently rekindled worldwide attention: "Ibn Fadlan's account has proved to be an invaluable source of information for modern scholars," Montgomery notes, "interested in, among other subjects, the birth and formation of the Russian state, in the Viking involvement in northern and eastern Europe, in the Slavs and the Khazars" ("Ibn Fadlan and the Rusiyyah," 1). In spite of the once heated debate over their real European identity, the Rus, in the view of Caroline Stone, are more and more acknowledged to be "one of the Scandinavian tribes," and "the most famous of these tribes were the Vikings" (4).[24]

Describing the circumstances of his historic encounter with the Rus, Ibn Fadlan tells us that he saw their encampments by the River Itel (Volga) while they were visiting the city of Bulghar for trade. The first thing that struck him was their perfect physique (al-Dahhan, ed., *Risalat Ibn Fadlan*, 149). Asserting with the utmost rhetorical force that he has never "seen people with a more developed bodily stature," he soon goes further to claim that they "are as tall as date palms, blond and ruddy" (Frye, *Ibn Fadlan's Journey to Russia*, 63). Especially intriguing here is Ibn Fadlan's reliance on the genuinely archetypal figure of the palm tree in his description of the physique of the Rus. The fact that the Quran and the Sunna are full of such similes adds greatly to the cultural and religious significance of this rhetorical borrowing.

Besides the numerous references to the tall, strong palm trees that God created for Man, among the rewards righteous believers will enjoy in *al-janna* (paradise) are "tall (and stately) palm trees, with shoots of fruit-stalks piled one over another" (Quran 50:10). In fact, the Quran and the Sunna, like the Bible, usually compare steadfast believers who endure all trials and tribulations to *al-shajara al-tayyiba* (the good tree), which is one of the Quranic appellations of the palm tree. However, it is, in the hadith narrated by ʿAbd Allah ibn ʿUmar, one of Muhammad's close companions, that this comparison is most directly addressed.[25] In light of these hadiths and other Quranic verses, Ibn Fadlan seems to construe the Other's rare familiarity through common topoi of his own culture.[26] It also shows the resonance of religious rhetoric in his portrayal of the Other(s) in general and his sketch of Rus defects, as will be shown later.

In contrast to their perfect physique, the first defect that loomed within the cultural horizon of Ibn Fadlan when it comes to the Rus was the semi-nakedness of their men and women. Ibn Fadlan notes with dissatisfaction that in contrast to the many weapons and metal items, Rus clothing is sparse and underdeveloped, defying Muslim and Eastern standards of clothing and challenging what he believed to be appropriate dress codes. Rus men wear neither tunics nor *kaftans* (cloaks), leaving half of their bodies uncovered. This makes some of their *ʿawrat*—that is, prohibited parts of the body—exposed to view (al-Dahhan, ed., *Risalat Ibn Fadlan*, 150).

More threatening, however, is the exotic and erotic metal-covered breasts and gold- and silver-adorned necks of the beautiful Viking women:

> Each of the women has fastened upon the two breasts a brooch of iron, silver, copper, or gold, in weight and value according to the wealth of her husband. Each brooch has a ring to which a knife is likewise fixed, and is hung upon the breast. Around the neck the women wear rings of gold and silver. (Frye, *Ibn Fadlan's Journey to Russia*, 63)

For Ibn Fadlan the *faqih*, who is enjoined to lower his gaze when seeing foreign women, the exotic and erotic Viking women proved too alluring to pass unnoticed. The temptation must have been inevitable for the pious Ibn Fadlan. In contrast to the Oghuz and the Bulghars, lack of appropriate clothing among the Rus reveals much when it comes to what he portrays as the unprecedented sexual shamelessness and promiscuity that dominate their life. Particularly appalling, however, is their disrespect of privacy and their "savage" sexual practices especially when it comes to their engagement in sexual intercourse in front of each other: "One of them may have sexual relations with his slave girl while his comrades look on. Sometimes a whole group of them may come together and engage in such action opposite each other," he relates (McKeithen, "The *Risala* of Ibn Fadlan," 131). It is to be noted that for a pious Muslim, which Ibn Fadlan appears to be, there is nothing more shameful for a man than having (legal) sex with one's wife or slave girl in front of other men or women.[27]

No less disturbing in Ibn Fadlan's eyes is Rus hygiene. Although they seem to have a closer relationship with water than the Oghuz, many of their hygiene customs appeared ultimately disgusting to him. In addition to the "always and already" reasons that make non-Muslim Others unclean, the Rus' practice of what Stone has identified as an ancient Germanic custom of communal bathing ("Ibn Fadlan and the Midnight Sun," 2) made them in Ibn Fadlan's eyes "the filthiest of God's creatures":

> Everyday, without fail, they wash their faces and heads in the filthiest and most foul water possible. A slave girl comes every morning carrying a large bowl filled with water. She presents it to her master, and he washes his hands and face, and the hair of his head which he also washes and combs into the bowl with a comb. Then he blows his nose and spits into it, and indeed there is no filthy deed that he refrains from doing in that water. When he has finished whatever is necessary, the girl carries the bowl to the one next him, who engages in the same activity as his colleague. She continues to pass it around from one to the other until she will have taken it to all those in the house, each one of them would in turn blow his nose, spit and wash his face and hair in it. (McKeithen, "The *Risala* of Ibn Fadlan," 132)

No doubt Ibn Fadlan's condemnation of Viking hygiene and his exaggeration concerning their filthiness are clearly a projection of his religion's conception of perfect hygiene and the importance of flowing water. This makes sense if one remembers as well that Ibn Rusta, for example, does not seem to be as appalled as Ibn Fadlan by their hygiene (Stone, "Ibn Fadlan and the Midnight Sun," 2).

Moreover, the Baghdadi Ibn Fadlan expresses his dissatisfaction with Rus medicine. The Rus, Ibn Fadlan implies, are not only incompetent but unreservedly backward in the art of medicine. If a Rus falls sick, the only thing they afford to him is to isolate him until he is cured or meets his destiny.[28] What is particularly strange to Ibn Fadlan, however, is the fact that the Rus conceived of visiting a sick person and the incineration of the dead as a class privilege (al-Dahhan, ed., *Risalat Ibn Fadlan*, 154–155). Reproachfully, he states that the Rus abandon a sick person, "[nor] do they speak to him. Rather they do not visit him throughout the period of his illness, especially if he happens to be poor or a slave" (McKeithen, "The *Risala* of Ibn Fadlan," 136). As pointed out by Caroline Stone, Ibn Fadlan—who comes from Baghdad, which at the time had not only several hospitals but also a number of medical schools—is appalled at the Rus' maltreatment of their sick, their ignorance of medical sciences, and their unawareness of the existence of an institution called the hospital. During this period, one must not forget, hospitals and medical colleges were commonplace in major cities east and west of *dar al-islam*.

Indeed, cities such as Baghdad and Cordoba possessed many *bimaristans* (hospitals) with thousands of beds, where physicians from different religious backgrounds and cultures took care of their patients. "Hospitals served all peoples irrespective of colour, religion, or background," writes Sharif K. al-Ghazal in "The Influence of Islamic Philosophy and Ethics on the Development of Medicine During the Islamic Renaissance," (2007). He goes on to explain that "the government ran them, as opposed to religious groups, and their directors were usually physicians who were assisted by persons who had no religious colour. In hospitals, physicians of all faiths worked together with one aim in common—the well-being of patients" (3). Patients were treated by highly qualified physicians. This was particularly true of physicians in the time of the caliph al-Muqtadir, who is credited with establishing two large hospitals in the city of Baghdad: Al-Sayyida Hospital, in reference to his mother, and the second, Al-Muqtadiri Hospital, which he named after himself (4).

Finally, Ibn Fadlan's detailed and accurate description of the funeral cremation of one of the Rus' chieftains and the concomitant sacrificial rituals has turned out to be perhaps the most invaluable and enduring anthropological information in the entire text. At the beginning of his report, Ibn Fadlan reveals to us that since the time he first heard that the Rus cremate their dead, he had been curious to witness such a strange custom with his own eyes. When the chance came, he did not hesitate to exploit it to the full. As he puts it, "I used to be told that at the time of death they do certain things to their chiefs, the least of which is burning. I was eager to find out about such matters" (McKeithen, "The *Risala* of Ibn Fadlan," 137). As much as this statement leaves no doubt as to the curiosity of Ibn Fadlan, it also convinces us that he was not a gullible collector of hearsay, especially when he assures us that on the day when the chief and female slave were to be cremated, he went to the river to witness with his own eyes the Rus' funeral rites (al-Dahhan, ed., *Risalat Ibn Fadlan*, 155). Ibn Fadlan proceeds to report to us every ritual performed by the Rus with an eye-catching interest in the most singular of the details, from the clothes of the dead chieftain, to the numerous animals they cut in two and throw into his boat, to the human sacrifice of the slave girl, which is the most dramatic episode of the entire account. "His oft-quoted description of this rite," asserts Stone, "is one of the most remarkable documents of the Viking Age, filled as it is with grim details of the dead leader laid out in his boat amid a treasury of expensive items" ("Ibn Fadlan and the Midnight Sun," 3). When the time for the human sacrifice comes, the slave girl is raised to the top of the boat. To bid farewell to her companions, she gets drunk and engages in singing. With fascinating detail, Ibn Fadlan has

movingly captured the macabre atmosphere that preceded the inevitable death of the poor slave girl:

> I saw her overcome with confusion. She wanted to enter the tent, but
> had inserted her head between it and the ship...Six men then entered
> the tent, all of whom had sexual intercourse with the girl. Then laid her
> down at the side of her master, and two of them seized her feet, and two of
> them her hands while the old woman, who is called the Angel of Death,
> placed a rope around her neck, the two ends of which pointed in opposite
> directions, and handed it to two men to pull on. She stepped forward,
> holding a dagger with a wide blade, and began sticking it in and pulling
> it out in different places between the ribs of the girl. Meanwhile, the two
> men were simultaneously strangling her with the rope until she was dead.
> (McKeithen, "The *Risala* of Ibn Fadlan," 147)

Notwithstanding the shameless *fuhsh* (lewdness/obscenity) that took place
inside the tent, the appalling paganism, the demonic Angel of Death,
and the utter savagery of the six Rus men, Ibn Fadlan seems to be more
concerned with the ineluctability of death. As a matter of fact, the hedo-
nistic festivities that preceded the killing of the slave girl, like the latter's
feigned willingness to be sacrificed, have done nothing to hide the petri-
fying subtext of death and Ibn Fadlan's overwhelming stress at witnessing
the distress of a dying human soul. As the passage strongly conveys, the
sheer human fear of death convinces us that, at least in the end, there is
more of humanity than alterity in the *Risala* of Ibn Fadlan.

No doubt Ibn Fadlan's *Risala* is a remarkable example of premodern
Arabic writings about the Other and one of the richest of its kind in world
literature. There is growing interest in its author and his account in the
West and the Middle East alike. At the same time, this tenth-century text
has negatively eclipsed many other accounts left to posterity by Arab travelers, captives, and envoys. This is true not only of other Mashriqi writers
but also and mainly of several Maghribi authors. This is the case with
several Andalusian travelers such as al-Ghazal (d. 864), Ibn Ya'qub (d. 999),
and al-Gharnati (d. 1170), as we shall see in the coming sections.

Medieval Andalusians in/and
the Heartland of Europe

Vikings in Andalusian Eyes: Diplomacy of Love in a
Ninth-Century Arab Account of the North

Lauded by the notable Andalusian historian Ibn Hayyan as *hakim
al-andalus* (the sage of Muslim Spain), the poet and diplomat Abu

Zakariyya Yahya ibn al-Hakam al-Bakri al-Jayyani (d. 864),[29] known as al-Ghazal (the gazelle) for his physical beauty and intellectual adroitness, traced his noble lineage to the powerful Arab tribe of Bakr ibn Wa'il (al-Kilani, *Surat Uruba Inda al-'Arab fi-l-'Asr al-Wasit*, 251).[30] Al-Hajji, a leading scholar in the field of Andalusian/Western relations, wrote, "Al-Ghazal was a distinguished and shrewd personality famous for his sociable nature, gaiety, smartness, adroitness, and quickness of wit" (*Andalusian Diplomatic Relations*, 167). Given these qualities, he was "a confidant," to use Judith Jesch's phrase, of five consecutive Umayyad emirs of Cordoba. Not surprisingly, two of them dispatched him for important diplomatic missions outside *dar al-islam*, the first of which was to Byzantium (Constantinople) in 840 and the second to the land of *al-majus* (the Vikings) in 845 (*Women in the Viking Age*, 92).

Interestingly enough, in his account of the life and achievements of al-Ghazal, the Andalusian chronicler Ibn Dihya (d. 1235) seemed to focus more on al-Ghazal's contribution to Andalusian history than on his poetry. Nowhere was this more evident than in *Al-Mutrib min Ash'ar Ahl al-Maghrib* (*The Melodious Compilation from the Poetry of the People of the West*), wherein Ibn Dihya described at length the strained relations between the Muslims of al-Andalus (Islamic Spain) and *al-majus*. As Sarah Pons-Sanz puts it, "The Vikings terrorised most of western Europe from the end of the eighth century to approximately the middle of the eleventh century. The Iberian Peninsula was no exception, though the Viking raids there were much less significant than those on the British Isles and Frankia" ("Whom Did Al-Ghazal Meet?," 5). Such was no doubt especially true of their series of assaults against many Andalusian towns along the Guadalquivir River in 844. As shown by Gwyn Jones in *A History of the Vikings* (2001), the main targets of these raids were the three affluent Muslim cities of Seville, Cadiz, and Cordoba (214). The most successful of the Viking campaigns was against Seville in August 844, when a score of their ships raided it by means of its river (Dietrich, "Al-Ghazal," 64).

Overwhelmed by the Vikings, the people of Seville fled their city, which was sacked and looted (Hmeida, *A'lam al-Jughrafiyyin al-'Arab*, 140).[31] "It was at this point," Neil Price wrote in "The Vikings in Spain, North Africa and the Mediterranean" (2008), that the Umayyad governor of al-Andalus 'Abd al-Rahman II "mobilised his forces, perhaps due to Seville's proximity to the capital at Cordoba" (464). Emboldened by their victories, the Vikings headed toward Cadiz and Cordoba, the capital of Muslim Spain. Cadiz fell easily to them; however, the Muslim fire catapults made a difference in Cordoba, where the battle ended in such a humiliating defeat for the Vikings that their king now feared the rage of his Muslim enemies. To avoid further humiliation, he opted for diplomacy by sending an embassy to Cordoba to negotiate for truce and peace (Hmeida, *A'lam al-Jughrafiyyin al-'Arab*, 141). Months later, in the year 845, 'Abd al-Rahman II deemed it advantageous to strengthen ties with the Vikings through ordering an embassy led by his chief diplomat al-Ghazal to accompany the Viking delegation back to where it came from (al-'Adawi, *Al-Sifarat al-Islamiyya ila Uruba fi-l-'Usur al-Wusta*, 21). As noted by Jones, "The next year, 845, 'Abd al-Rahman sent an embassy under al-Ghazal to the King of the Majus, with choice gifts for him and his queen. If the Vikings of the Guadalquivir were Danes, we judge that the embassy was to Horik in Denmark, if Norwegian to Turgeis in Ireland" (*A History of the Vikings*, 214).[32]

Introducing al-Ghazal's mission, Ibn Dihya mentioned that the Umayyad emir selected the poet for many reasons, not least of which were his "sharpness of mind, quickness of wit, skill in repartee, courage, and knowledge of how to behave in every situation" (al-Hajji, *Andalusian Diplomatic Relations*, 176). Certainly these qualities were in addition to the fact that he had "proved to have great diplomatic skills when he was sent to the Byzantine emperor Theophilus in 840" (Pons-Sanz, "Whom Did Al-Ghazal Meet?," 6). As W. E. D. Allen phrased it, "Al-Ghazal had the experience of his fifty years; and he was still ardent, quick witted and adventurous; a perfect choice for the perilous voyage to the Viking north" (*The Poet and the Spae-Wife*, 13).To secure this unprecedented mission, the emir presented al-Ghazal and his comrades with a stout ship loaded with provisions and regal gifts. Apart from the crew, al-Ghazal was accompanied mainly by an assistant named Yahya ibn Habib. Ibn Dihya and other historians record that the Viking envoys sailed back home on their Viking vessel from the same place and at the same time as their Andalusian colleagues. As stated by Dunlop, the two vessels sailed "from Silves, then the chief town and port of the province of Algarve (south-west Spain) in a ship specially built for them" (13).[33]

The narrative of Ibn Dihya, however, focused solely on the Andalusian ship. Without giving us much information about the circumstances of its departure, the introductory pages of the account are about the sea journey. Indeed, as soon as the ship left the port of Silves, troubles began. Most likely while sailing "past Cape Finnisterre" (Harvey, "Al-Ghazal," 486), a strong wind came up and the once-calm sea suddenly turned into a raging storm. This terrifying experience was captured by al-Ghazal in a poem he improvised, as his confidant the *wazir* Tammam ibn 'Alqama reported:

All of a sudden, Yahya told me what he thought:
Between waves like mountains we are caught!
Overwhelmed by winds from West and North,

That split the mast and tore the rope.
The Angel of Death toward us walked forth!
I saw at once our doom and fate.
As for our lives! O my poor mate!
Our kinfolk seemed to have no hope! (Ibn Dihya, *Al-Mutrib fi
    Ash'ar Ahl al-Maghrib*, 134; translation mine)

This short poem is remarkable in a number of respects, not least because it emphasizes the Arabic leitmotif of *al-khawf min-al-bahr* (the fear of the sea) quite common in classical Arabic literature and in *jahili* (pre-Islamic) poetry in particular.[34] Perhaps more remarkable is the poem's stress on the trope of the known/safe homeland versus the unknown/perilous land(s) of the Other(s), which not only emphasizes the Otherness of the remote and dangerous Viking lands but also serves as a perfect template for perpetuating the rhetoric of difference between the Muslim/Andalusian Self and the *Majus*/Viking Other. Al-Ghazal's use of the sea and the tempest as tropes of what Pons-Sanz has aptly called "the abandonment of the known territory and the entrance into the realms of the unknown" ("Whom Did Al-Ghazal Meet?," 22) is by no means unique. It is rather a universal theme that has been articulated often in literatures of travel, exploration, and colonialism. As Bennison has observed, "The world beyond Frankish and German territories was the most distant from Andalusi experience, and barely entered into their imagination before the Viking raids of the mid-ninth century" ("The Peoples of the North in the Eyes of the Muslims of Umayyad al-Andalus (711–1031)," 14).

Evocative of the Arabic genre of *al-faraj ba'd al-shidda* (relief after tension/hardship) and the story of Robinson Crusoe, at least in his miraculous survival and arrival upon an unknown island after a series of hardships at sea, al-Ghazal and his companion reached the first of the Viking islands "safe and sound."[35] After staying for several days to repair the ship and enjoy a little rest, the embassy continued on its way to meet the king of the Vikings, who was said to live on "a large island in the ocean, with flowing streams and gardens. The distance between it and the mainland [was] three days' sailing, that is three hundred miles" (al-Hajji, *Andalusian Diplomatic Relations with Western Europe during the Umayyad Period*, 177).

It is to be noted again that there has been much speculation and debate over the identification of this major northern island (or peninsula) and the northern people he met. The only explicit information given by al-Ghazal or rather recorded by Andalusian chroniclers was that this island, like the many small and large islands around it, was inhabited by *al-majus* (Vikings). More specific was the fact that the majority of these *al-majus*, with the exception of a number of tribes living on remote islands, had converted to Christianity. Of historical importance is al-Ghazal's indication that the Christianized Vikings used to attack and enslave the Vikings who chose to keep to their old faith (fire worship) and what al-Ghazal described as heinous practices in reference mainly to the incestuous marriages of brothers and sisters (Ibn Dihya, *Al-Mutrib fi Ash'ar Ahl al-Maghrib*, 136).[36]

As mentioned earlier, medieval (Andalusian) Muslims used the word *majus*, the same term their Eastern coreligionists used primarily in referring to Persian Zoroastrians, to describe all northern non-Christians who used fire so frequently in their religious rituals. This, in al-Hajji's view, makes it clear that although in theory it may well include the Swedes, the Norwegians, the Danes, and the Icelanders, the specific context of the embassy (peace negotiations)—in addition to several other historical realities about the different northern European *majus* (Vikings)—proved convincingly that al-Ghazal's final destination was the headquarters of King Horic (d. 854) in Denmark (*Andalusian Diplomatic Relations*, 157).[37] According to al-Hajji, historians of the Viking age concurred that Viking Swedes and Norwegians centralized most of their activities in eastern Europe, Scotland, and Ireland. In contrast, Danish Vikings were known for both their trades and raids in western Europe and the Iberian Peninsula (156). These facts convinced al-Hajji of the weakness of the view, advocated insistently by British scholars Allen and Dunlop, that the destination of al-Ghazal's embassy was Ireland. "All these arguments," al-Hajji wrote, "rule[d] out the hypothesis that the first attack and the embassy both came from the Norwegian Vikings in Ireland, where they locate[d] the embassy" (186).[38]

Knowing about their arrival, the Viking king gave an order to his advisers to meet these important Arab visitors and to show them Viking hospitality. At his command, a comfortable dwelling was provided for al-Ghazal and his companions. The first appearance of the Arab poet and his comrades proved dramatic. As mentioned by Ibn Dihya on the authority of al-Ghazal, the Vikings were taken by the encounter. Particularly significant, especially if one accepted as accurate Ibn Dihya's report of the arrival of the Andalusian embassy in the land of the Vikings, was their reaction to the appearance and dress of the Arabs. According to Ibn Dihya's text, "The Vikings thronged to look at [the Arabs], and they wondered at their appearance and their garb" (W. E. D. Allen, *The Poet and the Spae-Wife*, 20). Beyond the binary opposites of colonizer/colonized, civilized/barbarian, superior/inferior frequently present in early modern and modern encounters describing primarily the Western first gaze at and discovery of the Other, the Viking gaze and discovery of the Arab Other and vice versa seemed too "ideologically innocent" to conjure up, for instance, what Peter R. Beardsell has described as "the earliest example of a European casting his gaze upon America" (26), in reference to Columbus's first sight of the indigenous peoples on October 12, 1492.

Two days after its historic arrival in the land of the Vikings, the Arab embassy was summoned to meet the Viking king. Al-Ghazal did not accept the royal invitation until he was assured that the Viking king would not oblige him to kneel to him nor insist he engage in anything *haram* (forbidden). As stated in Ibn Dihya's text, the Viking king accepted al-Ghazal's conditions and requests. Through his delegates, he assured his Muslim guests that he and his people would be "culturally sensitive," to use the pertinent modern phrase. As demonstrated by Nabil Matar, one should perhaps acknowledge the reality of al-Ghazal's aforementioned demands in light of the numerous religious and cultural challenges medieval and early Muslim travelers had to confront while venturing outside *dar al-Islam* (*In the Lands of the Christians*, xxvi). It is no exaggeration to suggest that this medieval Muslim-Viking cultural encounter foretold in a way the ongoing debate over the significance of multicultural encounters in our contemporary world in general and in Western countries with huge immigrant populations.[39]

Not entirely convinced perhaps by this *"accommodement raisonnable"* with his Muslim guests, the Viking king opted for northern cunningness, or at least this is what al-Ghazal and later Andalusian chroniclers wanted their contemporaries to believe in order to show their strong attachment to their religion and homeland. When al-Ghazal tried to enter the royal court, he found that the Viking king had deliberately made the entrance door so low that his Muslim guests could enter only by kneeling in front of him. To the Viking's surprise, the "clever" Arab "was not easily browbeaten," (232) to quote Jonathan Wright's intriguing *The Ambassadors: From Ancient Greece to Renaissance Europe, the Men Who Introduced the World to Itself* (2006). Instead of kneeling, he "sat on the ground, and with feet foremost, slid forward on his posterior. Having passed through the door, he got up on his feet" (al-Hajji, *Andalusian Diplomatic Relations*, 178).

One does not need much imagination when it comes to the reaction of the Viking king. As stated in Ibn Dihya's text, the king was *bouche bée* and was said to have ordered his interpreter to praise the Arab envoy for his wisdom and intelligence. In front of his people, he avowed, "This [was] one of the wise and clever men of his people. We wished to humiliate him, and he displayed his shoes in our face" (178). As much as one may be surprised by Allen's assertion that "the story might express the mixture of arrogance and almost boyish buffoonery which was the humour of the Vikings" (*The Poet and the Spae-Wife*, 43), it seems that the underlying lesson of this fascinating anecdote is to show what Bennison aptly described as the Arab envoy's "sophistication and superior intelligence in his encounters with the Majus rulers" ("The Peoples of the North," 15). This would make more sense if we remember that, according to Ibn Dihya, al-Ghazal boasted that during his 20-month stay in the land of the Vikings, he met several Viking nobles and learned people with whom he engaged in religious and cultural debates (*Al-Mutrib*, 138).

Upon every occasion, al-Ghazal indicated that he not only had impressed his non-Muslim adversaries but had triumphed over them. Obviously al-Ghazal's self-aggrandizement was intended for home consumption by presenting his strong attachment to Islam and proving his success in advancing his country's political interest in the land of the Vikings. "Al-Ghazal," as noted by Lewis, was "at pains to show how he preserved his honour and that of Islam despite the attempt by his hosts to humble him" (*The Muslim Discovery of Europe*, 93). As such, Wright did not exaggerate when he described al-Ghazal's diplomatic maneuver as "an impressive display, a timeless example of an ambassador striving, in strained circumstances, to retain his honor and the honor of his culture" (*The Ambassadors*, 232). Al-Ghazal's rather frivolous self-promotion was neither peculiar to the Arab Muslim diplomatic tradition nor an idiosyncrasy of the premodern world.

Needless to say, the climax to al-Ghazal's journey to the North was his encounter and love affair with Nud, the beautiful and coquettish Viking queen. There has been a kind of consensus among scholars that the affair between the Arab poet and the Viking queen represented the single most moving episode of what was left of al-Ghazal's account of his embassy to the North. Not only was this true of its fascinating literary thread, which was reminiscent of several enduring Arabian love romances and tales; also, and perhaps more important, it told us of the "cultural work" of the earliest known journey of a Muslim traveler to western Europe. Introducing us to this encounter and affair, Ibn Dihya on the authority of Tammam gives the following information:

> When he went to the land of al-Majus, he was approaching fifty, and his hair was turning grey. He was strong, of straight body, and of handsome appearance. The King's wife, whose name was Nud, asked him one day what was his age, and he said in jest: "Twenty!" She said to the interpreter: "And how does he have grey hair at the age of twenty?" He said to the interpreter: "Why does she deny it? Has she never seen a foal with grey hair?" Nud laughed, and wondered at the words. Al-Ghazal extemporized on this occasion with a poem. (al-Hajji, *Andalusian Diplomatic Relations*, 181)

This poem turned out to be of impressive poetic genius. Fortunately, Allen's translation of the poem is no less brilliant:

> You are burned, O my heart, with a wearying passion
> With which you struggle as if with a lion.
> I am in love with a Viking woman.
> Who will not let the sun of beauty set.
> Who lives at the limit of God's world, where he
> Who goes towards her, finds no path.
> O Nud, O young and fair one,
> From whose buttons a star rises,
> O you, by my father, than whom I see
> None sweeter or pleasanter to my heart,
> If I should say one day that my eye has seen
> Any one like you, I would surely be lying.
> She said: "I see that your locks have turned white"
> In jest, she caused me to jest also,
> I answered: "by my father,
> The foal is born grey like this."
> And she laughed and admired my words
> —Which I only spoke that she might admire. (*The Poet and the Spae-Wife*, 24)

By most accounts, Ibn Dihya was not exaggerating when he noted that if this fascinating love poem was the work of an Eastern poet, "it would have been highly estimated" (24). Of course, Ibn Dihya's comment brings to our mind the previously discussed topoi of Andalucentricism especially as we saw Ibn Hazm and Ibn Bassam.

To return to our main topic, it should be noted, however, that contrary to the well-regarded Arabic tradition of *al-hub al-'udhri*—the equivalent of the Western tradition of courtly love, wherein chivalrous and powerful male poet-lovers fall in love with chaste, submissive, and beautiful (unmarried) females—the love affair of al-Ghazal and Nud challenged in a negative way several of the favorite tropes of the Arabic tradition of romantic love. This was true of the account's discursive emphasis upon the sexual forwardness of the Viking woman in contrast to famous Arab love heroines and the enduring 'Abla, Layla, and 'Azza in particular.[40]

Andalusian chroniclers such as Ibn Dihya and al-Maqqari after him—indeed many contemporary Arab scholars—tended to portray Nud's infatuation with al-Ghazal as more the physical lust of an unflatteringly promiscuous non-Muslim woman than anything else. Based on al-Ghazal's own version, they usually relate the *fitna* (sexual seduction and failure) of al-Ghazal both to the promiscuity of Viking women and to the sexual liberalism of Viking men. Between the lines, it was easy to understand the sexual nature of the affair between the Viking queen and the Arab poet in the libertine Viking court. On the authority of Tammam ibn ʿAlqama, Ibn Dihya wrote,

> The wife of the king of *al-majus* was infatuated with al-Ghazal, and could not pass a single day without sending for him. He used to stay with her, talking of the lives of the Muslims, their histories and their lands, and of the neighboring peoples. Never did he leave without her sending a gift after him as a sign of good-will, either a garment, some food or some perfume, until her relationship with him became notorious. His companions disapproved of it, and he was warned of it. (al-Hajji, *Andalusian Diplomatic Relations*, 180)

Had it not been for the intellectualism of the poet and his "talking of the Muslims, their histories and their lands, and of the neighboring peoples," one would have jumped to the conclusion that unlike the Venetian Desdemona, who was in many ways truthful when she used to avow that she saw "Othello's visage in his mind," the Viking Nud appeared to be satisfied with seeing al-Ghazal's mind in his visage, if not in his body. This image was evoked primarily by the plethora of physical, if not erotic, words that dominated Ibn Dihya's description of the nature of Nud's love of al-Ghazal.

As far as Nud's gifts of "good-will" are concerned, there is little doubt that those intimate gifts of garments, food, and perfume were signs of another type of will. Regarding the Arab culture of physical love, these objects were too intimate to be mere signs of "good-will." No wonder then that al-Ghazal's highly cultured companions were acutely aware of the *fitna* their Muslim fellow was subjected to. Somewhat analogous to the Quranic/biblical story of the seduction of the Prophet Yusuf, known in the Bible as Joseph, by the beautiful *imra't al-ʿaziz* (Potifar's wife), known also in some Islamic sources as Queen Zulaikha, the blame should have also, if not primarily, fallen on al-Ghazal. Unlike Yusuf, and mainly through his poetic moves, al-Ghazal was equally a seducer. Ibn Dihya and later Andalusian chroniclers seemed to have forgotten what al-Ghazal was obliged to do in such a situation, as Yusuf was reported to have said to Zulaikha: "Allah forbid! Truly (thy husband) is my lord! He made my sojourn agreeable! Truly to no good come those who do wrong!" (Quran 12:23). Judged by his own religious convictions, al-Ghazal proved unrighteous in not avoiding the *fitna* of the Viking woman.

Whether al-Ghazal's love, or rather sexual desire, for Nud was real or not, one cannot reach a definitive conclusion. His avowal that he flirted with the Viking queen for nothing but diplomatic ends was surely meant for home consumption. He must certainly have used the last line of the earlier poem as a poetic affidavit that his otherwise scandalous flirtations with Nud were nothing but intrigues made to serve his country's interest. This makes sense especially if we remember that as much as his affair with the Viking queen is surrounded by doubts, his poem is more ambiguous. In short, the licentious content and words might be seen as contradicting the initial image of a righteous and strict Muslim. Such a poem must have tempted many of his envious competitors to cast doubt on his moral integrity, a practice common in the cultural circles of medieval Islam. Whether one believes his record of the events or not, it is fascinating to see how the interaction among (successful) diplomacy, intrigues, and romantic/sexual affairs in his account conjured more contemporary accounts of diplomacy. It is unknown whether Nud's presumed seduction of al-Ghazal was a counter-diplomatic Viking intrigue aimed at securing Viking interests; if so, this would give French diplomat Rene Gallimard, as dramatized in David Henry Hwang's *M. Butterfly* (1993), a medieval precedent.

Close exploration of certain textual and cultural gaps in al-Ghazal's account may convince us that this Arab diplomat was by his own acknowledgment the real culprit in the affair with the married Viking queen. Nowhere was this clearer than in the report of their first meeting. As Ibn Dihya and al-Maqqari noted, as soon as al-Ghazal entered the queen's headquarters, he deliberately fixed his eyes on the queen's face. Islamically speaking, as we saw with Ibn Fadlan, this is an improper deed that goes against the Quranic injunction of lowering the gaze. Quite perplexed by his "gaze," the queen is said to have demanded her interpreter ask al-Ghazal about his meaning. Ignoring the specific requirement that Muslim males must avoid all indecent behavior with foreign women, al-Ghazal opted for emotional manipulation and inappropriate flirtation by ordering the interpreter to inform Nud that he was struck by her unmatched beauty. As might have been expected, the compliment weighed heavily on the heart of the Viking queen. As reported by Ibn Dihya,

> She said to her interpreter: "Ask him whether he is serious or jesting." He said: "I am in earnest." She said: "There is no beauty in their land." Al-Ghazal said: "show me some of your women so that I may compare them." The queen sent for women well-known for their beauty. They came, and he looked at them carefully up and down, and said: "There is beauty among them, but not like the beauty of the queen, for her beauty and fine attributes cannot be perceived by everyone, and can only be

expressed by poets. If the Queen wishes me to describe her beauty, her lineage and her intelligence in a poem to be recited throughout our land, then I shall do so." (al-Hajji, *Andalusian Diplomatic Relations*, 179)

To demonstrate her feelings, the evidently enamored queen ordered her enticer a gift, which he would not accept. This response saddened the queen and impelled her to ask about the reasons behind it. The manipulative al-Ghazal resorted once again to his wits and replied that "her present is indeed magnificent, and to accept it would be an honour, for she is a queen and the daughter of a king, but to look at her and to be received by her is an adequate gift for me" (180). It seems strange that the Andalusian chroniclers and many contemporary scholars such as al-Kilani and al-'Amri have tended to believe that al-Ghazal was a mere object of the Viking queen's lust. Al-Ghazal was said to have eventually accepted the warnings of his friends and, partway through the affair with Nud, to have determined to be more circumspect. When the latter noticed the change in her Arab lover, she reprimanded him. Al-Ghazal informed her about the warnings of his friends, and she laughed, saying, "We do not have such things in our religion, nor do we have such jealousy. Our women are with our men only of their own choice. A woman stays with her husband as long as it pleases her to do so, and leaves him if it no longer pleases her" (W. E. D. Allen, *The Poet and the Spae-Wife*, 23).

In the context of Arabic-Islamic views and perceptions of the Euro-Christians, Nud's statement is suggestive in two main respects. First, it captures perfectly the stereotypical image held by medieval Arab Muslims of Euro-Christian women as shamelessly accessible and characteristically forward. Second, it betrays typical Muslim views of Euro-Christian male jealousy that is still dominant today in the stereotyped perception of the West. Throughout the centuries, Muslims have noted with horror and condemnation but also in humorous contexts what they have deemed to be a lack of jealousy among Euro-Christian males. No Arab Muslim writer past or present has exploited this stereotype in Arabic-Islamic culture and literature so extensively as the writer and warrior Usamah ibn Munqidh (d. 1188), who did so through a plethora of short *qisas* (anecdotes) and *nawadir* (jokes) that he included in his popular *Kitab al-I'tibar* (*Book of Instructive Examples*).

Although Ibn Munqidh claimed that this *nadira* (joke) was a real *waqi'a* (event) that he witnessed when visiting the then Frankish-occupied city of Nablus, it is perhaps as powerful as the better-known anecdote of the Arab bath-keeper Salim and the Frankish knight and his wife in the Muslim public bath.[41] Ibn Munqidh recounted the story of his visits to Nablus, where he took lodgings in a house owned by a man named

Mu'iz, whose front neighbor was a Euro-Christian wine merchant. One day, according to Ibn Munqidh, the merchant found a strange man in bed with his wife. The presumed response of the Euro-Christian, as translated by Philip K. Hitti, is worth quoting:

> He asked him, "What could have made thee enter into my wife's room?" The man replied "I was tired, so I slept in it." "But," said he, "my wife was sleeping together with thee!" The other replied, "Well, the bed is hers. How could I therefore have prevented her from using her own bed?" "By the truth of my religion," said the husband, "if thou shouldst do it again, thou and I would have a quarrel." (*An Arab-Syrian Gentleman and Warrior in the Period of the Crusades*, 165)

Most significant in this quotation was indubitably Ibn Munqidh's highly ironical statement: "Such was for the Frank the entire expression of his disproval and the limit of his jealousy." This phrase not only captured the author's ridicule of Frankish honor but also reflected the sometimes extreme Levantine cultural understanding of family pride. Although it is doubtful that "honor killing" was quite as common among some Levantine Arabs during Ibn Munqidh's own age, the author and certainly many of his readers, at least in their "cultural horizons," would have considered the only satisfactory demonstration of male jealousy under such circumstances to be killing the wife and the man.[42]

It is now commonplace that Western writings about the Orient have made the "Oriental harem" one of the favorite topoi of cultural differences between the (Christian) West and the (Muslim) East. Perhaps the older Arabic writings about the West—as in the example of al-Ghazal's account, or let us say even in his invented story—have in turn made the "Occidental harem" one of their favorite sites through which they have not only explored themes of difference between the Self and the Other but also have constructed and perpetuated stereotypes and stock images about the Euro-Christian that are still dominant in the contemporary "learned" and "popular" Occidentalist (or *ifranjalist*) views and perceptions of the West.[43] As shown by al-Azmeh, in their attempts "to convey distinction by enumerating tokens of difference and implying inversions of order," Andalusi writers, just like their Mashriqi counterparts, "had long dwelt on the freedom of European (and other) women" ("Mortal Enemies, Invisible Neighbors," 267). Citing al-Ghazal and a few others, al-Azmeh added, "Most noteworthy, for these and other authors, was the lack of jealousy among the men and the sexual freedom of unmarried women" (267). Echoing al-Azmeh, Nadia Maria el-Cheikh noted, "The absence of jealousy on the part of a cuckolded husband [was] a constant accusation levelled against Byzantine men, as well as the Slavs and other Europeans, and later, the crusaders" (*Byzantium Viewed by the Arabs*, 182).

In sum, in spite of the exaggerated skepticism of some Western Arabists in regard to its authenticity and the heated debate over the final destination, what remains of al-Ghazal's account has recently drawn increasing attention. This is so not only because his is the earliest known Muslim account of medieval Europe, but also because it is a rare firsthand report of a Muslim visit most likely to ninth-century Denmark. One must acknowledge the fact that al-Ghazal's account, especially as preserved by Ibn Dihya, without doubting its great cultural and literary value, is lacking in the ethnographic and anthropological richness of not only the Easterner Ibn Fadlan's remarkable account of Western Vikings, but even those of his Andalusian successors, such as Ibn Ya'qub (d. 998) and al-Gharnati (d. 1080), as we shall delineate in the following sections. At times, one feels pushed to agree with the eminent Arabist André Miquel, who although accepting al-Ghazal's report as historical did not hide his perplexity at the impression that al-Ghazal's Vikings seem more like "*fantômes*" than real people (*La géographie humaine*, 345).

From Real Prague to the Fabulous "Town of Women": Northern Facts and Fables in the Remarkable Account of Ibn Ya'qub

Thanks mainly to the Andalusian geographers al-Bakri and al-'Udhri, some lengthy and important extracts of the tenth-century European *rihla* of Andalusian merchant, and probably diplomat, Ibrahim ibn Ya'qub al-Tartushi (d. 999)[44] have reached us.[45] Acknowledged to be one of the world's greatest premodern travelers and the author of "one of the best accounts of the period" (Levy, "Ibrahim ibn Ya'qub," 469), Ibn Ya'qub is said to have penetrated deep into Europe in a remarkable journey that took place between 961 and 967 (Constable, *Trade and Traders in Muslim Spain*, 79). Most likely Ibn Ya'qub set out around 961 from Almeria (Spain) to Marseilles in France. From there, he headed to Genoa and visited Rome.[46] After that, he crossed, either through the Adriatic Sea or the northern route by Venice, various Slavic countries (al-Hajji, *Andalusian Diplomatic Relations*, 245; and Nazmi, *Commercial Relations between Arabs and Slavs*, 40). He is said to have visited Hungary, Bohemia, Moravia, Poland, Holland, and Germany.[47] On his journey back home, he is said to have traversed the French towns of Verdun and Rouen and crossed the Pyrenees to northern Spain before arriving at Cordoba around 967 (al-Hajji, *Andalusian Diplomatic Relations*, 245; and Nazmi, *Commercial Relations between Arabs and Slavs*, 40).[48]

As shown by Petr Charvát in the introduction to *Ibrahim ibn Ya'qub at-Turtushi: Christianity, Islam and Judaism Meet in East-Central Europe, c. 800–1300 A.D.* (1996), there has been heated debate over the faith, profession, and the chief motivation behind Ibn Ya'qub's extensive travel mainly in the Carpathian basin and central Europe. For Charvát, although practically nothing is known of the life and family of the traveler because "personal data concerning him are so lamentably scarce," it is likely that he was born "in the course of the thirties" of the beginning of the tenth century (AD) in the Catalan town of Tortosa (17). To this town he owes the *nisba* (designation) of al-Tartushi by which he was mostly known in medieval Arabic sources. Nevertheless, the other *nisba* of al-Isra'ili, or the Israelite—which is used by some Andalusian chroniclers, among them al-Bakri—has encouraged a considerable number of Western Arabists to conclude that he was an Arab Jew, or as expressed by Charvát, " a cultivated descendant of an undoubtedly well-to-do Jewish family of Tortosa" (17).[49]

Citing the presence of the exclusively Muslim name Ahmad in his name, other scholars, mostly from the Middle East (including al-Hajji and Nazmi), have strongly contested this view, arguing rather that Ibn Ya'qub, although of Jewish origin, was in reality an Andalusian Muslim. In al-Hajji's own words, "The presence of Ahmad in his name indicates that he may have descended from a Muslim convert from Judaism or adopted Ahmad after embracing Islam" (*Andalusian Diplomatic Relations*, 230).[50] A minority of scholars, such as Lewis, have opted for a more reserved interpretation highlighting instead the insufficient biographical information about this Andalusian traveler. "There is some uncertainty to whether he was a professing Jew or a Muslim of Jewish origin," Lewis tells us before concluding that "the form of his name would allow either possibility" (*The Muslim Discovery of Europe*, 95).

Whether an Arab Jew or an Arab Muslim, a merchant or an envoy, a physician or a slave or mine trader, Ibn Ya'qub, as the erudite Rapoport once put it, must have been "a very trustworthy, learned and observant writer" ("On the Early Slavs, The Narrative of Ibrahim ibn Yakub," 333). In al-Hajji's view, "The detailed information about many Slav countries and his wide and first-hand knowledge of these countries suggest that he was a man of culture" (*Andalusian Diplomatic Relations*, 233). Commentary concerning his embassy to the German emperor Otto the Great and perhaps his meeting with Pope John XII, assuming such commentary existed and were recoverable, would have added greatly to the historical importance of Ibn Ya'qub. As Miquel writes, "The date of the original work and the quality of the fragments which survive, notably those about the Slavs, show how greatly to be regretted is the loss of so much of it" ("Ibn Ya'qub," 999).

Notwithstanding his remarkable reports on European regions, reports incorporated by some of the previously studied Arab scholars—especially as we saw with al-Bakri's account of the Prussians and the Bretons and his lengthy section on the Slavs (which we did not discuss)—scholars have agreed that Ibn Ya'qub has bequeathed to posterity one of the world's most valuable and reliable accounts of early Slavs inhabiting several central European Slavic countries, such as Poland and Bohemia-Moravia. These accounts are in addition to his brief but fascinating account of medieval Irish whalers and, as we shall see, his presumed dissemination in medieval Arabic *'aja'ib/ghara'ib* literature of the legend of *madinat/jazirat al-nisa'* (the town/island of women).[51]

It is worth stressing here yet again that similar to other vague terms with which medieval Arabs described Europeans (namely *al-rum* and *al-ifranja*) the term *al-saqaliba*, as Newman points out, "at times denoted Germanic, Finnish, Turkic, and other non-Slavic peoples" ("Arab Travelers to Europe," 12). Similarly, *ardh al-saqaliba* (the land of the Slavs) was vaguely located "somewhere beyond the land of the Byzantines or to the north of Muslim Spain" (Shboul, *Al-Mas'udi and His World*, 179). In contrast, Ibn Ya'qub's text marks an enormous advance especially through his concentration on the Slavonic countries that now make up modern Slavic states such as the Czech Republic, Slovakia, Slovenia, Bohemia, and Poland. "Ibrahim b. Ya'qub, qui visita l'Europe de l'ouest et centrale dans les années 345/965," writes Miquel, "nous a laissé un tableau des slaves occidentaux qui représente un incontestable progrès par rapport aux données de Mas'udi: époques et dates se lisent, enfin, à peu près en clair" (*La géographie humaine*, 316).

Indeed, on the authority of al-Bakri, Ibn Ya'qub confirms nearly all the general geographical information mentioned by al-Mas'udi in his earlier discussed section on the Slavs. Among other things, he states that their land stretches from *al-bahr al-shami*, that is, the Mediterranean Sea, up to *al-bahr al-muhit*, that is, the Atlantic Sea (al-Bakri, *Jughrafiyat al-Andalus wa Uruba*, 156). Ibn Ya'qub in general terms admired much of what he supposedly saw in the lands of the Slavs: wealth, agriculture, industry, trade, and military might. He mentions that the Slavs "inhabit countries very rich in dwellings and in provisions. They are diligent in agriculture and in other industries and in this they surpass all nations of the North. Their wares by land and sea reach the Rus" (Rapoport, "On the Early Slavs," 334).[52] Similarly, he refers with fascination to their exceptional bravery and prowess in war. All in all, had it not been for their destructive tribalism, the Slavs would have been the masters of the world. "If not for their disunion on account of their splitting into numerous branches and tribal dispersion," he asserts, "no nation in the world could equal them in power" (334).

Ibn Yaʿqub does, however, criticize some major Slavic tribes for not speaking their "national" language. Although he stressed the fact that several powerful Slavic tribes spoke Slavonic, many others preferred to speak the "foreign" languages of some neighboring enemy nations. He cites as examples the Slavic tribes of the Trshkin who preferred to speak Tedeski (German), the Ankli who speak Hungarian, and the Badjankia who speak the language of the Petchenegs (Turkic) (334). With these few statements, Ibn Yaʿqub seems to indicate that a unifying national language is essential for the rise and survival of a cohesive and strong nation.

Ibn Yaʿqub's observations on language in a way anticipated Johann Gottfried Herder's theory of "linguistic nationalism," still relevant in modern studies of nationalism and nation-building.[53] As Leigh Oakes remarks in *Language and National Identity: Comparing France and Sweden*, "For Johann Gottfried Herder, language was the core value of a people's *Volksgeist* (national spirit), so that to speak a foreign language was to lead an artificial life, detached from one's own spontaneous and distinctive personality" (22). Long before the German francophobe Herder called upon the Germans to speak German in *An Die Deutschen* (22), the Arab "Slavophone" Ibn Yaʿqub enticed the foreign Slavs to speak Slavonic and to be proud of their language.

Ibn Yaʿqub fills his report on the Slavs with other valuable ethnographic and anthropological details, especially regarding their preferred clothing, culinary habits, and musical instruments. Commenting on their dress, for instance, he notes that the Slavs prefer loose garments and only the lower part of their sleeves is narrow (Rapoport, "On the Early Slavs," 339). As for their food, he says that they enjoy eating the meat of cows and geese, but they avoid poultry in fear of erysipelas (339). As for liquids, he states that the Slavs are obsessed with drinking different varieties of mead beverages containing honey. As noted by a growing number of Slavists, Ibn Yaʿqub is arguably the first to mention in writing the popular Slavic mead, or honey-wine. As for Slav music, he noted that although the Slavs have various wind and string musical instruments, they enjoy two of them especially—a long flute and an eight-stringed lute whose inner side is flat and not convex. The latter could very well be a variant of the famous torban (339).

Even when it comes to hygiene and sanitary customs, against the grain of most medieval Arabic-Islamic writers about the Other, Ibn Yaʿqub portrays the Slavs as clean. He seems particularly taken by what he calls *al-atbba*. This is the word with which he refers to what one might describe as the Slavs' own version of the *hammam* (public bath). The description of this Slavic sanitary marvel is worth quoting at length:

> They have no bath houses, but they build a house of wood and caulk its chinks with some material which is obtained from their trees and is like a green marsh moss which they call *mokh*. Instead of tar they use it for their boats. Then they erect a stove of stones in one of the corners (of this house) and at the very top opposite the stove they open a window to let out the smoke. When the stove becomes red-hot they shut this window and close the doors, and in this house are kept basins with water which they pour over the red-hot stove, and then the steam rises. Each one holds in his arm a bundle of dried branches by which they move the air, opened and out of their body comes what is superfluous and rivers run out of them. And no traces of a rash or abscess are left on any of them. And they call this house *al-atbba*. (334)

In contrast to Western accounts of the Oriental *hammam*, Ibn Ya'qub has not only proved reticent in providing us with more specific details about the manners and behaviors of Slav men and women inside the *atba*'; he has also proved discursively disinterested in sensualizing this otherwise rich site of alterity. As Billie Melman has argued in *Women's Orients: English Women and the Middle East, 1718–1918*, Western (male) accounts, both real and imaginative, have portrayed Muslim *hammams* as quintessentially "*loci sensuales*" (89). "In western culture," Melman notes, the *hammams* "were identified as the erotically charged landscape of the Orient" and "came to apotheosize the sensual, effeminate Orient" (89).

The apparent disinterest in Slavic sexuality on the part of Ibn Ya'qub vanishes as soon as he turns to Slavic women. In a broader perspective, Ibn Ya'qub does not seem to add anything novel regarding the presumed moral inferiority and the alleged sexual promiscuity of Slavic women. In fact, he records with a sense of condemnation the premarital sexual freedom of young Slavic women. Ibn Ya'qub claims that Slavic women before marriage commit *zina*' (illegal intercourse) with as many men as they desire without having any religious, social, or familial qualms or inhibitions. In his own words, "when a girl falls in love with someone she goes to him and satisfies her passion with him" (Rapoport, "On the Early Slavs," 340).

Even more condemnable for Ibn Ya'qub is the fact that the Slavs are, in his eyes, gravely ignorant of the meaning of jealousy and shamelessly blind to the virtues of premarital virginity. Reminiscent of al-Ghazal's and Ibn Munqidh's notes on Viking and Frankish male jealousy, Ibn Ya'qub claims that "when a [Slav] man marries and finds his wife to be a virgin he says to her: 'If there was any good in you, men would love you and you would choose one who would possess you, and drives her away and renounces her'" (340).

In light of this, one is left with the impression that Ibn Yaʻqub's explicit comments on Slavic women quoted earlier lend themselves well to the overall Muslim attitude concerning non-Muslim women, but they also appear as Islamocentric as those of the more religiously conscious Ibn Fadlan, who commented on Oghuz and Viking women. This textual proof might tend to convince the reader that Ibn Yaʻqub, if not Muslim by faith, is Muslim by culture. Nevertheless, one can legitimately suggest that as much as the passage may reflect Muslim views of non-Muslim morality and sexuality, it may equally mirror then-current Jewish perceptions.

Of course, as much as there is a fairly close similarity between Judaism and Islam in regard to morality and sexuality, generally speaking, premarital virginity—the focus of Ibn Yaʻqub's notes on Slavic women—seems to be more emphasized in the Jewish tradition than in the Islamic one. Indeed, while there is a specific hadith interpreted to mean that it is *mustahabb* (preferable) for Muslim men to marry virgins, there are no texts in the Quran and the Sunna that prohibit them from marrying non-virgins.[54]

In fact, with the exception of ʻAʼisha, all of Prophet Muhammad's wives were non-virgin widows and one divorcée. This is certainly not the case with Jewish priests, who are not permitted to marry non-virgins. Roger Steven Evans acutely sums up this prohibition as follows: "The priests of Israel, the men who handled the things of God, i.e., sacrifices, incense, blood, showbread, etc., and who daily entered into the Holy place of the Sanctuary," were instructed to "take a wife in her virginity" (Lev. 21:13–14) (*Sex and Salvation*, 19). Evans adds, "The priests of God could not allow themselves to be 'one' sexually with a woman who had previously been 'one,' sexually, with another man" (19).

With remarkable attention to detail, Ibn Yaʻqub explores and observes the fauna and flora of the land of the Slavs. He was so much impressed by the wealth of the land—its agricultural resources, rich vegetation, varied fruit trees, and kinds of cattle—that he unhesitatingly described it as one of the richest in the world. He was particularly taken by two birds that he quite enigmatically called the *sba* and the *tra*:

And there is in their country a remarkable bird which on the upper part is dark green. It imitates all sounds of men and animals which it hears. Sometimes, they succeed in catching it; they hunt it and its name in Slavonic is *sba*. Then, there is a wild fowl which is called in Slavonic *tra* (wood-cock). Its flesh is tasty and its cries one hears from the tops of trees at a distance of one *farsang* (about 6 or 7 km) and more. There are two kinds of it; black and motley, which are more beautiful than peacocks. (Rapoport, "On the Early Slavs," 340)

Like other Arab travelers before and after him, Ibn Ya'qub has left a lively description of the unfamiliar northern climate, to which he devotes a relatively lengthy section. He noted with surprise the extreme ease with which the Slavs survive the unbearable cold and stated that since the Slavs are used to extreme cold, they cannot survive even the rather moderate heat of northern Italy (Lombardy). It is not surprising, he goes on to claim, that the Slavs do not dare to visit northern Italy (339). In a passage that recalls Ibn Fadlan's description of the cold of the city of Jurjaniyya (Urgench), Ibn Ya'qub tells us,

The countries of the Slavs are very cold, and the cold here is greatest when the nights are moonlit and the days clear. Then the cold increases and the frost get stronger. The soil becomes then like stone and all the liquids become frozen, and the well and the canal become covered as if with plaster so that they become like stone. And when people let water through their nose their beards become covered with a layer of ice as if with glass, so that one has to break them till one gets warm or enters the room. And when the nights are dark and the days foggy then the frost decreases and the cold weakens and at that time ships are broken and they who are on them perish, because out of the ice of the rivers in these countries get loose on them (on the ships) blocks like hard mountains. Sometimes a youth or a strong man is able to cling to such a block and to escape on it. (341)

Although there is nothing in the passage to suggest that Ibn Ya'qub is echoing the earlier mentioned dominant Arab Muslim geo-cosmographical views of barbarity and civilization, in this particular passage, he can be seen as offering further compelling evidence that medieval Arab writers, Maghribi and Mashriqi alike, conventionally perceived of difference in climate as one of the most critical markers of distance between the Self and the Other.

Ibn Ya'qub also provides a great deal of information concerning the political life of the Slavs. Bearing in mind what we already saw with al-Mas'udi, he states that before their division, the Slavs were ruled by a single king. After the death of one of these monarchs, major Slav tribes quarreled among themselves and fought each other. The result was the splitting of their once unified dominion into four independent kingdoms (334). Much as he expressed his disapproval of their disunity, Ibn Ya'qub was even more direct than al-Mas'udi in conveying his criticism, if not denunciation, of these kings, not least because of what he saw as their great wealth and luxurious lifestyle in comparison to the lives of the common people.

Reminiscent of some modern Western accounts of oriental potentates and most contemporary Western reports of some Middle Eastern rulers, Ibn Ya'qub was appalled by the fact that while Slav kings ride on big, high carts running on four wheels with frames wrapped with silk, "there is not so much" for Slav peasants and sick persons (341). In spite of this criticism, Ibn Ya'qub does not hide his overall admiration for what he calls in Arabic *bilad meshke* (Poland) and *bowima* (Bohemia).

Without doubt, Ibn Ya'qub has given us an intriguing description of Poland under Mieszko I (962–992), whom historians hail as one of the central figures in the history of Poland. Increasingly cited by a growing number of contemporary historians of Poland, Ibn Ya'qub has become an essential written source regarding this crucial period of Polish history and of the army of Mieszko I. On the authority of al-Bakri, Ibn Ya'qub tells us the following:

> Concerning the country of Meshke, it is the greatest of their [the Slavs'] countries. It is rich in bread and meat and honey and fish. The taxes which are collected by him (by Meshke) are paid in Byzantine money. They also (form) the salary of his men. Every month each of them receives a fixed number of *mitkals*. And he has 3000 men in armour, *and these are warriors of whom a hundred is equal to ten hundred of others* [italics mine]. And he gives to those men dress, horses, armament and everything they need. (336)

As exaggerated as the italicized comparison appears, the historians W. Sarnecki and D. Nicolle have recently shown in *Medieval Polish Armies 966–1500* that Mieszko I's soldiers proved to be powerful warriors in medieval Europe. Jerzy Lukowski and Hubert Zawadzki have noted that Mieszko's "retinue of warriors" did not only enable him to "annex Silesia from his former Bohemians in-Laws" and to "found the home port of Gdansk around 980," but also enabled his son Boleslaw I Chrobry (992–1026) "to impose his rule over Bohemia, Moravia, and much of modern day Slovakia" (*An Outline of the History of Poland*, 11). Luckily, Ibn Ya'qub had the chance to visit Bohemia and Moravia before they were conquered by Boleslaw, "the Valiant."

Recent scholarship has demonstrated that this Arab traveler bequeathed to posterity an exceptional account of the medieval Kingdom of Bohemia, now the modern-day Czech Republic. Ibn Ya'qub refers to Bohemia with the slightly distorted Arabic word *bowima*. He describes it as a wealthy country, large and bounteous, whose inhabitants enjoy a high standard of living, noting the excellence of its agriculture and the strength of its trade. He was especially impressed by its majestic capital city, which he calls in Arabic *fragha* (Prague). He mentions that its architecture is splendid and that most of its great buildings were made of stone and lime. Interestingly enough, he speaks of merchants and visitors who flocked to the bustling town not only from neighboring countries such as Hungary, Poland, and Russia but equally from the more distant al-Andalus and the Muslim East. These merchants, to quote Richter-Bernburg, "offered their wares including slaves, tin, furs, and 'marketable specie'" ("Ibrāhīm ibn Yaʿqūb al-Isrāʾīlī al-Ṭurṭūshī." 403).

As is the case with Krakow in Poland, some Slavists have argued not without some truth that Ibn Yaʿqub is the first to mention in writing the city of Prague. The Czech historian Eva Semotanová in *The Encyclopaedia of the Middle Ages* (2001), for example, has noted, "The rise of the town of Prague during the early Middle Ages is related in an account by the Arab-Jewish merchant Ibrahim ibn Jacoub (965–966)" ("Prague," 1177). Commenting on the importance and originality of Ibn Yaʿqub's section on Prague, the eminent Czech historian Lubos Kropacek states,

It has become an integral part of the general knowledge of the national history in this country. It has been incorporated into syllabi of courses of history in Czech secondary schools. A quotation of the famous paragraph saying that "the town of Frāgha is built of stone and lime and is the richest commercial centre, visited by Russians and Slavs from Cracovia with their goods etc." was placed in the historical section of the National Museum among the exhibits illustrating the rise of the Bohemian kingdom. On similar lines, the immediate following passage of the same text dealing with Muslim and Jewish traders was displayed at the very beginning of the elaborate exhibition on the history of Jews in Czechoslovakia held in Prague and some other towns in 1992. ("In Memory of I. Hrbek," 52)

Perhaps no less interesting to our study is Ibn Yaʿqub's observation that the Bohemians, contrary to other Europeans, were not fair of complexion. "It is strange that the Bohemians," he observes "have black hair and that fairness is a rarity among them" (Al-Bakri, *Jughrafiyat al-Andalus wa Uruba*, 167). In the absence of any single study of Ibn Yaʿqub's account of medieval Bohemia and the aforementioned statement, this observation remains a puzzle. Inasmuch as medieval Czechs, as demonstrated by Czech historians, were mainly of Slavic, Germanic, and Celtic origins, it seems unlikely that these dark-skinned men and women could be as dominant as recorded by Ibn Yaʿqub.

Conversely, owing to the existence of dark-skinned Roma with considerable numbers in medieval Bohemia, it is possible that Ibn Yaʿqub referred to none but the Gypsies. Yet this view is challenged by several prominent Slovak scholars, as we are told by Wadim Strielkowski of Charles University in Prague, who has argued that "the Roma first entered Bohemia via Hungary with the army of King Andrew II (1205–1235) after he returned from the Crusades in the Holy Lands in 1217–1218" ("Road Calls: Ethnic Origin and Migration," 6).[55] Perhaps it is time for these historians to reconsider the history of the Roma of Bohemia in light of Ibn Ya'qub's observations.

Last but not least, it is of crucial importance to mention that unlike many of his Arab (Muslim) predecessors and successors, Ibn Ya'qub never seems interested in flavoring his writing with fables and tall tales of the "strange and marvellous." Nevertheless, his name shows up not only in books of *'ajib/gharib* but also in a plethora of later geo-cosmographical works as the chief source of one of the most fantastic *'ajiba/ghariba* of classical Arabic-Islamic literature and culture, namely, the *madinat* or *jazirat al-nisa'*, or the town or island of women.[56]

In *Al-Masalik wa-l-Mamalik*, for example, al-Bakri (who is credited with preserving the most authentic fragments of Ibn Ya'qub's travel account) surprises us by claiming that during their presumed meeting, the German emperor Otto the Great told Ibn Ya'qub, "West to the land of the Rus [Bruss], there exists a city of women who rule over a vast territory and dominion" (169). "These women get pregnant by their own male slaves," Ibn Ya'qub is said to have added. "But, when they give birth to a male, they kill him. They also ride horses and fight in wars and they are known for their courage and braveness" (169).[57]

This is undoubtedly so Greek a *mirabilia* as to make one think of *The Arabian Nights* as a possible source, although Scheherazade would likely have enjoyed the idea of further threatening and taming the misogynist Shahrayar by empowering women in tales of the fearsome "*a-mazos* (without [one breast] or *a-masos* (not touching [men])" (Clements, *Marco Polo*, 87).[58] "In the earliest Greek accounts," Albrecht Rosenthal writes in his classic 1938 article "The Isle of the Amazons: A Marvel of Travelers," "the Amazons are a tribe of female warriors who have mutilated their right breasts to facilitate the use of the bow. This is supposed to be implied in their name: *a*=without, *mazos*=breast" (257). The Amazons, Rosenthal adds, "inhabited an exclusively female town which was surrounded by a river. Once a year they cross this river to mingle with neighboring men to have female children" (257).

No wonder then that the remaining details about these warrior women convince us that al-Bakri, rather than Ibn Ya'qub, was quoting verbatim from an Arabic translation of a Greek or possibly a Latin source.[59] Fortunately, if al-Bakri seems reluctant to acknowledge the

Greek origin of the fable he presented as fact, contrary to his account of the no-less-marvelous *jaza'ir al-sa'ada* (islands of happiness),[60] his Eastern contemporary al-Marwazi explained it all:

> Hippocrates has mentioned these women in some of his works. He calls them Amazuns, which means "those who possess but one breast," for they cut off the other, and they are only prevented from cutting off the race. The reason they cut off one breast is in order that it may not hamper them in shooting arrows on horseback. (Nazmi, *The Muslim Geographical Image*, 251)

Josine Block notes in *The Early Amazons: Modern and Ancient Perspectives on a Persistent Myth* that in spite of the long and seemingly never-ending debate over their origin, their possible existence in reality, and their various locations in the course of time, the Amazons have turned into a recurrent motif (Amazonology) in ancient culture in general and early Greek culture in particular (viii).

As Block has explained, although the Amazon motif in Greek was initially shown "to embody an otherness to the rest of masculinity and femininity in epic-heroic life," it became later imbued "with the meaning of ethnographic alterity" (vii). In other words, the Amazons became "an emblem of Otherness in its many guises" (vii), especially when it became commonplace among Greek writers to compare the Amazons with non-Greek peoples. "This ethnographic Amazonology was an attempt to give the Amazons a tangible form," Block goes on to conclude, "by connecting them with various peoples among whom the Greeks detected unusual customs, a high level of female mobility; sexual or marital which apparently failed to assign men authority over women and children; and the practice of horseriding and bearing arms by women" (85).

Constantly interested in conveying their own discourses of ethnographic alterity, medieval Arab Muslim writers had employed a foreign and initially subversive motif to consolidate the dominant poetics and politics of femininity and sexuality as they confronted it in the European panoply of lands and peoples beyond their borders. There should be no doubt that medieval Arab Muslim readers would have been shocked and appalled by the physique and *éthique* of these unnatural, abnormal, and masculine women who epitomized all that normative (Arab Muslim) womanhood was not. At the same time, *madinat/jazirat al-nisa'* would turn out to be, as mentioned by al-Azmeh in *Al-'Arab wa-l-Barabira*, the single most popular *khurafa* (legend) in the Arabic tradition of *'ajib/gharib* (202), as well as "the logical termini" of the typological motif of the "inversion of order" in Arabic writing ("Mortal Enemies," 267).

In my view, this "typological motif of the 'inversion of order'" is nowhere more clearly expressed in medieval Arabic literature than in the description of Frankish women warriors, the so-called "Amazons of the Crusades," by some Muslim chroniclers of the Crusades. Briefly stated, this is remarkably true of ʿImad al-Din al-Isfahani (d. 1201), Saladin's noted scribe and biographer, who in his *Kitab al-Barq al-Shami* related with shock and awe how the Frankish army included female warriors who

> rode into battle with cuirasses and helmets, dressed in men's clothes; who rode out into the thick of the fray and acted like brave men although they were but tender women, maintaining that all this was an act of piety, thinking to gain heavenly rewards by it, and making it their way of life. Praise be to him who led them into such error and out of the paths of wisdom! On the day of battle more than one woman rode out with them like a knight and showed (masculine) endurance in spite of the weakness (of her sex); clothed only in a coat of mail they were not recognized as women until they had been stripped of their arms. Some of them were discovered and sold as slaves. (Gabrieli, *Arab Historians of the Crusades*, 207)

By the same token, while the natural/normal/virtuous *al-madina al-fadhila*—that is, the virtuous city (utopia)—is quintessentially *madinat al-rijal* (a city of men), *madinat nisaʾ* is inherently a *madina fasida*, that is, a corrupt city (a dystopia). If it ever existed, one could never imagine it to have been within the confines of *dar al-islam*.

Another important point that springs to mind in connection with Ibn Yaʿqub's reference to the fantastic *madinat/jazirat al-nisaʾ* and its presumed existence in the (European) North is the tendency of some major medieval Arab Muslim writers to employ consciously or unconsciously the topoi of fables and legends as a template for the articulation of geo-cosmographical difference between *dar al-Islam* and the unknown and remote lands of the Other. Thabit Abdullah has even noted that some medieval Arab writers "believed that in the remote northern regions there lived monster-like creatures" ("Arab Views of Northern Europeans," 79). Citing al-Qazwini and Abu Hifs ibn Shahin, author of *Kitab al-ʿAjaʾib wa-l-Gharaʾib* (Book of Marvelous and Strange Things), Abdullah has maintained that whereas the former claimed the existence in the European North of a town named Kartanah where humans exist whose faces are differently colored, the latter mentions an island in the Atlantic Ocean named "*qlahat*" inhabited by humans with fishlike faces (79).

Medieval Arab Muslim writers did not hesitate to borrow creatively and to adapt culturally Greek geo-cosmographical legends and motifs as well as fables of marvelous and monstrous *juzur* (islands). In Nazmi's view, one is here speaking literally of dozens, such as *al-jazaʾir al-khalida* (the islands of the blest), *jaza'ir al-sa'ada* (the islands of happiness), and *jazirat al-waqwaq*, made popular by Ibn Battuta and identified by V. Minorsky and others as Japan. Interestingly, with the exception of the last and other African islands, most of these islands were imagined to exist in the North and the West (*The Muslim Geographical Image of the World*, 269).

Of course, writers and readers alike have always had a fascination with fables, myths, and legends. For reasons related mainly to the centrality of perceptions of Self and Other in these writings, it becomes evident that there is some truth in these texts when it comes to the discursive background of such accounts and their contribution in fashioning non-Muslim territory as territories of the fantastic and the abnormal, especially when we know that these *aja'ib/ghara'ib* were never located even in the remotest parts of *dar al-islam*. Like many of their medieval Western counterparts, strange islands imagined to exist in the North and West appear "to pander to a medieval audience's appetite for the strange and marvelous," to use Paul Smethurst's phrase. The strange and wondrous marvels of the East, as Smethurst and others have shown, were instrumental in mapping an East that is "either exotically different, or monstrously different," and presenting it as "other, populated by monsters, plants and strange human forms that belonged to a different system of Nature" ("Writing the East," 11), while the similar marvels of the North/West that one encounters in some medieval Arabic sources were also instrumental in fashioning and constructing a North/West no less different, exotic, or fabled. This is in several important respects what one finds in al-Gharnati's own record of his journey in twelfth-century central and eastern Europe.

Skiing, Giants, and Hungarian Maghribis: Marvelous Europe in the "Tall Tales" of Abu Hamid al-Gharnati

Long overshadowed by his two more world-famed "occidental" successors Ibn Jubayr (d. 1217) and Ibn Battuta (d. 1377), Abu Hamid ibn 'Abd al-Rahim al-Gharnati (d. 1169), once hailed by Lévi-Provençal as "the perfect type of the occidental *rahalla* [traveler/explorer]" ("Abu Hamid al-Gharnati," 125), has unquestionably surpassed both of them in bequeathing to posterity invaluable eyewitness accounts of several central and eastern European regions. Although not much is known about the early life of al-Gharnati, from a number of autobiographical references he incorporated in some of his works, he seems to have been born in 1080 AD in the city of Granada, to which he owes his designation al-Gharnati, that is, the Granadian (Nazmi, *Commercial Relations*, 40). This Occidental adventurer, as he used to identify himself in the Muslim East, tells us in *Al-Mu'rib 'an Ba'd 'Aja'ib al-Maghrib* with nearly the prevalent Andalucentric tone that he was born in the "extreme West, in an island called Andalus, which has forty cities" (el-Manssouri, "Abu-Hamid: The Twelfth Century Granadan Traveler," 43). After going through the "usual schooling available to a [Western] Muslim of his time," al-Gharnati, "fired by *wanderlust*," to use el-Manssouri's phrase, decided to embark on a long journey east and west of his native al-Andalus (43).

In all likelihood, al-Gharnati engaged in his first overseas trip, which took him to Egypt, starting in the year 1114. It was basically a *rihla fi talab al-'ilm*, that is, a journey in search of knowledge. Indeed, while in Egypt he attended the *durus* (lectures) of a number of scholars both in Cairo and Alexandria. He returned home but did not stay long since he journeyed back to Egypt in 1117 AD through Morocco, Algeria, Tunisia, Sardinia, and Sicily (Kratschkovsky, *Tarikh al-Adab al-Jughrafi al-'Arabi*, 295). Of great interest during this stage of his travels are his remarkable descriptions of the volcano of Mount Etna and the storied lighthouse of Alexandria. After spending almost five years in Cairo, he took the road to Damascus, where he stayed for a number of months before he decided to continue on to Baghdad, the capital of the East, which he reached in 1123. While in Baghdad, al-Gharnati attended the *durus* of several famous scholars and secured the patronage of a future *wazir* by the name of Yahya ibn Khabir al-Shaybani (Wahb, *Rihlat al-Gharnati*, 12). After a number of years in Baghdad, *wanderlust* took over again and pushed him to embark on what C. E. Dubler has called al-Gharnati's "Euro-Asian journey." After leaving Baghdad, he crossed Iran, and for more than 30 years he journeyed through the lands of the Turks, the Caucasus, Russia, Ukraine, the lands of the Bulghars, and at greater length the lands of the Magyars (Hungary). "Mais voilà que l'auteur traverse," Jean-Charles Ducène tells us, "la Caucase est passé près de trente ans de sa vie en Eurasie où il devient un témoin privilé-gié des populations Bulghares, turques, ouraliennes, slaves et hongroises" (*De Grenade à Bagdad*, 14).

As pointed out by Qasim Wahb in the introduction to the most recent, and indeed most comprehensive, Arabic edition of al-Gharnati's *rihla*, al-Gharnati, although not particularly known for his prolific production nor much appreciated for his language and style, left a number of interest-ing texts that, in spite of several "tall tales," are filled with accurate geo-graphical, historical, and ethnographical information (*Rihlat al-Gharnati*, 14). This is true not just of his somewhat unduly forgotten *récit de voyage*—for which he chose the title *Al-Mu'rib 'an ba'd 'Aja'ib al-Maghrib*, which could be translated as "On the Marvels of the West"[61]—but also of his *Tuhfat al-Albab wa-Nukhbat al-I'jab*, a compendium of wondrous information, news, and tales of different countries, towns, rivers, humans, non-humans, and animals.

We may perhaps appropriately begin by stating that al-Gharnati's attraction to *mirabilia* encouraged some of his contemporaries, notably the Damascene Ibn ʿAsakir (d. 1175), to castigate his works as books of *khawariq* (fables) and *asatir* (myths) unsuited for serious study (14). Conversely, and certainly against the perfunctory judgment of Ibn ʿAsakir and others, al-Gharnati has proved to be of great historical importance and pertinence, not least for a score of modern scholars who have found in al-Gahrnati's account of his European journey a "serious" document of twelfth-century central and eastern Europe.[62] This is particularly true of his records of the lands of the Bulghars and that of the Hungarians (Magyars), both of which, as we shall see, brim with plausible information and factual marvels: the fascinating reference to skiing as a medieval means of transport in Europe, the controversial issue of a witchcraft hunt as he witnessed it in the city of Kiev, and the mysterious Maghribi communities of Unquria (Hungary).

Al-Gharnati, like several of his Mashriqi and Maghribi predecessors such as Ibn Fadlan, al-Masʿudi, and Ibn Yaʿqub, had the chance to visit what medieval Muslims used to call in Arabic *ardh al-bilghar*, that is, the land of the Bulghars. The latter included the medieval Volga Bulghars, as well various other now-modern Russian territories. In the view of el-Manssouri, author of a rare and excellent English article on al-Gharnati, the land of the Bulghars in Arabic sources "extended westward to the Dnieper and the Kiev area and southward to the Caucasus" ("Abu-Hamid," 47). It included many modern east European towns such as Smirks, Kazan, Strakhan, and Kiev. Although not as detailed anthropologically speaking as that of the report of Ibn Fadlan, al-Gharnati's firsthand account of the socioeconomic and religious life of the Volga Bulghar state in the twelfth century and its then-Muslim capital, the city of Bulghar, has been of great value for modern scholarship.

Echoing Ibn Fadlan, among the conspicuous wonders of the lands of the Bulghars that al-Gharnati witnessed with his own eyes and experienced with his own body is the extreme *qisar* (shortness) of the night and the *buruda* (cold) of the weather. Al-Gharnati writes the following:

> And I've heard that in the City of the Bulghar—situated at the remote North of the Muslim lands—the day during the summer can last as many as twenty hours, whereas the night is only four hours. Since the weather is extremely cold, it is impossible to bury a dead person before the period of six months. This is mainly due to the fact that the earth becomes as hard as

iron. Therefore, no one is able to dig a grave. (*Tuḥfat al-Albab wa Nukhbat al-Iʿjab* [hereafter *Al-Tuḥfa*], 95; translation mine)

Inasmuch as this climate was an unquestionable marker of difference between the temperately warm to hot *dar al-islam*, both eastern and western, and this part of Europe, it represented in real life a religious challenge for these Muslim travelers who had to grapple daily not only with the extreme cold water indispensable for *wudu'* (ablution) and *ghusl* (bathing after sexual intercourse) but also with identifying the exact time of the five daily mandatory prayers. Of practical concern as well was the intermittent challenge of burying Muslims according to the prescribed rules and rituals of Islamic law.

This is what happened to al-Gharnati during his stay in the city of Bulghar, where the polygamous traveler lived for a number of years with his Bulghar wife, with whom, as he confesses, he had many children (el-Manssouri, "Abu-Hamid," 47). Because of the extreme cold, it is impossible to bury a dead person quickly. This is what he personally experienced when burying one of his sons. In fact, he tells us that he was obliged to wait three months to bury him (*Al-Tuḥfa*, 95).

Contrary to the theoretical geo-cosmographical views concerning the extreme cold of northern Europe (i.e., *ardh al-shamal*) as we saw with al-Masʿudi, with al-Gharnati and as a matter of fact Ibn Yaʿqub and other eyewitness travelers to the European heartlands, the issue was practical. Indeed, in the eyes of al-Gharnati, the cold weather is not to be taken as one of the ultimate markers of barbarity, as some "armchair" classical geo-cosmographers would have it. Al-Gharnati tells us with admiration that the extreme cold did not hinder the Bulghars from leading an active life. Shunning *al-kasal* (laziness), chastised in the Quran and the Sunna as not only one of the worst human attributes but as a proof of weakness of *iman* (faith), the industrious Bulghars, in addition to an excellent diet based mainly on honey and squirrel or horse meat, invented a marvelous instrument that facilitated their movement and filled their land with life.

In the course of this description of several tribes he encountered in the land of the Bulghars, he expresses his admiration for the *nashat* (vivacity) and *hayawiyya* (liveliness) of the northern tribes he met near a Bulghar region he called in Arabic *al-yura* and in particular the techniques used by these northern tribes to adapt to the cold weather and lead an active life in spite of the cold.[63] Al-Gharnati's total unfamiliarity with a certain wooden instrument widely used by these northern people did not prevent him from engaging in an attempt to describe what fits perfectly with a detailed description of the ski, especially when we know that the word *ski*, as explained by Peder Gammeltoft, finds its origin in the Old Norse *skíð*, which literally means a "split wooden board" ("Scandinavian Naming-Systems in the Hebrides," 488):

> The people make with their own hands wooden boards to walk with. Each board is one arm's length and a handbreadth wide. The beginning and the end of the board rise above the level of the ground. In the middle of it, there is a place where the walker can put his foot. On it there are a number of holes through which they fasten leather belts to their feet. The two sticks are tied on with a long strap similar to the one attached to the bridle of a horse. The walker holds the strap with his left hand. He also holds a stick as long as a man's leg. At the bottom of the stick there is a device that looks like a ball that is stuffed with wool as big as a man's head. The people rely on this stick to move on the snow by pushing it from behind like the paddling of the sailor. Were it not for this trick, none would be able to move for this snowy land is similar to sand and it does not harden. (*Al-Tuhfa*, 96; translation mine)

Al-Gharnati's complete unfamiliarity with this medieval European *'ajiba* (marvel) did not prevent him from bequeathing to us not just the first Arabic description of the ski but also one of the most original and plausible medieval reports on this wonderful instrument. It is perplexing that al-Gharnati is not referred to even in passing by perhaps the most comprehensive study on the history of skiing—E. John B. Allen's *The Culture and Sport of Skiing: From Antiquity to World War II* (2007)—especially when we know that Allen himself has deplored the dearth of documents that could have enhanced our knowledge of skiing (7).[64]

Needless to say, his precise account of the ski must have been hastily branded by al-Gharnati's contemporary Muslim critics as yet another unfounded *khurafa* (legend). Yet one cannot but share el-Manssouri's concern about the ongoing neglect of al-Gharnati's texts because of his "predilection for telling tall tales" ("Abu-Hamid," 57). Of course this neglect becomes less justifiable now that it is established that many of the "tall tales" were not as tall as his critics used to think.

Such severely cold weather did not discourage Muslim merchants from being active in Bulghar lands and the city itself. The latter is described by al-Gharnati as a Muslim town wherein he saw many big mosques and met several *fuqaha'* from both the Hanafi and Maliki schools of thought (el-Manssouri, "Abu-Hamid," 47). Here we should remember Ibn Fadlan's mission and the ensuing Islamicization of the Volga-Kama region after the decision of Almish to adopt Islam as we saw in a previous section. At that time, Z. Rorlich notes, Islam had become the dominant feature of Bulghar life. According to Rorlich, "Islam became the nucleus around which the spiritual life of the Bulghar state developed after the tenth century" ("The Bulghar State," 10), while Muslim merchants dominated much of the economic life of the city. From the East, they used to bring spices, precious stones, gold, and silver, which they traded for varied goods such as furs, grains, honey, beeswax, and leather items. This is in addition to trade in European slaves (6). The city of Bulghar was bustling with oriental-like *aswaq* (markets), *bazaris* (fairs), and *fanadiq* (inns) (10).

Al-Gharnati was also known for his fascination with what el-Manssouri aptly calls "tall tales," to which his account of the land of the Bulghars seems to testify. One such tale is about his presumed friendship with a giant Bulghar named Dange. In the words of al-Gharnati, this 14-foot-tall man was capable not only of holding a horse under his arm but also of breaking its body as a normal man would break a bundle of vegetables. His fantastic strength pushed the amir of the Bulghars to provide him with a monstrous shield, which used to be carried on a cart. His helmet was as big as a giant pot. In times of war, Dange fought with a great wooden bar made of oak, which he would hold easily in one hand; and when he struck with it, he could kill an elephant (*Al-Tuhfa*, 132).

Al-Gharnati insisted that not only did he see this giant with his own eyes but that he developed a strong friendship with him and his sister. Speaking about the kind of human being this otherwise "monstrous" giant was, al-Gharnati sympathetically reminds us that his friend was just a normal human being:

> He was very kind and modest. Indeed, every time he meets me he would greet me and treat me very generously. My head does not reach his groin. Throughout the land of the Bulghars, there is only one public bath that he can visit since it has a huge door. Undeniably, he was one of the most wonderful humans I have ever seen. Dange had a sister who was as huge as he whom I saw many times. Once, I was told by the Judge Ya'qub ibn al-Nu'man that this very tall woman killed her husband. The latter was called Adam and he, in turn, was one of the strongest men in the country. Once she hugged him until she broke his ribs and he passed away. (133; translation mine)

Although it is such "tall tales" that must have encouraged some medieval Muslim scholars to chastise al-Gharnati as a fabricator of lies and unfounded stories, it seems there may be some truth behind the story of the Bulghar giant. Dange could certainly be a reality. What seems rather "tall," perhaps, is the hyperbolic language and exaggerated metaphors with which al-Gharnati seasoned his description of Dange, most likely for literary purposes if one remembers the no-less-tall "horizons of expectation" of avid readers of the classical Arabic *ajib* genre, of which al-Gharnati was a master.

Al-Gharnati devotes an entire section to his journey to the land of the *saqaliba*, which as explained earlier was the vague term with which medieval Arabs, perhaps with the exception of Ibn Ya'qub, designated several eastern and central European countries. In the context of al-Gharnati's works, the main focus was upon what is now modern Ukraine.[65] After expressing his admiration for the country's varied fauna and flora, he informs us that it was particularly known for its agriculture. As with modern Ukraine, agriculture was the cornerstone of the Ukrainian economy in the twelfth century. Ukrainian farmers, we are told, grew mainly spelt, wheat, barley, and apples, and they also kept bees.

Along with this prosperity, there was a strong political system that guaranteed both Ukrainians and non-Ukrainians their fundamental rights and protected their personal property. Al-Gharnati does not see any religious or cultural taboo against praising Ukrainians for what he saw as just treatment of Muslims. Indeed, he emphasizes the fact that this Slavic country was a very safe place to live in, and above all, Muslims such as himself were treated equally. "Their country is very secure," he concludes, "and whenever a Slav transgresses financially upon a Muslim, he or one of his sons, or his house, is sold and the money is given back to the Muslim" (149).

In a language full of laudatory remarks when it comes to the rule and sanctity of law, al-Gharnati gives us a few specific examples of twelfth-century Ukrainian justice. Its most salient feature is its connection with slavery, which seems to be widespread among medieval Ukrainians, as was the case with other Slavonic races. For example, al-Gharnati mentions that every time a man transgresses upon another man's properties or relatives, he is obliged by law to pay a fixed fine. If he does not give the prescribed amount, the authorities will sell his sons or daughters to collect the fine. If, however, he does not have a family, he himself is sold and will stay a slave until he dies (146).

Twelfth-century Ukraine was not immune, however, from a number of social problems. Chief among them, as we are told by al-Gharnati, is the widespread practice of *sihr* (witchcraft) among their old women. After telling us that the Ukrainians, like most of the Slavs, are Melkite, he underlines the fact that many old women were seen to represent a persistent danger to their Christian society because of their pagan practices and propensity to witchcraft. "I was told that every ten years, witchcraft dramatically increases and witches muddle and harm their women," he reports before showing the kind of measures taken by the authorities (149).

The Ukrainians would arrest every old woman in their provinces and after tying their hands and feet, they would throw them in rivers. Every woman who sank in the water would be declared innocent and released. Those who floated, however, would be judged witches and burnt alive. Without being aware of what was known in early modern European countries as the Great Witch Hunt or the Burning Time, al-Gharnati left a valuable document on the possibly medieval precedent of this puzzling phenomenon that is still engendering a heated debate.[66] Although a further examination of this interesting subject goes beyond the scope of this work, al-Gharnati's description of the use in twelfth-century Ukraine of the ordeal by water—also known as the floatation test and the swimming of witches—should be seen in light of the comment made by William E. Burns in *Witch Hunts in Europe and America: An Encyclopedia* (2003):

> The water test was used in some English cases, particularly during the Matthew Hopkins witch-hunt. It was used only a few times in the English North American colonies and very little in Scotland. It had little impact in Italy, the Iberian Peninsula, or southern France. It had been used in Russia and the Ukraine during the Middle Ages, but was abandoned in the fourteenth century. Ukraine, but not Russia, began to use it again in the eighteenth century, continuing well into the nineteenth century. (94)

As is the case with his account of skiing, it is strange that al-Gharnati, who could unquestionably be an alternative source adding an outsider's point of view to the phenomenon, is still largely and unduly neglected in most recent studies, as in the example of Burns.[67]

Nonetheless, it is al-Gharnati's account of his three-year stay in the land of the Magyars (Hungarians), described by el-Manssouri as "the high-water of his career" ("Abu-Hamid," 48), that has proved most valuable, not least because it represents the single most important classical Arabic account of life in medieval Hungary.[68] This is in addition to the fact that it sheds light on the existence of thousands of Muslims, especially what he calls in Arabic *awlad al-maghariba* (Maghribis from al-Andalus and North Africa), in this European country; this phenomenon, if given its due importance in the growing field of Islam/West encounters, will certainly redraw several theoretical boundaries, especially when it comes to the claims discussed earlier that made medieval Europe a forbidden zone where medieval Muslims feared to tread.[69]

In the twelfth century, al-Gharnati encountered and lived in a Hungary that he described as not only affluent and rich but also exceptionally convivial for Muslims. With admiration and love, he recorded his pleasant sojourn in this medieval Christian kingdom that stretched over the Carpathian basin and, "in the 12th century, occupied a larger tract of territory than did the Byzantine Empire" (el-Manssouri, "Abu-Hamid," 48). In both *Al-Tuhfa* and *Al-Muʿrib*, he tells us that he lived three years in the country he interchangeably calls in Arabic *ardh al-bashghurd* and *anquria* (also *unkuriya*).[70] The former, as pointed out by Dubler, refers to the strongest of their founding tribes at the time of Hungaria Magna (*Abu Hamid*, 233), whereas the latter is a slight Arabic distortion of the word *Hungaria* itself.

Throughout the two accounts, al-Gharnati expresses his admiration for the Hungarians for their courage in wars and their civilized achievements and tolerance for Islam and Muslims. Hailing their great towns, he even dares to compare some of them to Baghdad and Isfahan. All in all, Hungary in al-Gharnati's eyes appears to be the most prosperous and most welcoming east-central European country he has visited during his long Euro-Asian journey.

Reminiscent in some ways of al-Tajir's description of ninth-century China, al-Gharnati portrays Hungary as a medieval utopia where he has enjoyed life to the full. With worldly satisfaction, he speaks more than once of the abundance of gold and silver; he cites the cheap prices of lamb, goat, and honey, traditionally thought to be among the favored delicacies in an Arab diet; and he speaks obsessively as well of the beauty of native women. With great joy, al-Gharnati praises the beautiful *jawari* (slave girls) he bought and sexually enjoyed, he implies, during his stay in Hungary. He writes that one can buy a beautiful and industrious slave girl for no more than ten *dinar*, and in times of war, the price can be as little as three *dinar* (*Al-Tuhfa*, 154). Al-Gharnati describes the situation in this way:

> I bought a young and beautiful slave girl from her master with the sum of ten *dinar*. Her father, mother, and sister are all alive. She was fifteen years old and was more beautiful than the moon with black hair and black eyes, yet, she was as white as camphor. She knew cooking, sewing, and writing. I bought also another eight-year old *rumiyya* (Roman/Byzantine) slave girl for only five *dinar*. She was so industrious that she used to extract five beeswax honeycombs as pure as gold from two clay pots of honey. When she gave birth to a boy who died I liberated her. I really wanted her to travel with me to Sejestin but I was afraid my Turkish wives would do her harm. (154; translation mine)

As much as modern readers may be disturbed by al-Gharnati's preferred themes, which do not sit comfortably with dominant worldviews, one has to remember that as the passage clearly shows, al-Gharnati is fashioned by and is fashioning a totally different worldview with its own values and its own standards.

It is of interest to mention here that, in Muslim law, when a concubine gives birth to a child (male or female), her legal status changes into that of the more prestigious *um-walad* (mother of child). In Sunni jurisprudence, upon the death of her master, she is automatically freed. However, an *um-walad* could be freed as soon as she gave birth to a child. That is exactly what al-Gharnati did with his slave girl in the previous passage. The latter also tells us much about the hidden competition between legal wives (maximum four) and what is known in classical Islamic law as *mulk al-ayman* (one's ownership), in reference to the female slaves that a Muslim male is allowed to have with precise conditions, a profound analysis of which is beyond the scope of the present volume.

In the larger context of the prosperity of Hungary in the twelfth century, there is much truth in al-Gharnati's account. As pointed out by the Hungarian historian Pál Engel in *The Realm of St Stephen: A History of Medieval Hungary, 895–1526* (2001), at that time in spite of the intermittent quarrels among the members of the royal family, Hungary reached the height of its military, economic, and cultural strengths. Similarly, Nora Berend in "Hungary in the Eleventh and Twelfth Century" in *The New Cambridge Medieval History* (2005) has maintained that during much of the twelfth century, thanks mainly to "Béla's strong regime and major reforms," Hungary was not only a rich and a powerful Christian kingdom, but also "an international power" (316). It is this good life full of abundance that seemed to encourage al-Gharnati's son Hamid and a surprising number of Muslims to settle there in the twelfth century. Thousands of Maghribi and Mashriqi Muslims chose to live in Hungary in harmony with the indigenous Christian population and under the direct protection and patronage of the Hungarian king. This makes al-Gharnati unique in reporting a premodern "season of migration" to the North, which was, however, different from the one eternalized by Tayyeb Saleh in *Mawsim al-Hijra il-a al-Shamal* (Season of Migration to the North).

As pointed out by el-Manssouri, "the question that remains unanswered in his [al-Gharnati's] narrative concerns the reason behind the presence of the Maghribis in the 12th century Hungary" ("Abu-Hamid," 48). Although this question is legitimate given the dominant view concerning the insularity of medieval Muslims in regard to Europe, and the dearth of research related to this interesting issue, the most compelling answer seems to be found in the narrative itself, a possibility that el-Manssouri does not seem to take into consideration—namely when she has suggested that these thousands of Muslims living in Hungarian towns and villages were all, as she puts it, "engaged in the lucrative and widespread *mamluk* trade exporting young Slavs, Teutons, Huns, Georgians, Greeks, Armenians, Khazars, Georgians, and Tartars" (50).[71] Still more surprising is her statement that her postulation is "self evident." "After all, would a contemporary author writing about Spain today," as she phrases it, "feel the need to explain why there is a large British community on the Costa del Sol" (50).

In short, although one cannot deny that some, or even many, of these Muslims, could have engaged in the *mamluk* trade, it is farfetched to conclude that all of them were "slave hunters." Indeed, as al-Gharnati implicitly acknowledged, most of these thousands of Muslims were rather military mercenaries whom the Hungarian kings recruited along with other fighters to ensure Hungary's interests in a century in which the country rose, as noted earlier, to the heights of international influence. One can also surmise, of course based on al-Gharnati's text, a possible twelfth-century Hungarian-Muslim alliance, or at least military cooperation, in the two peoples' struggle against Byzantium.[72] In fact, al-Gharnati appears to allude to this arrangement in his reference to jihad in the context of Muslim contributions in the wars of the Hungarians against the Byzantines. Speaking of his role and contribution as a pro-Hungarian propagandist, al-Gharnati tells us that the king was known for his assaults against Byzantium. He states proudly that he did his best to entice Muslims to engage in jihad along with the Hungarian king, assuring them that they would be rewarded for this. Al-Gharnati goes on to assert that hundreds of Muslims joined him in the attack on Constantinople and conceitedly claims that they ensured victory for the Hungarians (*Al-Tuhfa*, 155).

The immediacy and uncharacteristic directness of al-Gharnati when mentioning these events make it clear that many, if not the majority, of those thousands of Muslims had little to do with the *mamluk* trade. Their seeming willingness to fight for the king because of his tolerance of Islam and Muslims stands in contrast to the Byzantines, universally acknowledged by pre-Crusade Muslims as the archenemy of Islam. As Berend has pointed out, these Muslims belonged to the *hospites* (foreign settlers) who flocked to Hungary to enjoy a privileged status in Hungarian society. Living in royal lands and holding high-ranking military and political positions at the direct patronage of the king, these foreign settlers, Berend goes to explain, felt part and parcel of the *"gens Ungarorum"* ("Hungary in the Eleventh and Twelfth

Century," 314). The erudite Lewicki is worth quoting here:

> The Maghariba were like a great many of the Khawarizmians, war-
> riors, and Abu Hamid speaks of their participation in the war against
> Byzantium. They were very numerous, "thousands of people" according
> to the author, referring both to the crypto-Muslims and to the Muslims.
> ("Madjar, Madjaristan," 1018)

Perhaps more related to our purposes is al-Gharnati's confirmation that
foreign settlers and Muslims in particular enjoyed unprecedented cultural
and religious tolerance. Indeed, he writes that he was told by a number of
Muslims who fell captive to the Byzantines that they were asked by the
Byzantine emperor about the reasons that encouraged them to fight along
with the king. They all answered that they did so because—in contrast
to the Byzantines, who obliged Muslims to convert to Christianity—the
Hungarian king (Géza II) granted them the freedom to practice their
religion, and he built mosques for them (*Al-Tuhfa*, 155). This king is also
lauded by al-Gharnati for his presumed curiosity to learn about Islam
and his fascination with the author's *hikma* (wisdom). In the course of
al-Gharnati's account, the theological and political debate that had seemingly taken place between the two men is featured. Al-Gharnati tells
us that the king once summoned him to ask about the logic behind his
actions in encouraging Muslim *hospites* to practice polygamy while dis-
couraging them from drinking wine (155).

With a language full of conceit and self-advertisement—forgetting that
his statements could be seen as an indirect denigration of Muslims and
praise of Christians—al-Gharnati tells us that in his effort to vindicate
the superiority of Islamic law, he reminded the king that Muslims cannot
drink moderately. Indeed, as we shall see below, he stresses the fact that
Muslims when drunk lose their minds and behave more like beasts that
humans. The passage is worth quoting in full:

> When he heard that I have prohibited the Muslims from drinking wine,
> while allowing them to have four concubines and four wives, he said "This
> is not reasonable because wine strengthens the body while the multiplicity
> of women weakens it." So, I said to the translator: "Inform the king that
> Islamic law is different from that of the Christians: The Christen drinks
> wine (moderately) while feeding himself exactly as he does with water,
> that is why he does not get intoxicated and that makes him stronger. As
> for the Muslim who drinks, he does so to seek excessive intoxication. As
> a consequence, he loses his intellect and becomes like the insane person:
> fornicating, killing, and blaspheming. He turns into an evil person with
> no good in him: he gives away his arms and horse, squanders his money

in order to indulge in his own pleasures. Furthermore, the Muslims are your soldiers and if you order them to fight they will have neither horses, arms, nor money." (155)

When it comes to polygamy, al-Gharnati mentions that he told the king engaging in (legal) sexual relations with four wives and multiple concubines goes perfectly with what he phrases in Arabic as *hararati tiba'ihim*, that is, their inherent hot (sexual) temperament (155). The "wise" al-Gharnati goes on to make his case that the more children Muslim men will have, the more soldiers the Hungarian king will possess! What should one expect from such a scheherazadian tale of Arabian intrigue and wit except that the Hungarian Shahrayar will find himself not only convinced but utterly mesmerized by the tales of the Arabian shaykh? Indeed, with all possible pride and a reigning feeling of victory, al-Gharnati closes his account by informing his Arab readers that before the coming of the day, the Hungarian king had not only allowed his Muslim soldiers to practice polygamy but he had ordered his officers to disregard the orders of *al-qissisn*, that is, the priests, and has vowed to enjoy as many wives and concubines as, of course, his European temperament would allow (155).

CHAPTER 4

POETRY, FRONTIERS, AND ALTERITY: VIEWS AND PERCEPTIONS OF *AL-RUM* (BYZANTINES) AND *AL-IFRANJA* (FRANKS)

Byzantium and the Byzantines in Medieval Arabic Poetry: Abu Firas's *Al-Rumiyyat* and the Poetic Responses of Al-Qaffal and Ibn Hazm to Nicephorus Phocas's *Al-Qasida al-Arminiyya al-Mal'una* (The Armenian Cursed Ode)

Long before the rise of Islam in the seventh century, the Arabs had already established strong relations with *al-rum* (the Byzantines), who along with *al-furs* (the Persians) were considered to be the two most powerful empires of late antiquity. As masterfully demonstrated by Irfan Shahid in a number of studies on Arab-Byzantine relations before Islam, several Arab tribes were satisfied with a passive role—that is to say, accepting of the will of both these imperial powers in the *Oriens*—although many of the most influential tribes, owing mainly to religious affinities, favored the Christian Byzantines. In fact, mostly sedentary and Christian Arab tribes such as the Tanukhids, the Salihids, and the Ghassanids served as Byzantium's principal *foederati* (allies) in the *Oriens* (*Byzantium and the Arabs in the Fourth Century*, xvi). By signing a *foedus* (treaty) in return for *anonna* (allowances), the federate Arabs—especially the Ghassanids of the sixth and early seventh centuries—in addition to forming a "buffer zone" between their allies and their most antagonistic rivals the Persians, were expected to repel anti-Byzantine Arab raiders "from the Peninsula outside the *limes* [borders]."[1]

Understandably, pre-Islamic Arabs admired the Byzantines for their cultural achievements, military might, their "wonderful" artistry, and their excellent craftsmanship. According to Ahmad Shboul and N. M. el Cheikh, the Arabs' high esteem for Byzantine civilization was even alluded to in imagery used by a number of *jahili* (pre-Islamic) poets. Also among the most valued of these images were the Byzantine silver coins portraying scarce pools of water in the desert and gold coins depicting beautiful human faces (Shboul, *Al-Mas'udi and His World*, 46; and el-Cheikh, "Byzantium through the Islamic Prism," 56). The most striking imagery, however, lies in the comparison by some poets of their healthy she-camels to Byzantine bridges and palace arches (*Al-Mas'udi and His World*, 46). If on the one hand the Arabs were fully aware of the greatness of their Byzantine patrons, the civilized Byzantines, on the other, were equally conscious of their allies' *barbarismus*. "Whereas the Arabs saw the Byzantines as palace-dwellers and architects and builders *par excellence*," Shboul tells us, "the Byzantines thought conventionally of the pre-Islamic Arabs as nomads and tent-dwellers" (46). The "haughty" Byzantine perception of their *foederati* of the deserts would unquestionably change with the advent of Mohammed.

It should be mentioned from the outset that in spite of the Quran's initially positive view of *al-Rum* wherein the nascent Muslim community is divinely summoned to sympathize with the Byzantines by applauding a pending victory of the Byzantine *ahl al-kitab* (people of the Book) over the Persian *majus* (fire worshippers), the "physical" encounter between Muslims and Byzantines proved to be dramatically Huntingdonian.[2] This sympathy would vanish when Muslims and Byzantines found themselves competing for the vast area that makes up the entire modern Middle East and North Africa, thereby ushering in a new area of Muslim-Byzantine enmity that would color their relations until the dramatic conquest of Constantinople by the Ottomans in 1453. This was true in spite of intermittent truces, ransoms, exchanges of captives, and the ensuing diplomatic negotiations, as well as the "latent" manifestations of cultural influences represented on the Muslim side in the appreciation of Byzantine craftsmanship, architecture, and (fe)male beauty.[3] From the Byzantine side, it was most strongly felt in the Iconoclastic Controversy of the eighth and ninth centuries.[4]

As mentioned earlier, in 750 A.D. the Abbasids succeeded in ousting their archrivals the Umayyads. The latter, in spite of their wars with the Byzantines, had initially had strong cultural, diplomatic, and economic ties with them. Indeed, as mentioned in an earlier chapter, not only had the Umayyad retained Greek as their administrative language, but they had also learned from the Byzantines the arts of civil service and political governance by relying fully on Byzantine "administrative, legal, and numismatic traditions" (el-Cheikh, "Byzantium through the Islamic Prism," 55). In the words of el-Cheikh, "the administrative patterns and the political framework that were chosen by the Umayyad were Byzantine in origin" (55).

It is, however, in the domains of architecture and craftsmanship that the Byzantines were hailed by Muslims as the unequalled masters.[5] To the implied detriment of Byzantine science and philosophy, al-Jahiz's much quoted statement, for instance, sums it up well:[6] "In the domains of construction, carpentry, craftsmanship, and turnery, the Byzantines have no equal" (quoted in ibid, 109). In the example of al-Jahiz, "Arabic authors," Shboul remarks, "acknowledge this debt in various ways. Reporting traditions about Byzantine material and technical help in the building of some of the great early mosques of the Umayyad period is only one aspect of this" (*Al-Mas'udi and His World*, 52).

The Byzantines, contrary to their near defeat by the Umayyad troops who were twice on the verge of conquering Constantinople in 674–678 and 717–718, chose to attack by engaging in offensive skirmishes and sometimes full assaults across their southern borders. This pushed the early Abbasid caliphs, as demonstrated by Michael Bonner in *Aristocratic Violence and Holy War: Studies on the Jihad and the Arab-Byzantine Frontier* (1996), to invest in the strengthening of their positions along *al-thughur* through establishing strong "buffer towns," known in Arabic as *al-'awasim* in northern Syria (53).[7] These efforts were consolidated by the powerful caliphs/Ghazis (warriors) such as Harun al-Rashid, al-Ma'mun, and al-Mu'tasim. The latter's triumph over the Byzantines, for instance, in Amoriyya (Amorium) in 838 was celebrated by the poet Abu Tammam (d. 846) in a powerful *qasida* (long poem) in the Arabic genre of *madih* (panegyric-eulogy).[8]

Clearly, throughout the Abbasid era and irrespective of the internal strife that led to the rise of a number of independent dynasties and principalities, Muslim enmity with the Byzantines had never decreased.[9] One is left with no doubt that, at least until the Crusades, medieval Muslims (whether rulers or ruled) used to consider Byzantium and the Byzantines as the eternal archenemies of Islam and Muslims. This feeling was no better illustrated at the time than in the much quoted warning of the Abbasid polyvalent scholar, *katib* (official scribe), *naqid* (literary critic), and geo-political Abbasid strategist Qudama ibn Ja'far (d. 948). In *Al-Kharaj*, and after reminding Muslims that threats could emanate from all the *umam al-kufr* (nations of infidelity), he singled out the Byzantines as the hereditary enemy of the Islamic faith and the traditional opponents of Muslims (al-Kilani, *Surat Uruba Inda al-'Arab fi-l-'Asr al-Wasit*, 116).[10]

As with Qudama, Abbasid scholars motivated by the generous support of the caliphs initiated a systematic study of Byzantium's political, economic, and military systems both to comprehend the reasons that made Byzantium impregnable to Muslim armies and to contain any Byzantine danger looming from the *thughur* region. As el-Cheikh says, "Knowledge of Byzantium was imperative for the survival and prestige of the Islamic empire" (102). If seen from the same perspective as that from which Said saw the rise of Oriental studies in the West, one might posit that the Abbasid interest in Byzantium and the Byzantines anticipated the Western project of Orientalism. In any case, one cannot deny the fact that as Orientalism has actively participated in the construction of the Oriental as the Other of the early/modern European, this older medieval Muslim tradition indubitably bore a similar ideological responsibility in fashioning *al-rum* as the Muslim Other.

No wonder then that a close look at medieval Arabic literature and Arabic poetry in particular will convince us that *al-rum*, interchangeably called *banu al-asfar* (the Yellow Ones)—and derogatorily *'uluj*, plural *'ilj* (barbarians, unknown, and in some Arabic varieties, it is still used to denote a person with an unknown parent)—are depicted as *al-akhar* (the Other) par excellence.[11] Medieval Arabic poetry was the favorite "ideological apparatus" not only of the Abassid state but also of the common Muslim east and west of *dar al-islam* wherein the colloquial words *rumi* (masculine) and *rumiyya* (feminine) in many Arabic dialects, especially in the Maghreb, still denote the non-Muslim European Other whether German, French, Italian, Spanish, English, or Scandinavian. Abbasid literature, certainly in its Hamdanid branch, and poetry in particular, waged an ideological war against political and military archrivals. Anti-Byzantine poetry, in the words of Shboul, "may be seen as an interesting illustration of Muslim public opinion, with no small amount of the mass media flavor especially when one considers the Arabs' appreciation of poetry" (*Al-Mas'udi and His World*, 54).

Throughout these times, a highly emotional type of poetry that encompassed almost all the classical genres—such as *madih* (eulogy-panegyrics), *hija'* (lampoon-invective), *munaqadhat* (polemics-debates), *ritha'* (elegy), *fakhr* (praise), and *hanin ila al-awtan* (homesickness)—became so culturally and politically à la mode that court poets competed ferociously to come up with the most impressive *madih* of Muslim notables who had engaged in fighting the Byzantine "infidels." "The preoccupation with the Byzantines as the Arabs' chief enemy," Shboul asserts, "is particularly reflected in Arabic poetry of the late seventh, eighth, and tenth century. This poetry is mainly in praise of Muslim caliphs, emirs or generals who waged war against the Byzantines and restored the prestige of Islam" (55).

This war poetry came to be known in most medieval Arabic critical circles as *Al-Rumiyyat* (poems about *al-rum*), and "Byzantinesques,"
in my view, could be an excellent translation.[12] Other critics, however, preferred to describe it with the no less suggestive appellation of
al-thuguriyyat, or poems about borders. Although this type of poetry
deals predominately with the *gesta* of Muslim leaders who engaged in
jihad against the Byzantines, many of the poems written in this tradition focus on the "common people" and either deal directly with the
life of Muslims in *mudun al-thughur*—or the border towns, especially
Tarsus—or narrate the plight of *al-asra al-muslimin* (Muslim captives), as
is the case with the majority of Abu Firas's *Rumiyyat*.

The middle of the ninth century witnessed an increasing decline
in the central power of the Abbasid caliphate over its vast territories.
Mentioned earlier, this led to the rise of a number of independent and
semi-independent dynasties and principalities. Chief among these was
the Hamdanid Emirate of Aleppo, founded by the Hamdanid prince Sayf
al-Dawla in 944. In addition to his patronage of learning and poetry,
which made his court a magnet for the greatest poets of his time such
as al-Mutanabbi, Abu Firas, and others, Sayf al-Dawla is remembered
for his wars with the Byzantines. Because of his principality's proximity to the Byzantine frontiers, Sayf al-Dawla, in the words of Mahmud
Ibrahim, "found himself playing the role of defending the lands of Islam
against Byzantium, the historical enemy of the Muslims since the days of
Heraclius" (*Songs of an Arab Prince*, 17).

The challenge was daunting since the Byzantines he was confront-
ing were already enjoying an unprecedented military resurgence, which
reached its apogee with Nicephorus Phocas (d. 969), the very personification of the Byzantine Other in medieval Arabic-Islamic poetry and
hija' (invective/lampoon) in particular, as will be seen in a number of
Abu Firas's poems and in al-Qaffal's and Ibn Hazm's poetic responses to
the vituperative assault on Islam in the poem attributed to him known
in some Muslim chronicles as *Al-Qasida al-Arminiyya al Mal'una*, or the
Armenian Cursed Ode.

Abu Firas's **Al-Rumiyyat:** *Or the Byzantines Are Coming!*

As Shboul correctly observed, it is misleading to think that the majority
of "professional" poets of *Al-Rumiyyat*—who wrote predominately in the
madih (eulogy-panegyric) genre, "in praise of caliphs, emirs, or generals"
(*Al-Mas'udi and His World*, 54)—were ideologically engaged and wholeheartedly committed to their patrons' "divine mission" of defending the
thugur of *dar al-islam* from the Byzantines and their *tawaghit*, or their ungodly

leaders (4).[13] Many of them, if not the majority, "used and abused their muses" to gain their livelihood and provide for "their bread and butter," to borrow A. F. L. Beeston's phrase (*Selections from the Poetry of Bashshār*, 3). Beeston describes the setbacks that the *badi'* (innovative) poet Bashar (d. 784) had to face because of his challenge to many of the prevailing norms of poetry in the early Abbasid period through his extensive usage of new rhetorical devices and poetic styles invented by him and other later *muhdath* (modern) poets, such as Abu Tammam and Ibn al-Mu'taz (d. 908).[14]

It would be apposite to affirm that some of those poets, especially the ones who were not in dire need of patronage, which is the case of the prince/poet Abu Firas al-Hamdani (d. 968), found themselves deep in the mayhem of Arab-Byzantine rivalry. This does not mean, however, that this second type of poet of *Al-Rumiyyat* was engaged through litera-ture in the modernist sense of *l'engagment littéraire* especially as delineated by Jean-Paul Sartre, for it cannot be denied that those poets "*restent quand meme des poètes*" in a culture that traditionally adores poets. This is certainly true of Abu Firas, contrary to the majority of the panegyrists such as his archrival al-Mutanabbi, who were characteristically covet-ous of money and power. Abu Firas wrote his *Al-Rumiyyat* to record the excruciating experience of captivity at the hands of those he consciously called *akhwaī* (my maternal uncles) in reference to his Byzantine mother, who after giving birth to him was manumitted through gaining the legal status of *um-walad*, which as we saw earlier literally means the mother of a child (Farrukh, *Abu Firas, a Knight and Romantic Poet*, 23).[15]

Abu Firas was born most probably in the city of Mosul in northern mod-ern Iraq in 932. He belonged to the famous Arab tribe of Bani Hamdan, who came to legendary fame through the poet's cousin, mentor, and brother-in-law Sayf al-Dawla, founder of the Hamdanid dynasty and one of the most admired emirs in medieval Arabic war poetry for the impres-sive bravery he showed during his numerous struggles with the Byzantines (Ibrahim, *Songs of an Arab Prince: Verses from the Poetry of Abu Firas al-Ham-dani*, 12).[16] At a very young age, Abu Firas demonstrated extraordinary aptitude in the arts of poetry and war. As A. el-Tayib pointed out, "In appre-ciation of his valour and brilliance," his cousin Sayf al-Dawla appointed him governor of the town of Manbej when he was only 16 ("Abu Firas al-Hamdani," 317). It is in this town that he fell captive to the Byzantines. This captivity at the hands of his *akhwal* represented the turning point of his short life, for he died in 968 at the age of 34. In fact, captivity was the impetus behind his most famous poems, known as *Rumiyyat*. "It is to the so well documented captivity of 962," observes el-Tayib, "that we owe the group of *qasa'id* [poems] called *Al-Rumiyyat*, in which is to be found some of Abu Firas' finest poetry" (317).

It comes as no surprise, then, that in addition to the emotional thrust that inspired Abu Firas to produce some of the finest poems of the period, the experience of captivity at the hands of the Byzantines also supplied the poet with the ideological mindset that made him stereotypical in his portrayal of the Byzantine as not only the Hamdanids' military archrivals but as the *umma*'s (Muslim nation's) religious Other par excellence.[17] The impact of the poet's captivity in Constantinople and its literary manifestation invokes in many ways not only that of Cervantes's much talked about five-year captivity in Algiers and his description of the Moors in *El Trato de Argel* and *Don Quixote* but also, and regardless of the heated debate over the authenticity of his account, the Byzantine John Cameniates, who was captured by the Arabs in 904 during their sack of Thessaloniki.[18]

Needless to say that in Abu Firas's *Al-Rumiyyat*, one can find many poems that succinctly illustrate the captive's feelings of estrangement in the Byzantine lands. The two texts "Mother of the Captive" and "The Cooing of a Dove" are the most moving in their description of the emotional turmoil inflicted upon the captive. In my view, however, it is Abu Firas's *qita'* (short poems), such as "A Captive's Suffering" and "Separation," both love poems; "The Byzantines Are Coming," a *tahridh* (literally instigation, call to revenge); and "How Dare You Claim," a *hija'* (invective-lampoon) of the Byzantine emperor Nicephorus Phocas, that should draw our attention if we want to explore the poet's anti-Byzantine rhetoric of alterity.

Very simple in structure and economical in diction, yet rhetorically and thematically robust, "A Captive's Suffering" and "Separation" successfully utilize a number of conventional topoi of the classical Arabic *qasida* in the poet's effort to depict *ardh al-rum* (the land of the Byzantine) as not only inherently foreign and unfamiliar, indubitably in the negative sense, but also as a space of *ightirab* (alienation) and *firaq* (separation):

> In captivity, a lover suffers in disgrace.
> And tears flood down his lonely face.
> In Byzantine land, his body must reside.
> Though in Syrian land his heart does still abide.
> A lonesome stranger and out of place!
> Where none with love may him embrace. (*Diwan Abu Firas al-Hamdani*, 31)

And:

> In the past, separation, I could not withstand.
> Although with a camel's swiftest space,
> At will, it was easy to find your trace.
> But now, what separates us is Byzantine land.
> And hope of reunion never looms in my face! (31)[19]

Unlike the traditional *nasib* or introductory passage of the *qasida* in which poets would conventionally weep over *al-atlal* (abandoned campsites) of their absent beloved in a nostalgically laden setting evocative of the Western *ubi sunt* formula, Abu Firas, while keeping the nostalgic mood of the *nasib* by referring to his captivity at the hands of the Byzantines, has opted not only for a more realistic and historical setting but also for a highly political content.[20]

The *nasib*'s nostalgic emphasis on the lover's *ghiyab* (absence), *firaq* (separation), and the longing for *wisal* (reunion), which represent the gist of this topos, is powerfully captured by Abu Firas's rapid reference to his captivity in the *sadr* (literally front), or the first hemistich, of the first *bayt* (literally tent) or couplet of the first *qit'a*. In the second poem, it is strongly centralized also through the powerful imagery of the camel in *al-'ajuz* (literally back), while the second hemistich of the second *bayt* of the second *qit'a* is most commonly used in Arabic literature to denote *al-safar* (travel), *al-rahil* (leaving), and *al-mawt* (death). The traditional metaphorical use of *nasib* imagery is of paramount importance in these two poems especially when it comes to Abu Firas's playing on the concepts of *al-zaman* (time), *al-makan* (place), *hudhur* (presence) and *ghiyab* (absence), and *al-shi'r* (poetry) itself, especially when one remembers that the Arabic word is derived from *al-shuhur*, which means emotions, whose power is, by itself, a hymn to *al-ana*, the "I" or the "self."

Most of the time, the metaphors of *al-madhi* (past) are driven by the mnemotopic power of the Arabic language itself, which is forcefully translated in the linguistic *jians* (paronomasia) that connect a number of lexical items belonging to the semantic fields of memory, such as *al-tadhakkur* (the faculty of memory), *al-dhakira* (memory), and *al-dhikra* (souvenir or remembrance). The outcome for the reader, or at least what S. B. Yeats would call "the discerning reader," would be to find himself/herself consciously or unconsciously a captive of the poem's antithetical fluctuation between *al-waqi'* (reality) and *al-khayal* (fiction/illusion), especially when the love poem through its intermittent flashbacks dramatizes the poet/ lover's fear of *al-nihaya* (the end) of his *hayat* (life) owing to his *shakk* (doubt) concerning *al-wisal* (reunion) with his beloved.

The absence of the loved one is the thematic leitmotif that provides the perfect mood for the *hanin* (nostalgia) for the known land, that is, *dar al-islam* and Syria in particular. Of rhetorical importance in this regard is the poet's reliance on *tibaq* (antithesis) between physical existence and emotional states. The striking thing, however, is that the poet moves so quickly to emphasize the fact that, unlike the conventional absence of the loved one in such poems that denotes an eternal absence, the lover in this poem is aware that absence is temporary. In other words, the abode of the beloved could be regained in reality if the poet/lover succeeds in convincing his cousin Sayf al-Dawla to ransom him. Contrary to the conventional *nasib* of love poems wherein the physical place represents the poetic locus, it is clear, and owing to the strong *tibaq* between body/heart and Byzantine/Syrian lands, Abu Firas's emphasis here falls rather on the excruciating experience of *ghurba* (foreignness), which is in essence a temporary experience. Whereas the physical locus of conventional love poetry is a place that is well known and familiar, in these love poems, the foreignness and unfamiliarity of *al-makan* adds surely to the poet's depression and alienation.

By virtue of the rhetorical importance of *tadhmin* (implication of meaning)—which refers to the fact that the accurate meaning of the current *bayt* is to be found in the following one—in both *qit'a*, the poet appears to juxtapose masterfully the traditional *'udhal* (adversaries/denouncers) of the poet/lover (in)famous in classical Arabic love poetry to the historical enemies of the captive/lover.[21] This dramatizes the antagonistic nature of *al-makan* and the people (*al-rum*) who are implied to represent the prime cause of *firaq* (separation).

If the apparent dominant theme is the recurring love motifs of lost happiness, lovesickness, and longings for *al-mahbub* (the beloved), the poet's implied emphasis on the Byzantine lands as the barrier between him and his beloved makes it clear that there is more than the traditional topos of *firaq* in these poems. Likewise, the archetypal enmity of *al-habib* (the lover) to *al-'udhal*, who do everything to ruin his relationship with his *mahbub*, is brilliantly transfigured to depict the captive's *karaha* (hatred) toward his captors. By implication, the Byzantines are plotting against Muslims in the same way that *al-'udhal* plot against lovers. If lovers in the classical *qasida*, however, are most of the time alert to the plots of their enemies, Muslims in the poet's view are not. It is his duty, therefore, to remind them of the danger looming from these foreign and inimical lands. This is the explicit and straightforward message of the following lines:

> As many a Byzantine troop is rolling towards your land.
> Cheering infidelity and raising crosses in the hand.
> Their horses carry nothing but injustice full of hate.
> And injustice is man's most destructive trait.
> They are staunch and committed! So you must understand!
> For the unprepared, only their like can them withstand!
> If you do not rise in anger for God's true faith,
> No swords for its sake shall be drawn. (*Diwan Abu Firas al-Hamdani*, 51)

Conspicuous as it is, this powerful *tahridh* (instigation to revenge/war) is replete with expressions of *mubalagha* (hyperbole) and *ziyadat* (exaggerations), especially when it comes to the number of the Byzantine troops and their diabolical plots to invade Muslim lands and destroy the *din* (religion) of Allah (God).

Of rhetorical importance also is the effective and appropriate *tikrar* (repetition) of the word *ghayy* (injustice/wrong/transgression), which the poet deliberately employs as a *kinaya* (metonymy) not only to depict the Byzantines' deeds but also to describe their most idiosyncratic feature. Certainly, the striking *majaz* (metaphor) of Byzantine horses carrying their masters' *ghayy* to the Muslim land, in addition to the powerful *ḥikma* (aphorism) "and injustice is man's most destructive trait," proves extremely effective in conveying this message. In this way, the Byzantine Other becomes an allegory of Otherness. He represents all that is contrary to the Muslim Self. He is depicted as the agent of *kufr* (infidelity), and he is associated with *sharr* (evil) and *fasad* (corruption).

Abu Firas's "hyperbolic accounting," to use Jonathan Burton's phrase, of the Byzantine forces finds a strong echo in Western medieval and early modern depictions of the raging Saracen and Turkish armies. As a matter of fact, it is unexpectedly expressed by Elizabethan dramatist Christopher Marlowe in *Tamburlaine*. The following lines are, comparatively speaking, analogous:

> As many circumcised Turks we have,
> And warlike bands of Christians renied,
> As hath the ocean or the Terrene sea
> Small drops of water, when the moon begins
> To join in one her semi-circled horns. (III.1.8–12)

Certainly Abu Firas's hyperbolic description of Byzantine troops in his effort to warn Muslims of the impending "Yellow Peril" is comparable to Marlowe's description of the Turkish Bajazeth's Muslim troops as "the drops of the ocean" in his attempt to alert Europe to "the raging and expansionist Turk" (Burton, *Traffic and Turning*, 73). Abu Firas's stress upon the religious identity of the approaching Byzantine troops through the figure of the Cross, the principal icon of Christianity, is very similar to Marlowe's foregrounding of the figures of the circumcised Turk, the Christian renegades, and the crescent moon. This, according to Jonathan Burton, not only "confirm[s] European fears of immense Ottoman armies," but it steadily broadcast "Bajazeth's Islamism and his threat to European Christendom" (73).

Abu Firas's deep belief in the Manichaean division between Muslims and Byzantines and his stereotypical demonization of the Byzantines would become especially evident in his *hija'* of Nicephorus Phocas, one of the most loathsome figures in medieval Arabic-Islamic writing. The opening lines of this *hija'* are a challenge:

> How dare you claim!
> Oh you huge-throated rogue,
> That we lions of war,
> Are ignorant of wars! (*Diwan al-Amir Abu Firas al-Hamdani*, 34)

Both uncharacteristic of his chivalrous character and unrepresentative of his "romantic" poetry, Abu Firas's facetious assault on Nicephorus sums up neatly the mood of nervousness that must have characterized the Hamdanids' response to the military threats of Nicephorus and his "raging army." This can be easily discerned from the absurd invective and abusive ad hominem argument in the following lines, which have certainly compromised the otherwise highly poetic *Al-Rumiyyat*:

> How dare you threaten us with wars?
> As though our hearts and yours,
> Have never been tied at their cores!
> Indeed, both of us in wars did meet,
> Every time, we were lions,
> Whereas you proved a dog! (34)

Abu Firas unprincely and unpoetically resorts to *fuhsh* (impropriety) and *batha'a* (vulgar language), especially through his shocking *tashbih* (comparison) of Nicephorus to a dog, an animal that denotes *najasa* (uncleanness) and *haqara* (baseness) in Arabic-Islamic culture. In this, the dog is second only to the pig. In calling Nicephorus "a dog," the prince Abu Firas had a predecessor who is none other than Harun al-Rashid.[22] Abu Firas's lack of decorum is perhaps understandable if one remembers his almost xenophobic Arabism and extreme self-pride evocative of the pre-Islamic *jahili* culture. His assault seems to be a direct reaction to Nicephorus's provocative denigration of the Arabs in his presence. As many medieval Arabic sources mention, Abu Firas wrote his *hija'* of Nicephorus most probably as a later response to the latter's derisive remark while visiting Abu Firas in his captivity, during which he said to the captive that contrary to the Byzantines, "the Arabs are born for pens and not for swords." This is reflected in the closing lines of the poem:

> Was it then our pens,
> Or perhaps our swords!
> That made you shiver in your holes!
> In the midst of the desert,

You hid your face
Like a jerboa burrowing in the earth. (34)

Paradoxically, if seen from a modern perspective, it seems that Nicephorus was indirectly praising the Arabs. But in the medieval age of the sword and in the context of Muslim/Byzantine enmity, Nicephorus's remark, if as reported, was certainly an invective, which proved enormously successful.

Without the powerful figures of speech dominant in the previous poems, Abu Firas's focus in this lampoon of Nicephorus falls directly on a number of *mathalib* (demerits) and *'uyub* (shortcomings) of the Byzantines, such as *qubh* (ugliness), *kibr* (pride), *ta'ali* (arrogance), *kadhib* (lies), and *jubn* (cowardice). These negative characteristics conjure up the figure of the *shaytan* (the devil). Abu Firas through his vicious *hija'* of Nicephorus sums it all up as he denigrates the *mahju* (object of invective) and strips him of any "Arab" quality. The antithetical symmetry between Arab/Muslim on the one hand and Byzantine/Christian on the other is the ethos and telos of the poem, if not the entire *Rumiyyat*. In other words, Abu Firas wants to convey the message that the Byzantines stand for everything that Muslims do not stand for. In this, the poet has implemented literally what medieval Arabic critics theorized when it comes to the power of *hija'* in not only degrading the Other but utterly negating him/her.

Abu Firas's *hija'* of Nicephorus will serve as an introduction to the more compact polemical invectives directed against Nicephorus and the Byzantines that dominate the poetic responses of al-Qaffal (d. 946) and Ibn Hazm to a poetic diatribe against Islam and its prophet attributed to Nicephorus. Because of the length and complexity of the texts in question, a full exploration of the poems' rhetoric of Otherness is beyond the scope of this discussion. Accordingly, the focus will be on the poets' use of the Islamic division of *tahara* (purity) of the Self versus the *najasa* (impurity/pollution/contamination) of the Other, their anti-Christian polemics, their assertion of the political and military domination of Muslims over Byzantines, and their foregrounding of the religious motif of the Other as the scourge of God.

The Impure Scourge of God: The Byzantines in the Poetic Responses of al-Qaffal and Ibn Hazm to Nicephorus's **Al-Qasida al-Mal'una**

In addition to the obsessive interest in *al-naqfur* (Arabic for Nicephorus) that dominates a number of medieval Muslim texts on Byzantine/Muslim relations, it is the bizarre name of *Al-Qasida al-Mal'una* that haunts several others. This is true, for instance, of Ibn Kathir's entry on Nicephorus. Ibn

Kathir devotes many pages to the poem, which he calls *mal'una* (cursed), a word that not only captures vividly the rage felt by Muslims in knowing about this poem but also shows perfectly the efficacy of Nicephorus's propaganda in his psychological war against his enemies. "This cursed *naqfur*," Ibn Kathir angrily informs his readers, "sent a poem to the caliph al-Muti' in which he defames Islam, derides the Prophet, and vows to conquer all the lands of Islam and turn them into Christian dominions" (*Al-Bidaya wa-l-Nihaya*, 260).[23] Unfamiliar with the response of al-Qaffal, Ibn Kathir proceeds to comment that no Muslim had ever before written a response to the poem until the Andalusian Ibn Hazm penned a poem he described as *al-farida al-islamiyya al-mansura al-maymuna*, that is, the unmatched and triumphant Islamic masterpiece.[24]

As demonstrated by al-Munajjid, *Al-Qasida al-Arminiyya* is well structured since it can easily be divided into five sections. In the first section, the poet-proxy catalogs the deeds and victories of Nicephorus and his ancestors in Muslim lands. Of particular significance is the focus on the humiliation of Muslims especially through dramatizing the capture of Muslim women, a claim that is insulting and dishonoring for Muslims. In the second section, the poet strongly vows that Christian knights will continue their assaults on Muslim lands until they have subdued Egypt, Arabia, Iraq, Persia, and Yemen. No doubt, however, the most serious threat is the conquest of Mecca and the extermination of Muslims from the face of the earth. In the third section, the poet is surprising since he attributes the defeat of Muslims to their imperfect practice of Islam's tenets.

Although the reader was expecting that the poet would link the Christian victories to the truth of their faith and their courage, he relates it intrinsically to the moral depravity of Muslims. It is as if God chastised them after their ruler and judges had transgressed the Islamic laws of governorship and justice. Section four is another pledge to propagate Christianity with the power of the sword. Finally, the last section is in praise of Christianity and Jesus and a diatribe against Islam and its prophet. The opening and closing lines of this long poem summarize it well:

> From Nicephorus, the pure Christian king to
>   the remnant of the Hashimites.
> His Excellency al Mutee, who is doomed to endless plights.
> Haven't your ears heard what I've been doing in recent fights!
> Or too feeble you are to act the unyielding knight!
> If, however, you know, yet deliberately uncaring,
> I'm sleepless planning what I'm planning. (Al-Munajjid,
>   *Qasidat 'Imbratur al-Rum Naqfur Fuqas fi-Hija'*
>   *al-Islam wa-l-Rad 'Alaih*, 11)

And:

> East and west of God's earth shall be mine.
> Christianity will triumph with my sword.
> Jesus is exulted and his crown sits high in the heavens.
> Victorious is the one who sides with the Lord.
> While your prophet is dead in the earth.
> And his disciples' reputations are torn and soiled. (22)

The anti-Islamic rhetoric and the crusading spirit of this poem made it notorious in Baghdad. It is said that the first response to the poem in the Mashriq came from the *faqih* Abu Bakr al-Qaffal, who must have been taken by religious zeal upon hearing the anti-Islamic propaganda and the assault on his prophet. The opening lines of al-Qaffal's *qasida* are powerful, especially when it comes to capturing the highly "othering" religious rhetoric *of al-ana al-tahira* (the pure Self) versus *al-akhar al-najis* (the impure Other):[25]

> News came to me of a man who, in times of quarrels,
> Is ill-bred in the arts of the word.
> Pompously claiming titles he has not.
> And great deeds he has never done.
> Calling himself pure when, in truth,
> He is an infidel, most impure.
> His garments are polluted with impurity.
> Pretending to be a good Christian. In fact, he is not! (28)

As a non-Muslim Other, Nicephorus, who in turn attributes to himself his own religious purity (from the pure Christian), is depicted by al-Qaffal as grouping three types of *najasa* (impurity/pollution/uncleanness).

The first one is Islamically speaking the most revolting, for it is synonymous with *kufr* (infidelity/unbelief) and *shirk* (associationism/polytheism). It is perceived as *najasa ma'nawiyya* (abstract impurity), and it denotes the uncompromisingly Other of the pure monotheistic and submissive Self. Second, *al-najasa al-hissiyya* (physical/tangible), which is perfectly alluded to in al-Qaffal's reference to Nicephorus's unclean/polluted garments, is one of the most recurring topoi of differences in medieval Muslim writing about the Other. Most often it deals with the issues of *al-tahara al-kubra* (major purity) after sexual intercourse and menstruation for women.[26] The third one, it seems, is the invention of al-Qaffal, and it refers to *al-najasa al-akhlaqiyya* (moral/ethical uncleanness), through which al-Qaffal alludes to the cruelty of the Byzantines during their wars. This was to become very much the central theme in Muslims' perception of *al-ifranj* during the Crusades, as we shall see in the coming section.

The distinction of the pure Self versus the impure Other is not unique to the religious-cultural consciousness of Islam.[27] Indeed, it is universal. However, this polarity has maintained a dominant place in the religious discourses of Judaism, Christianity, and Islam. In *Jewish Identity in Early Rabbinic Writings* (1994), for instance, Sacha Stern has demonstrated the paramount importance of the polarity of the pure Jew versus the impure non-Jew in the construction of Jewishness and concomitant dialectics of Self and Other.

In Western literature in general and English literature in particular, the polarity of purity and impurity is strongly echoed in numerous medieval and early modern works. In Elizabeth Carey's *The Tragedy of Mariam, the Fair Queen of Jewry* (originally published in 1613) for example, this polarity is central in the religious and racial discourse of the first English play ever to be published by an English woman. In order to delineate the doomed marriage of a pure Christian woman represented by the protagonist of the play to an impure non-Christian, the antagonist Herod, the playwright designs a tragic encounter of the Arab Silleus and the half-Jewish Salome. After he discovers the love affair of his wife Salome and her intention to leave him for Silleus, the Jewish Constabarus's words illustrate this opposition explicitly:

> Oh Salome, how much you wrong your name,
> Your race, your country, and your husband most!
> A stranger's private conference is shame,
> I blush for you, that have your blushing lost.
> Oft have I found, and found you to my grief
> Consulted with this base Arabian here
> Heavens knows that you have been my grief
> Then do not now my greater plague appear. (I.6.1–6)

In short, as a Jewish husband, Constabarus is concerned with his name and honor. Nonetheless, as he reveals it, his "greater plague" lies in the fact that his wife has given him up, he who is a pure Jew, for the sake of an impure gentile, a stranger, a "base Arabian," as he bluntly puts it.

Like Constabarus, al-Qaffal in his poetic process of self-assertion and self-identification highlights the impurity/pollution of the Other, an impurity that does not only denote the religious-cultural inferiority of the Byzantine but also invokes their baseness and lack of human compassion. In this, they are the same both in times of war and peace. The primary contrast that the poet creates is between the insatiable cruelty of the Byzantines and the humane heroism of Muslims, as in the following lines:

> Our power and pride lie in our faith.
> By God, soon our birds will fly over in your lands.
> The number of our captured women you did overplay.
> Forgetting that thousands of yours are in our hands.
> We are the most merciful when we triumph in the fray.
> But you are the cruelest when you win the day. (Al-Munajjid,
>   *Qasidat 'Imbratur al-Rum Naqfur Fuqas fi-Hija' al-Islam*
>   *wa-l-Rad 'Alaih*, 30)

Ibn Hazm's polemical invective is strikingly similar to that of al-Qaffal.[28] Although there is nothing to indicate that Ibn Hazm might have been familiar with al Qaffal's response, it is clear that the religious background and fervor of both poets were the foremost motivation behind their poems. This is illustrated largely by their assault on the theological foundations of Christianity. Ibn Hazm writes,

> How dare you brag of a Trinitarian faith?
> So removed from reason, so out of place.
> Worshipping a being who has a worshipping face!
> Woe to you! Where is your sanity and brain?
> Your gospels are tampered with in every place.
> And in them, words of truth are often slain.
> You bow still to a wooden cross.
> Woe to you! Where is your sanity and brain? (53)

In Ibn Hazm's view, because of their adherence to Christianity, the Byzantines are irrational and intellectually feeble. Reason, he argues, does not seem to have any place for the Byzantines when, as he maintains, the basic tenet of their "faulty" religion (i.e., the Trinity) is essentially removed from reason. This message is consolidated by questioning rhetorically their worship of Jesus, who (in Muslim understanding), although a venerated prophet and source of many miracles, worships in turn his Creator.

The *hija'* of the Christian Byzantines and their faith shifts to *madih* whenever Ibn Hazm—and by the same token al-Qaffal—refers to the Muslim faith or the Prophet of Islam. Evidently, ridicule of Christianity and the ensuing denial of the Other are ultimately an indirect celebration of Islam and a final affirmation of the Self. "Thus while the surface elements of the *hija'* are the opposite of those in *iftikhar* [praise]," S. P. Stetkevych asserts, "the ultimate purpose is the reaffirmation of those same values" (*Abū Tammām and the Poetics of the 'Abbāsid Age*, 335).

With Ibn Hazm and al-Qaffal, when it comes to the *mahju* (object of invective), the main rhetorical and ideological focus of *hija'* lies in the description of their Otherness with a special insistence on their religious *dhalal* (misguidance), moral inferiority, and the ensuing military and cultural weaknesses. In contrast, the Muslim *mamduh* (the praised one) is cherished for his/her religious truthfulness and moral superiority and the resulting military and cultural achievement, which should be thought of as divine proof of these qualities. Certainly when the reality of the battlefield indicates otherwise, as we will see later, there is always the universal idea of God's affliction and disapproval.

As demonstrated by a number of scholars, in the Arabic literary tradition, especially in times of wars and enmities, *hija'* has been part and parcel of conflicts. It was, for example, the most effective weapon in the tribal wars and rivalries of the Arabs before Islam. Similarly, since the time Prophet Muhammad called his poets to attack their enemies with their words, it has become central in the propaganda of jihad. Given that, it seems clear why Ibn Hazm and al-Qaffal have foregrounded the links between the explicit *hija'* concerning the Byzantines and their religion and the implicit *madih* of the Arabs and their religion. S. P. Stetkevych's reference to Ibn-Rashiq's explanation of the underlying function of *hija'* is worth considering:

> According to medieval critic ibn Rashiq, *hija'* (invective) can be termed the censure, blame, or ridicule for the absence of those virtues. The dictum "all poetry can be summed up in three phrases:...When you praise, you say 'you are'; when you lampoon, you say 'you are not,' and when you elegize you say 'you were'" is worth repeating here. (335)

Furthermore, it should be remembered here that within the thematic and rhetorical battle of the Self and the Other, the obsessive reference to the other *tahrim* (womenfolk) is crucial in understanding the nature of Muslim/Byzantine rivalry and the underlying topoi of the medieval Arabic-Islamic rhetoric of alterity.

The emphasis on capturing, enslaving, and—implicitly—sexually enjoying the Other's women is central to this alterity. It all starts with Nicephorus's, Islamically speaking, insulting reference to "the noble and sumptuous ladies descendents of your Prophet" who according to the poem attributed to Nicephorus "were captured and gave themselves without contracts and dowries." Unsurprisingly, al-Qaffal and

Ibn Hazm responded with a defensive rhetoric of apology that reveals the success of Nicephorus's psychological war and his deep knowledge of the Muslim psyche. Echoing al-Qaffal, Ibn Hazm writes,

> Of our women, you did not capture many.
> Whereas of yours, we have as many as the drops of rain.
> Indeed, counting them is an endless task.
> Like a man counting the pigeons' feathers.

And:

> Your emperors' daughters, we herded with our hands,
> As a hunter herds a desert's deer to his own field.
> Ask Heraclius about our deeds in your Lands.
> And other kings of yours who were made to yield.
> For they can tell you about our troops deployed
> And the countless Byzantine women we have enjoyed. (Al-Munajjid,
>   *Qasidat 'Imbratur al-Rum Naqfur Fuqas fi-Hija'*
>   *al-Islam wa-l-Rad 'Alaih*, 46)

Echoing several other *Rumiyyat*, especially those texts of Abu Tammam's *madih* of al-Mu'tasim's *fath* (opening, conquest) of Amuriyya (Amorium) and al-Mutanabbi's *madih* of Sayf al-Dawla, the previous lines of al-Qaffal and of Ibn Hazm illustrate the central role played by "the sexual gender-based imagery," to borrow S. P. Stetkevych's phrase in the description of Muslim military and political domination of the Byzantine Other (*The Poetics of Islamic Legitimacy*, 176). Although there is no explicit reference to rape, as is the case with Abu Tammam and others, the references to the sexual enjoyment of female Byzantine captives can be seen as metaphors for the poets' final declaration and ultimate celebration of Muslim superiority over the Byzantine Other. As S. P. Stetkevych puts it, "The image of sexually defiled womanhood, however, varied in detail and powerfully achieved is the conventional means for expressing the ultimate (male) dishonor and degradation" (176).

Last but not least is the poets' use of the trope of the infidel Other as the "scourge of God" in their efforts to justify the Byzantine threat and to downplay the military, even temporary, superiority of the Other. If the Byzantines defeated the Muslims, it is neither because they are believers in the true faith nor because they are militarily superior, let alone invincible. Rather, they are used by God to alert Muslims to their neglect and transgression of Muslim values. Confirming Nicephorus's criticism of

Muslim corruption, al-Qaffal replies,

> You triumphed thanks to our leaders' misconduct.
> Indeed, that is exactly what you said,
> If so! That is a proof of the accuracy of our faith;
> For it is a law when we transgress,
> We are transgressed upon. (Al-Munajjid, *Qasidat 'Imbratur al-Rum*
>   *Naqfur Fuqas fi-Hija' al-Islam wa-l-Rad 'Alaih*, 30)

The recurrence of this theme made Ibn Hazm transfer his lampoon of the Byzantines not only to Kafur but also and unexpectedly to the Hamdanids in spite of all their efforts in fighting the Byzantines: "With the Hamdanids and Kafur you triumphed / Who were but ill-bred, impure and weak" (Ibid, 47). The Umayyad Ibn Hazm does not let the chance go by to attack his political opponents. It is clear that in his view, the Byzantine resurgence is a direct and severe punishment from God precisely because those who fight in his name are in essence usurpers, if not heretics.

From another perspective, al-Qaffal's and Ibn Hazm's perception of the "Byzantine Peril" as a scourge inflicted by Allah on disobedient Muslims recalls the Western medieval and early modern tradition of the "Infidel Saracen/Turk" as a scourge of God and that of the sixteenth- and seventeenth-century German anti-Turkish pamphlets known as the *Türkenbüchlein*. In short, as shown by John W. Bohnstedt, these German Lutheran and Catholic pamphleteers interpreted "the Turkish peril as a scourge inflicted by God upon a sinful Christendom and many of them seem to have been more concerned with the sins of the Christians than with the Turkish danger *per se*" (*The Infidel Scourge of God*, 3).[29]

The three aforementioned forgotten poems, and to a lesser degree Abu Firas's texts, are characteristically violent in tone, if not indeed sadistic. This very violence, however, does capture well the nature of the historical and religious enmity between Islam and Byzantium during the Middle Ages. Undoubtedly a modern reader, in spite of the ongoing wars of the moment, will be perplexed by the apparent enjoyment of violence in these works. Nevertheless, if one approaches the "Cursed Poem" in relation to al-Qaffal's and Ibn Hazm's responses within their historical context and literary form, one can better appreciate their content. It must be remembered also that what we consider nowadays useless violence was, as the poems suggest, based in examples of courage and heroism.

The texts studied here are reminiscent of classical epics east and west such as *Gilgamesh*, *The Iliad*, *The Odyssey*, *Beowulf*, the *Chansons de Geste*, the Arthurian romances, and the popular *hamasa* genre in the Arabic tradition

such as *Sirat 'Antar*, as well as the poetry of Abu Tammam and al-Buhturi.[30]
The Western epic and Arabic-Islamic *hamasa* poems are founded upon
the veneration of heroism, chivalry, courage, and sacrifice for one's faith,
country, friends, and lovers. Many of these qualities cannot be realized
without invoking violence in some form. Certainly, the Western epic and
to a lesser degree the Arabic-Islamic tradition of *hamasa* have also been
often related to legendary battles and combats where the hero has had to
fight gods, monsters, dragons, and the like. This is not the case with the
poem attributed to Nicephorus and the responses of al-Qaffal and Ibn
Hazm for the very reason that they were most often describing violence
that was historical and real. The players in this violence and the recipro-
cal demonization of the Other, in spite of some instances of ruptures and
negotiations, intensified with the coming of the Crusades and changed
with time. Indeed, as we shall see in the following section, *al-ifranja* would
take the place of *al-rum* as the Other, interestingly, in the same manner
that Turks had taken the place of Saracens in European literature with the
rise of the Ottomans and the ensuing danger they represented for early
modern Europe.

Ifranjalism: Crusades and Crusaders in Arabic Medieval Poetry, Stereotypes and Ruptures: Ibn al-Qaysarani as a Case Study

> I fell enamored to a Frankish woman.
> Who sweetens the fragrance's breeze.
> In her robe, there is a tender branch,
> And her crown glimmers like a shining moon.
> And if her eyes are, indeed, azure,
> So are the heads of the spears! Ibn al-Qaysarani (Kilani, *Al-Hurub
>   al-Salibiyya wa Atharuha fi-l-Adab al-'Arabi fi-Misr wa-l-Sham*,
>   57; translation mine)

The Crusades did not only usher in what Sari J. Nasir once described as the
"beginning of a period of direct contact between Arabs and Europeans"
(*The English and the Arabs*, 7), but they also provided both sides of the
conflict with an unprecedented opportunity to experiment culturally and
literarily with "the always and already" issues of the Self and the Other.[31]
Indeed, as Hillenbrand explains it aptly, the Crusades "shaped western
European perceptions of the Muslim world just as decisively as they
formed Muslim views of the West" (*The Crusades*, 3). Needless to say, in
the Western world, the Crusades were well recorded in a number of Euro-
Christian chronicles, such as Fulcher of Chartres's *History of the Expedition
to Jerusalem*, Raymond d'Aguilers's *The Deeds of the Franks*, William of

Tyre's *History of Deeds Done beyond the Sea*, and Guibert de Nogent's *The Deeds of God through the Franks*.

Even more remarkable, however, was the literary manifestation and, in many ways, the historical transfiguration of the Crusades in medieval Western literature and in French and English epics/romances in particular. Contrary to the dominant view held by a number of Western scholars, in the "Saracen" world the picture was not that different. Unfortunately, some of these scholars, as much as they have incessantly deplored the lack of medieval Arabic historical and literary sources on the Crusades, have even more emphatically claimed that, in contrast to Europeans, Muslims were characteristically uninterested in this major historical phenomenon. Nowhere is this clearer than in Thomas F. Madden's book *The New Concise History of the Crusades* (2005). Among several other surprising statements, Madden has claimed: "The first Arabic history of the [C]rusades was not written until 1899"; "In the Islamic grand sweeps of Islamic history the [C]rusades simply did not matter"; and "The [C]rusades were virtually unknown in the Muslim world even a century ago" (218). These claims made him perfunctorily conclude that "although the [C]rusades were of monumental importance to Europeans, they were a minor, largely insignificant thing to the Muslim world" (218).[32]

There can be no doubt that Arabic historical and literary sources dealing with the Crusades were never as sparse as these scholars have claimed. The existence of a series of personal memoirs, travel accounts, diplomatic reports, religious (polemical) epistles, official letters, and, most important for this thesis, poetry clearly proves that this claim is untrue. As we shall see through argument and example, Arabic poetry of the Crusades, very similar to its medieval Western (epic) counterpart, was animated by the spirit of jihad and driven by strong anti-Christian propaganda (Khattab, *Das Bild der Franken in der arabischen Literatur des Mittelalters*, 23). The result was not only a demonic depiction à la Saracen of the European Crusaders but also a zealous call to annihilate them à la Kurtz, thus echoing one of the Crusaders' most cherished slogans: "To kill the Muslim Arab was to slay for God's love" (Nasir, *The English and the Arabs*, 7).

The Crusades resulted not only in the occupation of Jerusalem and the humiliating defilement of al-Aqsa mosque but also in the massacre of thousands of Muslims (Hillenbrand, *The Crusades*, 75). Those who survived had no other choice but to flee to cities that had not been attacked by the Crusaders, such as Aleppo and Damascus in Syria, Mosul and Baghdad in Iraq, and Cairo in Egypt (75). Indeed, chroniclers—both

Muslim and paradoxically Euro-Christian—have movingly transmitted to us, albeit sometimes with exaggeration, the plight of Muslims
in the wake of the Crusaders' sacking of Jerusalem in 1099. Raymond
d'Aguilers, an eyewitness chronicler of the First Crusade, wrote the
following:

> When our men took the main defences, we saw then some astonishing
> things amongst Saracens. Some were beheaded, and that's the least that
> could happen to them…We could see in the roads and in the places of
> Jerusalem bits and pieces of heads, hands and feet…But all that was only
> little…There was so much blood in the old temple of Solomon that dead
> corpses swam in it. We could see hands floating and arms that went to glue
> themselves to bodies that were not theirs; we could not distinguish which
> arm belonged to which body. (G. Le Bon, *La Civilisation des Arabs*, 249)

His contemporary Radulph of Caen does not only admit this genocide
but also adds with pride the following horrifying words: "In Ma'arra our
troops boiled pagan adults in cooking pots; they impaled children on
spits and devoured them grilled" (Maalouf, *The Crusades through Arab
Eyes*, 26). The chronicler Albert of Aix, who took part in the carnage of
Maarra, in turn acknowledges that "[not] only did our troops not shrink
from eating dead Turks and Saracens [Arabs]; they also ate dogs!" (26).[33]
No wonder then that the Muslim chronicler Ibn al-Athir's record of
the onslaught on Jerusalem would be by no means the invention of his
fertile mind:

> The population of the holy city was put to the sword, and the Firanj spent
> a week massacring Muslims. They killed more than seventy thousand
> people in Al-Aqsa Mosque. The Jews had gathered in their synagogue
> and the crusaders burned them alive. They also destroyed the monuments
> of saints, the mosque of Umar and the tomb of Abraham, may peace be
> upon him. (34)

Quite conventionally, in their attempts to capture the first Muslim responses
to the Crusades and the ensuing shock that engulfed *dar al-islam*, medieval
Muslim chroniclers could not find a more moving entry than the speech
uttered by the Damascene *qadhi al-qudhat* (supreme judge) al-Harawi
(d. 1124) in the caliphate court of Baghdad. As several sources mention,
after the stunning subjugation of several Levantine towns, a delegation of
Sunni luminaries led by al-Harawi left Damascus for Baghdad to "prick the
conscience" of the then weak caliph al-Mustadhir (1078–1118) and his military chiefs (Kilani, *Al-Hurub al-Salibiyya*, 123). It is said that the delegation
members were so touched by what had befallen their religious fellows that as

soon as they were led into the caliphal court they wept bitterly and made the listeners weep (al-Sarisi, *Nusus min-Adab 'Asr al-Hurub al-Salibiyya*, 24).

The climax of the meeting, however, was al-Harawi's stirring sermon in which he reminded the Abbasid dignitaries and officers of their religious duty toward their Levantine brethren. He also warned them of the imminent disaster that would befall Islam and Muslims if they did not act firmly and swiftly. In addition to the quotations from the Quran and the Sunna, al-Harawi peppered his speech with lines from a heartbreaking poem that most scholars attribute to the contemporary Iraqi poet al-Abiwardi (d. 1113). It is this particular poem that is of interest to us since it movingly captures early Muslim responses to the Crusades.

The opening stanza of the poem depicts the state of shock and disbelief that struck contemporary Muslims, who, as the poet implies, instead of fighting back responded with pity and tears in a time of swords and deeds:

We mixed blood with flooding tears,
Until we were bereft of mourning words!
Tears are a man's weakest arms,
When flames of war are kindled,
With the thrusts of mighty swords! (ibid., 24; translation mine)

Alerting the dignitaries to their religious duty of defending the faith and honor of their Levantine brethren who had been witness to all types of humiliation at the hands of the Crusaders, the poet skillfully utilizes the trope of *tibaq* (antithesis) to prick the conscience of Muslims and to juxtapose the frivolous life they were leading so joyously with the fate of their Muslim brothers:

Woe to you Muslims! For ahead of you,
Are unruly challenges and intractable deals!
Have you opted for slumber in coziness and peace?
Like garden flowers in the shade of the trees!
While in the Levant, your brethren are lying,
On the backs of slaughter boards and in the bellies of beasts!
The base Franks tyrannize them and tease!
While you enjoy a life of comfort and ease! (24; translation mine)

What is needed, therefore, is a concrete response, a jihad to stop the misery of their brethren and to expel the invaders. If Iraqi Muslims, whether Arabs or Persians, are not agitated enough to rise up out of religious obligation, he reminds them, their culture ought to stir them to action. Indeed, it is the ultimate shame for an Arab not to fight for family honor since this is an absolute duty. So it should and must be the task of the chivalrous Arab to do the deed:

> Our arrows fly past the forms of the foe.
> And our faith is so weak in this moment of woe.
> Avoiding fire and fearing death are now the law!
> And in our thoughts, honor has fallen so low.
> Have the great Arabs yielded to humiliation and shame!
> Have the great Persians accepted dishonor and stain!
> If we've lost the fervor to fight for our faith,
> Let us unleash our swords for our family name! (26; translation mine)

Here the poet cleverly invokes the classical codes of *al-furussiya*, in which fighting for one's tribe and family honor is highly praised. Sacrificing one's life in order to save the reputation and honor of *al-harim* (women) is especially heroic.

Not only did Arabic poetry, this true record of the Arabs in the example of the previous poem and the following ones, capture with power the general shock felt by Muslims; it also recorded the plight of the Muslims of the Levant. Other poets, some of whom preferred to write anonymously, flavored their poetry with the emotional and melancholic tradition of *al-buka' 'ala al-atlal* (weeping over the ruins/standing over the ruins). The following poem attributed to Ibn al-Mujawir (d. 1204) is an example:

> Oh my eyes do not stop your tears!
> With weeping and cries,
> Weave your mornings into your nights!
> Let the flowing tears soothe the sigh,
> And rekindle the embers of the heart.
> For the lost al-Aqsa mosque.
> Place of prayers, most venerable site.
> Let all the Muslim lands mourn Jerusalem,
> And declare their grief over its plight. (Kilani,
>   *Al-Hurub al-Salibiyya*, 290; translation mine)

Intensely morose and meticulous in depicting the defilement of Muslim (holy) places, massacring of men, and dishonoring of Muslim women, Arabic poetry of the Crusades employs the convention of *al-buka' 'ala al-atlal*, the equivalent of the Latin *ubi sunt* tradition. Here the leitmotifs of *buka'* (wailing), *huzn* (sorrow), and *khawf* (fear) from the present condense a wide array of religious and sociocultural alienations, longings, and nostalgias and alert the reader to the threat of a totally catastrophic future if Muslims do not accept the challenge seriously and rise up for jihad.

This is the case with the following anonymous poem as well, once described in passing by Emmanuel Sivan in his classic *L'islam et la croisade: Idéologie et propagande dans les réactions musulmanes aux croisades* (1968) as extremely moving and powerful (53). Thanks to Ibn Taghrbardi (d. 1470) and other late chroniclers, however, it is still available to us:

> The infidels have inflicted an unprecedented injustice upon Islam!
> That for long we shall wail in excruciating pain.
> A lost right, a defiled land.
> A scourging sword, and running blood.
> Many a Muslim man they wronged,
> Many a Muslim woman they dishonored.
> Many a mosque they converted into churches,
> In prayer niches, they erected their crosses[34]
> With the blood of pigs they filled them!
> With burning Qurans, they perfumed the air!
> If a pondering child some reason seeks,
> White hairs will soon hide his youthful cheeks! (al-Sarisi, *Nusus min-Adab 'Asr al-Hurub al-Salibiyya*, 27–28; translation mine)

Of paramount rhetorical importance in the text is the poet's subtle and frequent use of hyperbole, paronomasia, and antithesis. Indeed, through these rhetorical devices, he has not only succeeded in drawing the attention of his audience to the horrifying state of their Levantine co-religionists but also, and indeed more emphatically, in highlighting the "barbarity" of their assaulters and their indescribable enmity to Islam.

Closely associated with the previous poem is the following poem by Ibn al-Khayyat (d. 1120), who asserts truculently,

> For how long will you stay unmoved!
> While the infidels are streaming as a tide.
> As massive as an ocean wide!
> Huge armies, like collapsing mountains
> Are moving from the Frankish side.
> For how long will you accept oppression?
> Overlooking those whose currency is war!
> You sleep in comfort, ignore the foe,
> In times of sorrow and tinged with woe! (Kilani, *Al-Hurub al-Salibiyya*, 301; translation mine)

The Crusaders, he reminds his audience, have flocked from *ardh al-ifranja*, that is, the lands of the Franks, with a definite aim, which is the humiliation of Islam and the extermination of Muslims. The

Franks, he wants them to believe, speak only the language of war. Driven by a natural propensity to evil, they are determined not only to spread their *shirk* in the monotheistic lands of Islam but also to spread all types of *fasad* (vice/evil):

> The infidels do not forbid vice,
> Nor do they set a limit to what is wrong.
> When killing, they do not spare a soul.
> Nor do they show mercy at all. (301; translation mine)

The overriding images and metaphors of war and destruction effectively project doom for Muslims if they do not assume their religious obligation to defend their faith and honor in the face of an enemy who is inherently evil. By continuously highlighting their religious identity and constantly invoking their *shirk*, Ibn al-Khayyat alerts Muslims to the real nature of the enemy. The Crusaders not only came en masse to pillage and plunder Muslim and Jewish sites they meet on their way; they flocked to *dar al-islam* "to exterminate all the Brutes," to use Joseph Conrad's revelatory phrase. Indeed he utilizes brilliantly *al-tibaq* (antithesis/paradox), a highly regarded figure of speech in Arabic poetry, to place the Frankish *fasad* in the binary context of us versus them and posits the Otherness of the Franks within the framework of the clash between truth and falsehood. Obviously the stock image used by these poets when speaking of *al-ifranja* was negative and related to a Manichaean-like understanding of the (Muslim) Self and the non-Muslim Other.

Muslims, however, had gradually begun to forget about the shock of the fall of Jerusalem, for they had come to the conclusion that what they needed was a rekindling of the flame of the religious fervor of Muslim rulers by reminding them of the value of jihad. Most likely, it was the historian/poet Ibn al-Adhimi who inaugurated this poetic tradition, which dominated much of the literary expression of Arab Muslims throughout the Crusades. Disappointed with the defeatism and fatalism of many Muslims, al-Adhimi (d. 1160) addressed the once "libertine" governor of Mardin, Najm al-Din ibn Artuq (1107–1122), urged him to raise the banner of jihad, and called upon him to take revenge on the polytheistic tyrants. He says, "The polytheistic tyrants must soon know / that you will seek revenge and more" (Kilani, *Al-Hurub al-Salibiyya*, 312). These lines of poetry, we are told by a number of chroniclers, had deeply touched the once indifferent ruler of Aleppo before engaging the Crusaders in a major battle between the Crusader principality of Antioch and Aleppo in 1119. The result was the first major victory for Muslims at the battle known in

Arabic sources as *sahat al-dam* (field of blood) and in Western sources as the Battle of Ager Sanguinis.

With this battle, hope was restored and the future loomed much brighter for Muslims. It is not surprising, therefore, that the most optimistic poem of Arabic medieval poetry came to the surface. It is the poem known as *Al-Qasida al-Munfarija* (An Ode of Hope) and attributed to Ibn al-Nahawi (d. 1119). The popular first lines begin,

> The starker a crisis gets,
> The closer it is to the end!
> When the night gets most dark,
> The day looms most bright.
> And the black clouds breed pure rain,
> When the storm comes in sight.
> God's decrees are but lessons,
> That soothe our hearts and brains. (Kilani,
>   *Al-Hurub al-Salibiyya*, 312; translation mine)

Such a hope was rekindled by a call to jihad. Contemporary poets played a leading role in this call by enticing Levantine emirs to embrace the cause of jihad and fulfill their religious and moral obligation to help their brethren in need. Through their eloquent words, contemporary poets helped foster the jihadist spirit and furnished the ideal setting for it by extolling and idealizing the jihadist rulers.

Addressing 'Imad al-Din Zangi (1127–1146) after his liberation of Edessa, the poet Ibn al-Qaysarani (d. 1154), whom we will return to later, extolled him for using force against a bloodthirsty enemy that in his view understood nothing but the language of the sword:

> Nothing empowers a man,
> Like the thrusts of the sword!
> Nothing protects one's land!
> If the sword isn't in one's hand. (275; translation mine)

In a style and diction that are reminiscent of Abu Tammam's earlier mentioned line of *hamasa* poetry—*al-sayfu asdaqu anba'an min al-kutubi* (the sword is truer in telling than the books)—the verses of Ibn al-Qaysarani have now become among the most quoted lines of medieval Arabic-Islamic poetry of the Crusades.

Perplexed by what he sees as an inherent religious gullibility, Ibn al-Qaysarani, at least in this poem, depicts the Franks as *asra al-dhalala* (prisoners of misguidance). According to him, they (the Franks) are not able to draw lessons from previous Muslim-Christian conflicts. This is in addition to the actual signs that, he believes, predict the failure of the Crusades and the imminent humiliation of the Cross. God has already chosen the side that professes the true faith. The liberation of *al-Raha* (Edessa) is the turning point:

> Verily in the liberation of Edessa
> There are miraculous signs that belie,
> All that the *'uluj* have believed.
> In the birth(day) of the son of Mary,
> They have expected victories and glories.
> When nothing has miraculously changed! (275; translation mine)

For our study, however, the most important word in these lines is the insulting *al-'uluj* (barbarians/uncivilized), for it tells us much when it comes to Ibn al-Qaysarani's early stereotyping of the Franks and the ensuing perception of their *mathalib* (demerits). Unexpectedly, however, Ibn al-Qaysarani would refute many of these stereotypes when he came into direct contact with the Franks during his real encounter with them in the town of Antioch.

Glorification of jihad and the idealization of *al-mujahid* (holy warrior) became the dominant themes of jihadist poets as a consequence of these events. Only godly emirs were capable of engaging in God's mission.[35] No wonder then that poets of the period filled their lines with images of major battles and heroes of early Islam wherein the *mujahidin* are depicted as envoys of God come to defend *al-bilad al-tahira* (the pure land) from the *shirk* (polytheism) and *najasa* (impurity) of the *kuffar* (unbelievers). A poet named Shihab al-Halabi addressed Salah al-Din Yusuf ibn Ayyub (1174–1193), widely known in the west as Saladin, after the liberation of Akka (Acre) and said,

> All praises are due to the only God!
> By whose grace, the state of the Cross is lost.
> And at the hands of the brave Turks,
> The religion of the Arab Prophet has carried the fray.
> A thing that was so beyond our scope.
> That even as a dream in the night,
> One would not dare to hope! (Abdulmahdi, *Bayt al-Maqdis fi Adab al-Hurub al-Salibiyya*, 104; translation mine)

The emphasis on the *na'im* (delights) that await the *shahid* in the hereafter is also of paramount importance.[36] As D. Ephrat and M. D. Kabha put it, "Long passages, composed during the sixth/twelfth and seventh/twelfth centuries, are devoted to depicting paradise: its castles, gates, buildings, tents, gardens and inhabitants, especially the women awaiting Muslim martyrs" ("Muslim Reactions to the Frankish Presence in *Bilād al-Shām*," 31).

Medieval Western literature, in turn, had played a no less significant propagandist role during the centuries of the Crusades. According to Ziaddin Sardar, medieval Western writers "gave the contemporary Crusades a history, locating their motifs, concerns, and rationale by harking back to the time of Charlemagne when the Muslim tide had been turned back from the heart of Europe" (*Orientalism*, 37). This is particularly true with regard to their role in fashioning and perpetuating a demonic image of Islam and Muslims.

Although a comprehensive analysis of medieval Western views of Islam and Muslims is beyond the scope of the present argument, it should be noted that since the appearance of the pioneering work of Norman Daniel in *Islam and the West: The Making of an Image* (1960) and Richard Southern's *Western Views of Islam in the Middle Ages* (1962), numerous scholars from different backgrounds and interests have convincingly argued that medieval Europe was in many ways haunted by the specter of the Saracens (Muslims). The Saracens, as Dorothee Metlitzki once eloquently phrased it, became "a crucial public theme" that permeated the religious, political, military, and social life of Christian Europe (*The Matter of Araby in Medieval England*, 116).

A growing number of scholars have demonstrated that during the Middle Ages, Christian "discourse" had dominated the literary texts and had thus actively participated in the actual Crusades.[37] In *Empire of Magic: Medieval Romance and the Politics of Cultural Fantasy* (2003), Geraldine Heng has shown that throughout the Middle Ages, the Crusades were obsessively produced, revised, and copied in "biographies, national and regional histories, and texts" (41). This may be seen in such medieval masterpieces as the *Chanson de Roland*, *L'entrée de Spagne*, *Chanson de Jerusalem*, *Richard Coer de Lion*, *Sir Ferumbras*, *Sowdone of Babylone*, *King Horn*, and *The King Alisaunder*, to name but a few.

Through her examination of the depictions of Muslims as idolaters in some of these texts and others, such as *Le Jeu de saint Nicholas* and the *Digby Mary Magdalen* play, Suzanne Conklin Akbari has come to the conclusion that "the depiction of Muslims in western European texts is designed to hold up a mirror to medieval Christian practice, showing the readers of those texts what they are *not* so that they may understand what they *are*" ("Imagining Islam," 20). Echoing Akbari, Leona F. Cordery in "The Saracens in Middle English Literature: A Definition of Otherness" has convincingly argued that medieval Western attempts to construct a crusading identity were dependent on the literary fashioning of a

physically and spiritually vilified and threatening Saracen. As she put
it, "The Saracens, who were the chosen enemy of Christendom, were
seen to be both a physical and spiritual threat to Christendom. Physical
because they represented a ferocious enemy in battle and spiritual because
should the Saracens be victorious then the very souls of the Christians
would be in mortal peril" (89).

John V. Tolan has argued in *Saracens: Islam in the Medieval European
Imagination* (2002) that nowhere was this more emotionally captured than
in the following "prose monologue" by the thirteenth-century Florentine
traveler and missionary Riccoldo da Montecroce:

> Suddenly, in this sadness, swept up into an unaccustomed astonishment, I
> began, stupefied, to ponder God's judgment concerning the government
> of the world, especially concerning the Saracens and the Christians. What
> could be the cause of such massacre and such degradation of the Christian
> people? Of so much worldly prosperity for the perfidious Saracen people?
> Since I could not simply be amazed, nor could I find a solution to this
> problem, I decided to write to God and his celestial court, to express the
> cause of my astonishment, to open my desire through prayer, so that God
> might confirm me in the truth and sincerity of the Faith, that he quickly
> put an end to the law, or rather, the perfidy, of the Saracens, and more
> than anything else that he liberate the Christian captives from the hands
> of the enemies. (xiii)

Nevertheless, as we shall see with Ibn al-Qaysarani's questioning and dis-
ruption of medieval Arabic dominant views of the Franks, there did exist in
medieval Western literature as well some literary and cultural negotiation
of the dominant Euro-Christian views of the Saracens. Not least because
of what she considers to be a "monolithic and monologic" interpretation of the role of the Saracens in medieval Western literatures, Sharon
Kinoshita in a provocative book, *Medieval Boundaries: Rethinking Difference
in Old French Literature* (2006), and an essay, "Discrepant Medievalisms:
Deprovincializing the Middle Ages," has called for "acknowledging the
historical complexities of the Middle Ages" against what she describes
as "the dominant discourse of postcolonial medievalism" ("Discrepant
Medievalisms," 80).

In Kinoshita's view, medieval Iberian literature—which according
to her was "at best addressed only in passing in some central works of
the emerging field of postcolonial medievalism"—can be suggested as a
possible "privileged site from which to disrupt reductive notions of the
'European' Middle Ages" (80). Citing the "little 'orientalism' in medieval Spain's posturing toward the Moors" and the absence of "overriding

compulsion towards abjection," Kinoshita has gone so far as to contend that the Spanish medieval masterpiece *Cantar de Mio Cid*, "retrospectively constructed as the Spanish national epic," contained rather "a pragmatic give-and-take that lines itself up only exceptionally along the battle lines of crusade." In *Cantar de Mio Cid*, she goes on to explain, it is not the Muslims who are portrayed as "the protagonist's most troublesome enemies." The latter in her view are rather "his sons-in law, the counts of Carrion" (85).

In light of what Kinoshita has suggested and in spite of the tense religious atmosphere that dominated much of the encounter between Levantine Muslims and Euro-Christians during the Crusades, a number of Muslim writers exhibited a readiness to revise many of the stereotypes and prejudices they themselves had for a long time embraced, endorsed, and perpetuated. This was the outcome of direct contact with the Other and his/her "real" culture, and as a consequence, many of these writers dared to cast doubt openly on some of these prejudices and stereotypes.

Such was no doubt true of Ibn al-Qaysarani, whose direct contact with the Franks of Antioch had driven him to reconsider certain of the stereotypes he had himself propagated in a number of earlier jihadist poems.[38] Literarily speaking, this encounter culminated in a *diwan* (collection of poems) for which he chose the title *Al-Thaghriyyat* (Borderlands or Poems Written in Borderlands). Indeed, after crossing the territorial borders, Ibn al-Qaysarani found himself obliged to disavow several of his culture's proscriptions. Nowhere is this more evident than in his encounter with the "real" Frankish women whom he had imprisoned in a "jezebel stereotype."

As early as the moment he reached the first Frankish town of 'Azzaz (60 kilometers north of Aleppo, Syria), Ibn al-Qaysarani found no reason not to reveal his stereotypical perception of Frankish women. Upon meeting the very first "herd" of them, as he says, he directs his scopophilic/voyeuristic eyes upon them, thus turning them into mere objects of erotic desire:

> While passing by the Frankish town of 'Azzaz
> I recalled my bygone youth with weeping eyes.
> For I stalked a herd of lively Frankish gazelles
> Young and slender, they were gracefully quick.
> With their scent, the air was pleasurably thick.
> Their languid eyes as mesmerizing as the past.
> Their busts are perfect with perfect size.
> And above them, let fall a liquid kiss,
> As sweet as the sugar of the Ahwaz.

If their faces give signs of bliss to come,
The ultimate miracle lies in their comely bums! (*Shi'r Ibn al-Qaysarani*,
    249; translation mine)

The poem begins with the conventional comparison of women's beauty
to gazelles. Indeed, in medieval Arabic poetry of *ghazal* (love) in particular, the gazelle/antelope is one of the most common archetypal epithets/
similes used to celebrate a woman's physical beauty. Swiftly, however,
the poem turns into an overtly erotic piece wherein the Frankish women
become mere objects of sexual desire and stimulation. The graphic focus
on Frankish women's erogenous parts and the poet's usage of somewhat
licentious diction convince us of his initial views and perceptions of
Frankish women.

Ibn al-Qaysarani would thus portray the realm of the Franks, at least
in the beginning, as a world of moral wantonness, bacchic escapism,
and sexual adventurism. Nowhere is this more evident than in the following poem:

If one must drink and sin!
Let the hands that serve the fest,
Be those of the waitress of the Jisr's Inn!
A waitress from whose swelling breast,
A white palm pith does show itself in quest!
When she is not within my sight,
The drink is not empowered in its true might.
She brings to the moon the sun's full light.
And when she approaches with her lovely face,
Her eyes turn wine useless and a waste.
And if I'm there, so well placed,
With my hand and in great haste,
I play the belt around her waist. (239; translation mine)

In his quest for sexual gratification in the territory of the Other, Ibn
al-Qaysarani seems to have in mind what some European travelers had
centuries later while physically or imaginatively crossing the borderlands
into the Orient. As Said put it in *Orientalism*, albeit too generally, "[So] the
Orient was a place where one could look for sexual experience unobtain-
able in Europe. Virtually no European writer who wrote on or traveled to
the orient in the period after 1800 exempted himself or herself from this
quest" (190).

The eroticization of Frankish women and the "Orientalization" of the
Frankish land would vanish as soon as Ibn al-Qaysarani found himself in
the town of Antioch. It is there that the Arab Muslim poet had a perfect

chance to encounter a real Christian woman, one completely antithetical to those he initially fantasized about and presumably conquered sexually. It comes as no surprise then that the angelic image of the Christian Maria came to reign in his heart, ushering in a radical change in the poet's perception of Frankish women. The chastity and purity of this Christian woman would make her worthy of nothing but *al-hub al-'udhri* (platonic/romantic love). No doubt the poet's infatuation with Maria is a pure experience of *al-hub al-'udhri*:

> Every time I visit Maria,
> I feel pure bliss when her I see.
> A maid that resembles the Ben-oil tree,
> With her youth and vigor.
> She has so Christian a face,
> It brings life to a dead figure! (*Shi'r Ibn al-Qaysarani*,
>   431; translation mine)

The poet's fascination with Christian Maria became the impetus behind his interest in the Christian town and the Christian symbols, which, in turn, have a direct impact on the diction as poet. Now in every Christian woman he sees Maria, the epitome of piety, purity, and love:

> In churches, many a chaste virgin does reside!
> Like antelopes, in their shyness their beauties lie!
> To Mary's icon in devotion they bow,
> If, themselves, hung, to them the icons would bow!
> Slender necked and short-waisted in saintly poses.
> On whose cheeks, timidity has planted roses,
> Whose branches they water with their
>   innocent eyes. (215; translation mine)

Taken by what he saw in the Frankish churches, at one point he hesitatingly suggested, "Had it not been for my religion's sake! / To them, I would have appeared in my hooded cloak / And emotively, I would have orchestrated their mass!" (215; translation mine). More daring, however, is his open acknowledgment that during his stay in the town of Antioch, he attended a mass at a church called *dir sam'an* (the abbey of Sam'an):

> Haven't you heard of *dir sam'an*!
> And the marvels that delight the eye!
> I'm still wondering about its sanctuary!
> Is it a place of worship or Beauty's nursery!
> That night! How shall I forget!

Wherein my fire with their own had met.
Fire and light illuminated the night,
By that which shone on the Son of 'Imran.
Till daylight invaded the churches.
Revealing male and female worshippers,
Fully enjoying their spiritual delight. (405; translation mine)

No doubt the Muslim poet's absolute immersion in this Christian ambiance must have been considered at least unorthodox, if not heretical. Describing his sadness at the ending of the celebration, he says,

My soul departed, to my regret!
With every departing Christian I met.
Indeed, so beautiful was the Cross's fete!
That I pray my life be filled with Christian feasts. (405; translation mine)

The previous poems are remarkable in a number of respects, not least because they lend themselves to different, if not oppositional, interpretations. Of course, if read from an orthodox Muslim theological perspective, Ibn al-Qaysarani would have certainly been chastised, if not "excommunicated," for declaring his love for the enemies of Islam and revealing his *ta'dhim* (veneration) of their religious festivities, icons, and holy places. Conversely, a more esoteric approach would perhaps lead us to an association of Ibn al-Qaysarani with the then growing Unitarian Sufism that highlighted the absolute unity of all creatures believed to be the ultimate manifestations of God and emphasized love of all beings as the most important proof of attachment to God. Perhaps even before the Sufi Ibn 'Arabi (d. 1240) had written on this subject, Ibn al-Qaysarani's heart, if not "for every form," had become capable of embracing everything Christian he encountered in the then Frankish town of Antioch.[39]

Ibn al-Qaysarani had in several respects lived an epiphanous moment with the Franks whom he once demonized to the point of calling for their utter annihilation. This change of heart manifested itself in the form of an emotional bond with a real Frankish woman. The latter, in turn, drove him to embrace many of the Franks' thoughts and feelings and, at least metaphorically, their religion. Said differently, Ibn Al-Qaysarani, who had initially been very prejudicial of the Franks, had wholeheartedly edged their *un-heimlishe* (unfamiliar) culture after a visit to the city of Antioch, then under Frankish rule. This visit led him not only to touch the Frankish manners and values but also—and through the fascination with Maria, the chaste Christian woman—to become so intimate with the Franks' idiosyncratic and utterly un-Islamic "cultural complexes."

Be it as it may, one is tempted to conclude by stressing that the value of the previous poems lies not so much in how they document the poet's personal experience with the Franks but rather in the documentation of the array of the medieval Arab views and perceptions of the Euro-Christians. Indeed—bearing in mind the paramount importance of the Crusades within the history of relations between Islam and the West past and present and in spite of the tense religious atmosphere that dominated much of the encounter between Levantine Muslims and Euro-Christians during the Crusades and the ensuing demonization of the Franks in medieval Arabic literature and Arabic poetry in particular—a number of Muslim writers exhibited a readiness to question many of the stereotypes and prejudices they themselves had for a long time embraced, endorsed, and perpetuated. In several important respects, this was mainly the outcome of direct contact with the Other and his/her "real" culture. After this direct contact, some of these writers not only dared to cast doubt on several of the prejudices and stereotypes they held concerning *al-ifranja*, but they, metaphorically at least, embraced their most salient features of Otherness.

CONCLUSION

All mankind is from Adam and Eve, an Arab has no superiority over a non-Arab nor a non-Arab has any superiority over an Arab: also white man has no superiority over a black nor a black has no superiority over white except by piety and good action.

Rogerson, *The Prophet Muhammad*, 208

This quotation from Prophet Muhammad's last sermon seems to make it clear that, at least in theory, the binary prism through which the Self views the Other is *al-mutabaqa* (sameness) or *al-ikhtilaf* (difference) of *al-din* (religion), expressed herein by the Arabic word *al-taqwa* (piety). The latter is not only a central landscape feature of the Muslim community; it is rather the *significant* marker that shapes its identity, maintains its boundaries, and ensures its existence.

In a sense, all other common markers such as *al-qawmiyya* (nationalism), *al'irq* (ethnicity/race), *al-jins* (gender), *al-lawn* (color), *al-watan* (homeland), *al-nasab* (ancestry), and *al-hasab* (class) are considered *jahili* (un-Islamic). When compared with the religious marker described in the Quran and the Sunna as *taqwa* (piety), they all pale into insignificance. As Carolyn Moxley Rouse puts it in *Engaged Surrender: African American Women and Islam* (2004):

> Many Muslims believe that instead of privileging racial/ethnic, gender or class identity, their faith is the umbrella under which all their identities can be expressed without coming into conflict. At the women's entrance to Masjid al-Mutaqim there were always several copies of Prophet Muhammad's last sermon, and the continual availability of the sermon is no accident. The sermon resonates so powerfully with this community that it is used to represent the essence of the faith to both new and old converts. (101)

To a varying extent, therefore, the Muslim *umma* (community/nation), especially during the period studied in the present book, was thought to be exclusively faith-based.[1] In fact, so long as Islam, as fashioned in the Quran and the Sunna, is a divine message to all humans irrespective of their differences, those who accept it become *al-ana* (the Self), whereas those who reject it are doomed to embody *al-akhar* (the Other) par excellence.[2]

This message is far from imagining a community that is based on territory, history, race, language, common customs, or socioeconomic interests, especially as delineated by a number of contemporary Western theorists of nationalism and nation-building such as Elie Kedourie, Anthony D. Smith, E. J. Hobsbawm, Benedict Anderson, Earnest Gellner, and Dudley Seers, to name but a few. Paradoxically, in light of his controversial views of Islam, it seems that Ernest Renan's older concept of "un plebiscite de tous les jours" (a daily plebiscite) Islamically speaking makes more sense, especially if one considers answering *al-adhan*, or the call to the five obligatory prayers, as a daily proclamation of the plebiscite described by Renan.[3]

Yet as much as the Quran and the Sunna acknowledge that Muslims differ in their sameness in light of their differences in the degree of attachment to their faith and practice of its teachings, non-Muslims, in turn, are not the same. As a matter of fact, their difference or Otherness from the Muslim Self is proportional to the degree of their *kufr* (disbelief) and their *'ida'* (enmity) to the faith and its adherents.[4] In other words, if what makes the Self is the level of *iman* (belief) and its implementation in *a'mal* (deeds), what makes the Other is the level of departure from Islam and its implementation in deeds. This can range from conspiring against Muslims to fighting them. On this basis, the *kuffar* (literally, those from whom the truth [Islam] is hidden) are divided into two categories: those who fight Muslims and those who do not.

This distinction is extremely important for a better understanding of the growing polemic over an alleged Muslim binary, if not Manichaean, division of the world into two eternally warring spheres: *dar al-islam* (the abode of Islam) versus *dar al-harb* (the abode of war). In broader terms, the picture is much more multifaceted and complex. In fact, contrary to the dominant monolithic views espoused by Muslim jihadists and certain Western experts of the Middle East, the majority of classical Muslim jurisprudents, as well as contemporary ones, have argued that the binary division of the world into *dar al-islam* versus *dar al-harb* is not only an *ijtihad* (legal choice) on the part of a number of Hanafi jurisprudents but also a *ra'y marjuh* (a weak view).

This is regardless of the fact that for many, *dar al-harb* (abode of war) could well mean a Muslim country in the same way that *dar al-islam* could in some circumstances mean a non-Muslim country. As demonstrated by Hilmi Zawati in *Is Jihād a Just War? War, Peace, and Human*

Rights under Islamic and Public International Law (2001), major Muslim jurisprudents (jurists) who wrote about this particular issue—such as Ibn Qutayba, al-Mawardi, Ibn-Qudama, al-Ghazali, Ibn al-Qayyim, and al-Shawkani, to name but a few—opted for and adopted the more flexible and complex triple division of the world.[5] As Zawati puts it,

> In discussing the *jihād* theory, Muslim jurists divided the world into three parts: the territory of Islam (*dār al-Islām* or *dār al-salām* or *dār al-'adl*); the territory of covenant (*dār al-'ahd* or *dār al-muwāda'a* or *dār al-ṣulḥ*); and the territory of war (*dār al-ḥarb* or *dār al-jawr*)…In this respect, al-Shawkāni argues that a territory can be considered *dār al-Islām*…as long as a Muslim can reside there in safety and freely fulfil his religious obligations.
>
> Conversely, *dār al-ḥarb*, which stands in opposition to *dār al-Islam*, can be defined as a territory which does not apply Islamic rules, and where a Muslim cannot publicly adhere to ritual practices of his faith. (50)

As I have tried to show throughout the chapters of this book, medieval Muslim writers, some of whom as we saw were not only pious persons but also distinguished jurisprudents, in their accounts of non-Muslim Others they imagined and encountered in their textual and physical journeys, seemed to go beyond these religious markers and jurisprudential views of the division of the world. People such as al-Mas'udi, al-Biruni, al-Tajir, al-Bakri, al-Ghazal, Ibn Fadlan, Ibn Yahya, Ibn Yaq'ub, and al-Gharnati built their perceptions and attitudes of non-Muslims rather on anthropo-ethnographic and sociocultural blueprints: civilization, climatic ethnology, environmental determinism, character, physical appearance, women, language, hygiene, dress, dietary rules, education, justice, social services, and political systems.

Of course, like all other cultural meetings, medieval Muslims' encounters with the Other in general and the Euro-Christian in particular brought out some elements of prejudice, exaggeration, and in some cases, whether consciously or unconsciously, tropes of ethnocentrism that made some writers judge the Other in relation to their own cultural notions and conceptions. As we saw through the course of the chapters—notwithstanding *al-qaswa* (cruelty) that, for example, served as the most common denominator between *al-rum* (Byzantines) and *al-ifranja* (European Crusaders), as reflected in medieval Arabic poetry—Muslims were duly struck by what they conceived as lack of hygiene among medieval Europeans, sexual freedom of their women, and absence of jealousy among their men. No wonder then these specific European features served as the most common denominators of the overall Muslim views and perception of the otherwise heterogeneous European *ajnas*.

In spite of this, however, the most important lesson that one learns from the texts studied in this book is that medieval Muslims were curious to know about alien *thaqafat* (cultures) and willing to appreciate them. As I have shown in the first chapter, this curiosity and willingness to study and appreciate foreign cultures was the main impetus behind *harakat al-tarjama* (the movement of translation) by which, as al-Jahiz records in *Al-Hayawan* (On Animals), not only *hikmat al-ighriq* (Greek wisdom) but also *adab al-furs* (Persian literature) and *kutub al-hind* (Indian books) were ardently translated into Arabic.

Perhaps a no less important conclusion is the fact that more than a handful of medieval Muslims were textually and physically interested in medieval Europe.[6] As I demonstrated in the second and third chapters, generally speaking there was no shortage of Muslims who cast curious eyes and minds toward Europe and the Europeans. Contrary to the assumptions of some, medieval Muslim scholars did not appear to see the entire European continent as "an outer darkness of barbarism" or as an "African jungle," and at no moment did we come across a single Muslim writer who felt the need to apologize to his readers "for devoting some attention" to Europe and the Europeans (Lewis, *A Middle East Mosaic*, 24).

By most accounts, and notwithstanding the much more publicized enmities, conflicts, and wars, there were negotiations, embassies, truces, exchanges of captives, ransoms, and even (as we saw with al-Ghazal and the Viking queen) love and romance. It is of interest to propose that perhaps the proximity of Arab Muslims of al-Andalus to the Euro-Christians created its own record of deeds and discoveries. Faithful to their spirit of tolerance and multiculturalism, the former appeared more adventurous, if not bolder, in their encounters with the Other. It is not surprising, therefore, that from the very land of Europe, medieval Arab Muslims drew some of the most detailed accounts of Europe and the Euro-Christians during the pre-Crusade encounter between Islam and the West.

Even the Byzantines and the Franks, in the dominant views and perceptions expressed in medieval Arabic literature, as I tried to show in the fourth chapter, resemble in several respects those of the Saracens and Moors (Turks) as found in Western medieval and early modern literature, which made both of them *al-akhar* (the Other). Be that as it may, several Muslim writers acknowledged a number of their *fada'il* (qualities/virtues). In addition to Byzantine and Frankish beauty, this was true especially of craftsmanship and architecture for the former and courage and perseverance for the latter.

In connection to the important period of the Crusades within the history of relations between Islam and the West past and present, it is not going too far to say that in spite of the tense religious atmosphere that dominated much of the encounter between Levantine Muslims and Euro-Christians during the Crusades and the ensuing demonization of the Franks in medieval Arabic literature, a number of Muslim writers exhibited a readiness to question religiously and culturally many of the stereotypes and prejudices they themselves had for a long time embraced, endorsed, and perpetuated.

As we saw with the once celebrated poet of jihad against the Franks Ibn al-Qaysarani, this was mainly the outcome of direct contact with the Other and his/her "real" culture. After this direct contact, some of these writers not only dared to cast doubt on several of the prejudices and stereotypes they held concerning *al-ifranja*, but they, metaphorically at least, embraced their most salient features of Otherness.

In the same vein, and akin to their early modern successors, medieval Muslims were no less eager "to ask questions about *bilad al-nasara* and to record answers—and then to turn their impressions into documents" (Matar, *In the Lands of the Christians*, xxii). Without question, Arabs did not wait until the years following 1831 to write "the first influential Arab account of a European country," as Lewis asserted in *From Babel to Dragomans: Interpreting the Middle East* (128).[7]

It is my contention, therefore, that almost 900 years before the date suggested by Lewis and others, Ibn Fadlan had already done so. Indeed, I will always remember how, a few years ago, a Tunisian friend of mine found himself in my room, where he read through the edge titles of the books that I had. Among the titles that caught his attention was Richard Frye's *Ibn Fadlan's Journey to Russia* (2005). Not able to understand the time of the journey without the subtitle, my friend thought that Ibn Fadlan was the alias of a contemporary Arab writer who had recently visited Russia.[8] When I introduced him to the man and his tenth-century European journey and spoke to him about Ibn Fadlan's encounter with the Vikings, he grew more cynical. In fact, quite mockingly, he replied to me by posing the following questions: How was he able to reach Russia at that time and how come the Vikings did not "eat" him?

Could it be that the medieval world with all its shortcomings and despite decades, if not centuries, of bad publicity was not that barbaric! Perhaps the answer(s) will be found if, as has been the main objective of the present study, we steer ourselves toward the shores of undiscovered non-Western equivalents of Orientalism in general and medieval Arabic traditions of alterity in particular. I have coined the word Ifranjalism hoping to provoke not only more interest but further work by others in this neglected direction.

In several important respects, however, statements such as the one quoted further in this paragraph by the versatile tenth-century Baghdadi *adib* (litterateur) Abu Hayyan al-Tawhidi are tantalizingly inviting.[9] Replying to a *wazir* who asked him whether he favors the Arabs over non-Arabs or vice versa, al-Tawhidi—as one may read in his great literary work *Al-Imta' wa-l Mu'anasa* (Enjoyment and Conviviality)—had this to say:

> In essence, all nations have merits and demerits in the same way that they have always shared many common things and concepts of life. Yet each nation has cultivated some specific traits that its sister has not. Of course, in what they share, there is the good and there is the bad. Needless to remember the commonplace that every nation has its merits and virtues. *Thorough research, sharp understanding, and deep thought are characteristic of the Greeks. By contrast, Indians are known for their fertile imagination, perception, wisdom, tricks, and magic. As for the Arabs, they excelled in rhetoric, eloquence, encyclopedism, and the magic of the tongue. The Persians are the best when it comes to moderation, manners, politics, order, drawing, and servitude [to God]. As for the Turks, they are famous for courage and bravery.* (25; translation and italics mine)

Al-Tawhidi's statement is significant, not least because it betrays a spontaneous acknowledgment of cultural relativism and a courageous recognition of the Other. In a sense, Tarif Khalidi was not exaggerating when he stated, in his short but indispensable article "Islamic Views of the West in the Middle Ages," that classical Muslim civilization was characterized by "an unparalleled capacity to learn from other cultures, an open and oft-expressed willingness to acknowledge its cultural debt to Indians, Persians, Greeks, and so forth" (36).

In light of al-Tawhidi's views, perhaps it is time to acknowledge and recognize the fact that casting one's curious eye toward the Other is too universal to be construed as an exclusive virtue of one particular culture. Indeed, one should be convinced that throughout the course of human history, different cultures across the globe have produced their own curious writers and travelers who ventured textually and physically into alien worlds and foreign words.

APPENDIX OF TRANSLATED POETRY

1. Abu Dulaf

ومن كان من الأحرا ر يسلو سلوة الحر***ولاسيما في الغربة أودى أكثر العمر

وشاهدت أعاجيبا وألوانا من الدهر *** ابت بالنوى نفسي على الإمساك والفطر

فنحن الناس كل النا س في البر و في البحر*** أخذنا جزية الخلق من الصين إلى مصر

إلى طنجة،بل في كل أرض خيلنا تسري *** إذا ضاق بنا قطر نزل عنه إلى قطر

لنا الدنيا بما فيها من الإسلام والكفر ***فنصطاف على الثلج ونشتو بلد التمر

2. Al-Ghazal

قال لي يحي وصرنا بين موج كالجبال *** وتولتنا رياح من دبور و شمال

شقت القلعين وانبتت عرى تلك الحبال *** وتمطى ملك الموت إلينا عن حيال

فرأيت الموت رأي العين حالا بعد حال *** لم يكن للقوم فينا يا رفيقي رأس مال

3. Abu al-'Arab

البحرللروم لا تجري السفين به *** إلا على غرر والبر للعرب

4. Abu Firas

A. "A Captive's Suffering"

إنَّ في الأسرِلَصَبّاً***دَمعُهُ في الخَدِّ صَبُّ

هُوَ في الروم مُقيمٌ***وَلَهُ في الشام قلبُ

مُستَجِدّاً لَم يُصادِف***عِوَضاً مِمَّن يُحِبُّ

B. "Separation"

لقد كنت أشكو البعد منك وبين* بلاد إذا ماشئت قرّبها الوخد

فكيف وفيما بيننا ملك قيصر ّ*** ولا أمل يحي النفوس ولاوعد

C. "The Byzantines Are Coming!"

هذه الجيوش تجيش نحو بلادكم***محفوفة بالكفر والصّلبان

لبغي أكثر ما تفلّ خيولهم***والبغي شرّ مصاحب الإنسان

ليسوا ينون فلاتنوا في أمركم***لاينهض الواني لغير الواني

غضبا لدين الله إن لاتغضبوا***لم يشتهر في نصره سيفان

D. Selected lines from the hija' of Nicephorus Phocas

أتزعم يا ضخم اللغاديد أننا *** ونحن أسود الحرب لا نعرف الحربا

أتوعدنا بالحرب حتى كأننا *** وإياك لم يعصب بها قلبنا عصبا

لقد جمعتنا الحرب من قبل هذه *** فكنا بها أسدا وكنت بها كلبا

بأقلامنا أحجرت أم بسيوفنا *** وأسد الشرى قدنا إليك أم الكتبا

تركناك في بطن الفلاة تجوبها *** كما انتفق اليربوع يلتثم الترب

5. Selections from *Al-Qasida al-Mal'una* (The Cursed Poem)

A.

من الملك الطهر المسيحي مالك *** الى خلف الاملاك من ال هاشم

الى الملك الفضيل المطيع اخي العلا***ومن يرتجى للمعضلات العظائم

اما سمعت اذناك ما انا صانع *** ولكن دهاك الوهن عن فعل حازم

فان تك عما قد تقلدت نائمًا ****فاني عما همني غير نائم

B.

سافتح ارض الله شرقًا ومغربًا *** وانشر دينًا للصليب بصارمي

فعيسى علا فوق السموات عرشه *** يفوز الذي والاه يوم التخاصم

وصاحبكم بالتراب اودى به الثرى *** فصار رفاتًا بين تلك الرمائم

تناولتم اصحابه بعد موته *** بسبّ وقذف وانتهاك المحارم

6. Selections from the Response of al-Qaffal to *Al-Qasida al-Mal'una*

A.

أتاني مقال لإمرئ غير عالم *** بطرق مجاري القول عند التخاصم

تخرّص ألقابا له جدّ كاذب *** وعدّد آثارا له جدّ واهم

تسمّى بطهر وهو أنجس مشرك***مدّنسة أثوابه بالمداسم

وقال مسيحي وليس كذاكم *** أخو قسوة لايحتذي فعل راحم.-

B.

نحن على فضل بما في أكفنا *** وفخر عليكم بالأصول الجسائم

ونرجو وشيكا أن يسهّل ربّنا *** لردّ خوافي الرّيش تحت القوادم

وعظّمتَ من أمر النّساء وعندنا *** لكم ألف ألف من إماء وخادم

ولكن كرُمنا إذا ظفرنا وأنتم *** ظفرتم فكنتم قدوة للألائم

C.

وقلت ملكناكم بجور قضاتكم *** وبيعهم أحكامهم بالدّراهم.

وفي ذاك إقرار بصحّة ديننا *** وأنا ظلمنا فابتلينا

7. Selections from the Response of Ibn Hazm

A.

أتقرن يا مخذول دينا مثلثا *** بعيدا عن المعقول بادي المآثم

تدين لمخلوق يدين لغيره *** فيا لك سحقا ليس بخفي لعالم

أنا جيلكم مصنوعة قد تشابهت*** كلام الأولى فيها أتوا بالعظائم

وعود صليب ما تزالون سجدا *** له يا عقول الهاملات السوائم

B.

سبيتم سبايا يحصر العدو دونها *** وسبيكم فينا كقطر الغمائم

خلق عدها رام معجزا *** وأتى بتعداد لرش الحمائم فلو رام

ليالي قادوكم كما اقتادكم *** أقيال جرجان بحز الحلاقم

رسل بنات ملوككم *** سبايا كما سيقت ظباء الصرائم وساقوا على

C.

لكم من ملوك مكرمين قماقم *** ولكن سلوا عنا هرقلا ومن خلى

كرائم يخبركم عنا التنوخ وقيصر *** وكم قد سبينا من نساء

وعما فتحنا من منيع بلادكم *** وعما أقمنا فيكم من مآتم

8. Arabic Poetry of the Crusades

A. Al-Abiwardi's poem

مزجنا دماء بالدموع السواجم *** فلم يبق منا عرضة للمراحم

وشر سلاح المرء دمع يفيضه *** إذا الحرب شبّت نارها بالصوارم

فإيها بني الإسلام إن وراءكم *** وقائع يلحقن الذرى بالمناسم

أتهويمة في ظل أمن وغبطة *** وعيش كنوار الخميلة ناعم

وإخوانكم بالشام أضحى مقيلهم *** ظهور المذاكي أو بطون القشاعم

تسومهم الروم الهوان وأنتم *** تجرون ذيل الخفض فعل المسالم

أرى أمتي لا يشرعون إلى العدى *** رماحهم والدين واهي الدعائم

ويجتنبون النار خوفا من الردى *** ولا يحسبون العار ضربة لازم

أيرضى صناديد الأعاريب بالأذى *** ويغضي إلى ذل كماة الأعاجم

فليتهمو إذ لم يذودوا حمية *** عن الدين ضنّوا غيرة بالمحارم

B. Ibn al-Mujawir's poem

أعيني لا ترقي من العبرات *** صلي في البكا الآصال بالبكرات

لعل سيول الدمع يطفئ فيضها *** توقد ما في القلب من جمرات

على المسجد الأقصى الذي جل قدره *** على موطن الإخبات والصلوات

لتبك على القدس البلاد بأسرها *** وتعلن بالأحزان والترحات

C. Anonymous poem

أحل الكفر بالإسلام ضيم *** يطول عليه للدين النحيب

فحق ضائع وحمى مباح *** وسيف قاطع ودم صبيب

وكم من مسلم أمسى سليبا *** ومسلمة لها حرم سليب

وكم من مسجد جعلوه ديرا *** على محرابه نصب الصليب

دم الخنزير فيه لهم خلوق *** وتحريق المصاحف فيه طيب

أمورٌ لو تأملهن طفل *** لطقّل في عوارضه المشيب

D. Ibn al-Khayyat's poem

إلى كم وقد زخر المشركون *** بسيل يهال له السيل مدّا

وقد جال في أرض إفرنجة *** جيوش كمثل جبال تردّى

تراخون من يجتري شدة *** وتنسون من يجعل الحرب نقدا

أنوماً على مثل هذا الصفا *** وهزلا وقد أصبح اليوم جدّا

بنو الشرك لا ينكرون الفساد *** ولا يعرفون مع الجور قصدا

ولا يردعون عن القتل نفسا *** ولا يتركون من الفتك جهدا

E. Selections from **Al-Qasida al-Munfarija**
(An Ode of Hope)

اشتدي أزمة تنفرجي *** قد آذن ليلك بالبلج

وظلام الليل له سرج *** حتى يغشاه أبو السرج

وسحاب الخير لها مطر *** فإذا جاء الإبان تجي

وفوائد مولانا جمل *** لسروح الأنفس والمهج

F. Selections from Ibn al-Qaysarani's poem on
the liberation of Edessa

هو السيف لا يغنيك إلا جلاده *** وهل طوق الأملاك إلا نجاده

لقد كان في فتح الرهاء دلاله *** على غير ما عند العلوج اعتقاده

ولم يغن عند القوم عنه ولاده *** يرجون ميلاد ابن مريم نصرة

G. Shihab al-Halabi on the liberation of 'Akka

الحمد لله ذلت دولة الصّلب *** وعزّ بالترك دين المصطفى العربي

هذا الذي كانت الآمال لو طلبت *** رؤياه في النوم لاستحيت من الطلب

H. Ibn al-Qaysarani on the Franks

I. "I Fell Enamored to a Frankish Woman"

لقد فتنتني فرنجية**** نسيم العبير بها يعبق

ففي ثوبها غصن ناعم*** وفي تاجها قمر مشرق

وإن تك في عينها زرقة*** فإن سنان القنا أزرق

II. "In the City of ʿAzzaz"

أين عزّي من روحتي بعزاز *** وجوازي على الظّباء الجوازي

واليعافير ساحبات المغافي*** رّ علينا كالرّبرب المجتاز

بعيون كالمرهفات المواضي *** وقدود مثل القنا الهزّاز

ونحور تقلّدت بثغور *** ريقها ذوب سكر الأهواز

ووجوه لها نبوّة *** غير أنّ الإعجاز في الأعجاز

III. "The Frankish Waitress"

إن كان لابدّ من السّكر *** فمن يديْ خمّارة الجس

خمّارةٌ تُطلعُ من نَحْرها *** جُمّارةٌ بيضاءَ من نَحْر

تُمسي فتُمسي الرّاحُ في راحها *** تهدي سَنا الشّمْس إلى البّدر

حتّى إذا دارَت على شَرْبها *** ألحاظها أغْنَتْ عن الخَمْر

ما زرتُها إلّا وباتَتْ يدي *** أوْلى من الزّنار بالخصر

IV. "On Maria"

إذا ما زرت ماريّا *** فما سعدي وماريّا

فتاة كقضيب البا***ن يثنيها الصّبا طيّا

لها وجه مسيحيّ *** ترى الميت به حيّا

V. "The Virgins of the Church"

كم بالكنائس من مبتلـة *** مثل المهـاة يزينها الخفر

من كل ساجدة لصورتها *** لو ألصقت سجدت لها الصور

قديسـة في حبل عاتقها *** طول وفي زنارها قصر

غرس الحياء بصحن وجنتها *** ورداسقى أغصانـه النظـر

VI. "Wish"

فلولا التحَرّج في ملّتي *** طلعت عليهنّ في برنس

وقمت ألحّن قدّاسهنّ *** غير بليد ولا أخرس

ولم تك فرسانها في الطعان *** بأشجع منّي ولا أفرس

VII. "On Dir Sam'an"

يا هل سمعتم بدير سمعان *** وما به للعيون من عان
أموقف للصلاة هيكله *** أم منبت من منابت البان
في ليلة لم تزل بها حرقي *** تلفح نيرانهم بنيران
نار ونور كأنّ إنسهما *** في الليل ما آنس ابن عمران
حتى انجلى الصبح في كنائسها *** عن كلّ نشوانة و نشوان
وانصرفوا والفؤاد أفئدة *** مع كلّ نصرانة ونصران
ياحسن عيد الصليب لو أن كا *** نَ الدّهر فيهم أعياد صلبان

NOTES

Introduction: Be(yond)fore Orientalism; Medieval Muslims and the Other

1. For the details, see Bernard Lewis, *A Middle East Mosaic: Fragments of Life, Letters, and History* (New York: Random House, 2000), 27–34.

2. The Iranian historian Mohamad Tavakoli-Targhi in *Refashioning Iran: Orientalism, Occidentalism, and Historiography* (New York: Palgrave Macmillan, 2001) was among the first to criticize Said for assuming that "Orientalism had no corresponding equivalent in the Orient" and for viewing it "as a one way exchange" (19).

3. The German scholar Isolde Kurz seems to be among the earliest to call for an end to this intellectual cul-de-sac. As she puts it in the conclusion of her book *Vom Umgang Mit Dem Anderen: Die Orientalismus-Debatte zwischen Alteritätsdiskurs und interkultureller Kommunikation* (Wurzburg: Ergon, 2000): "Zwanzig Jahre Orientalismus-Debatte und kein Ende. Wo stehen wir? Wie denken wir heute den 'anderen'? Der Konsens des alten Orientalismus ist zerstört—aber gibt es einen neuen?" (229).

4. Inspired by Sadiq Jalal al-'Azm, others have opted for *al-istishraq ma'kusan* (Orientalism in reverse).

5. Ian Buruma and Avishai Margalit, to cite an example in *Occidentalism: The West in the Eyes of Its Enemies* (New York: Penguin, 2004), suggest that Occidentalism/anti-Westernism has manifested itself in different forms: "From Counter-Reformation to the Counter-Enlightenment in Europe, to the many varieties of nationalism and social fascism in East and West, to anti-capitalism and anti-globalization, and finally to religious extremism that rages in so many places today" (11).

6. Until the present day, North African Arabs and Berbers, including myself, identify themselves as *maghariba* (Occidentals/Westerners) in contrast to *mashariqa*, or Arabs of the East.

7. Before the Crusades, it was more common to use the word *al-rum* (Romans/Byzantines). This is in addition to purely religious words such as *al-nasara* (Christians), *ahl al-kitab* (People of the Book), *al-kuffar* (non-believers), and *al-muhrikun* (polytheists).

1 Translation, Travel, and the Other: The Fascination with Greek and Oriental Cultures

1. Quoted in Tim Mackintosh-Smith, *The Travels of Ibn Battutah* (London: Macmillan, 2002), x.
2. Abdullah Ibrahim, in his somewhat "anachronistically postcolonial" *Al-Markaziyya al-Islamiyya: Al-Akhar fi al-Adab al-'Arabi al-Wasit* (Beirut: Dar al-Baida, 2001), speaks of a "manifest and latent" *markaziyya islamiyya* (Islamocentrism) in the same way that Said speaks of Eurocentrism. Ibrahim appears to be more interested in enforcing some of the most radical postcolonial views and Said's in particular on classical Arabic writings. By most accounts, the result is evocative of Said's interpretation of Jane Austen's *Mansfield Park*.
3. As Mathew Arnold once defined culture in his seminal *Culture and Anarchy: An Essay in Political and Social Criticism* (London: Smith Elder, 1869).
4. For an English translation, see *The Fihrist of [Ibn] al-Nadim: A Tenth-Century Survey of Muslim Culture*, ed. and trans. Bayard Dodge (New York: Columbia University Press, 1970).
5. Greek remained the official language of the Umayyad *diwan* (administration) until it was replaced by Arabic during the reign of Abd al-Malik ibn Marwan. At the order of the latter, the translator Sulayman ibn Sa'id translated the whole *diwan* into Arabic.
6. For a comprehensive English list of the works translated from Greek into Arabic, see R. Walzer's *Greek into Arabic* (Cambridge, MA: Harvard University Press, 1962).
7. Ibn al-Nadim and other medieval historians mention that Aristotle came to al-Ma'mun in a dream, urging him to diffuse Greek philosophy and science in his empire (Richard A. Mollin, *Codes: The Guide to Secrecy from Ancient to Modern Times* [Boca Raton, FL: Chapman and Hall, 2005], 46).
8. In reference to the three erudite brothers who were instrumental in promoting scientific research and played a notable role in *bayt al-hikma*. Their names were Hasan, Ahmad, and Muhammad.
9. They called themselves *ahl al-'adl wa-l-tawhid* (people of justice and monotheism). For more, see Gavin Picken's brief but comprehensive entry "Mu'tazilim" in *Encyclopedia of Islamic Civilization and Religion*, ed. Ian R. Netton (London: Routledge, 2008), 472–473.
10. For example, their assertion that the Quran was *makhluq* (created) and *ghayr azali* (not eternal).
11. *Kitab al-Rad 'ala al-Mantiqiyyin* (Refutation of the Logicians).
12. This chapter is entitled "Fasl fi-Ibtal al-Falsafa wa-Fasad Muntahiliha" (Refutation of philosophy and the corruption of its adherent). Although acknowledging that *al-falsafa* (philosophy) has *thamra wahida* (one single fruit), which is *shahn al-dhihn fi tartib al-adilla wa-l-hujaj* (training the intellect in using arguments and proofs), it is inherently suppositious and erroneous. Because of this, *al-falsafa* is all *dharar* (harm) especially, as was the case of al-Farabi and Ibn Sina—whom he singles out in the

chapter—when used to interpret theological issues. Ibn Khaldun concludes his chapter by calling upon fellow Muslim scholars to champion *al-naql* (tradition) and satisfy themselves with the Quran and the Sunna in understanding the fundamentals of faith.

13. It is noteworthy that the backlash against Greek culture and philosophy was the main impetus behind the rise of a number of influential theological and intellectual schools, such as *al-ash'ariyya* and *al-maturidiyya* in theology and the *al-ishraqiyya* movement in mysticism, to name but a few. For more information on these groups and others, see Tim Winter, ed., *The Cambridge Companion to Classical Islamic Theology* (Cambridge: Cambridge University Press, 2008).

14. Peter S. Groff has noted, "Words directly meaning knowledge or *'ilm* appear twenty-seven times in the Qur'an, and *'alim* (knower) 140 times. There are 704 references in the book to words that come from *'ilm*" (Groff and Leaman, *Islamic Philosophy A-Z*, 33).

15. The two sayings attributed to Muhammad—"Seek knowledge even in China" and "Seek knowledge from the cradle to the grave"—are among the most quoted references in Arabic-Islamic culture. Interestingly, despite the quasi-legendary fame of these two sayings, the majority of Sunni *muhaddithin* (expert scholars of hadith) declared both of them as either *dha'if* (weak) or *mawdu'* (fabricated). An example of a *sahih* (authentic) hadith that highlights the virtue of travel for the sake of knowledge is the following:

    "If anyone travels on a road in search of knowledge, Allah will cause him to travel on one of the roads of Paradise. The angels will lower their wings in their great pleasure with one who seeks knowledge, the inhabitants of the heavens and the Earth and the fish in the deep waters will ask forgiveness for the learned man. The superiority of the learned man over the devout is like that of the moon, on the night when it is full, over the rest of the stars. The learned are the heirs of the Prophets, and the Prophets leave neither *dinar* nor *dirham*, leaving only knowledge, and he who takes it takes an abundant portion" (*Sunan Abu Dawud, Book of Knowledge*, no. 3634, p. 1034).

16. This said, one should be left with no doubt that there is no dearth of cases wherein several famous travelers undertook their long journeys "for a specific religious purpose which had the pilgrimage to Mecca as its heart and goal," as Ian R. Netton phrases it in "Basic Structures and Signs of Alienation in the Rihla of Ibn Jubayr," in *Golden Roads: Migration, Pilgrimage and Travel in Mediaeval and Modern Islam*, ed. Ian R. Netton (Richmond, UK: Curzon Press, 1993), 57.

17. As we will see in the second chapter, in his major works al-Mas'udi, "drawing upon a variety of sources," marshaled "historical, geographic and ethnographic information on peoples from the west (Frankish kings), north (slavs), and east (Indian kings and Chinese emperors)," as Chase F. Robinson has eloquently phrased it in his book *Islamic Historiography* ([Cambridge: Cambridge University Press, 2003], 137) while commenting on al-Mas'udi's magnum opus, *Muruj al-Dhahab*.

18. As Khalidi has shown, al-Mas'udi used to interview "a great number of people from all walks of life whom he met on his travels. Merchants, seamen, and travellers provided him with geographical and historical information untapped by earlier historians" (*Islamic Historiography: The Histories of al-Mas'udi* [Albany: State University of New York Press, 1975], 3).

19. In *Minute on Education* (1835) (*Macaulay, Prose and Poetry, selected by G. M. Young* [Cambridge MA: Harvard University Press, 1957]), Lord Macaulay wrote the following: "I have no knowledge of either Sanskrit or Arabic. But I have done what I could to form a correct estimate of their value. I have read translations of the most celebrated Arabic and Sanskrit works. I have conversed both here and at home with men distinguished by their proficiency in the Eastern tongues. *I am quite ready to take the Oriental learning at the valuation of the Orientalists themselves. I have never found one among them who could deny that a single shelf of a good European library was worth the whole native literature of India and Arabia*" (722, italics mine).

20. As scholars have suggested, the interest in other religions found its origin in the Quran and the Sunna. Before al-Nawbakhti, however, there was no shortage of scholars who were keenly interested not only in different Jewish and Christian sects but equally in the religious views of the ancient Greeks, Zoroastrians, the Sabians of Harran, Hindus, and Buddhists. For more on this, see David Thomas's entry "Heresiographical Works," in *Encyclopedia of Islamic Civilization and Religion*, ed. Ian Richard Netton (London: Routledge, 2008), 226–229.

21. For a study of some of these writers, see Jacques Waardenberg's "Muslim Studies of Other Religions," in *The Middle East and Europe: Encounters and Exchanges*, ed. Geert Jan Van Gelder and Ed de Moor (Amsterdam: Orientations, 1992), 10–38, and his edited book *Muslim Perceptions of Other Religions: A Historical Survey* (Oxford: Oxford University Press, 1999).

22. For the original French essay, see Jacques Le Goff, "L'occident médiéval et l'océan Indien: un horizon onirique," in *Pour un autre Moyen Age: temps, travail et culture en Occident: 18 Essais*, ed. Jacques Le Goff (Paris: NRF-Gallimard, 1977).

23. Scholars such as De Goje, Blachère, Kratschkovsky, Kimble, Miquel, Achoy, Gibe, Palencia, Reinaud, Bartold, Wussienfeld, and Sarton.

24. Abu Dulaf was a poet and a traveler named by Ibn al-Nadim and other medieval chroniclers as a *jawwala*, or globe-trotter. In spite of the debate over its authenticity, he is thought to be the author of his own account of India. This account was published with a Latin translation in Berlin in 1845 (Ahmad, 115).

25. As demonstrated by Hourani in his classic *Arab Seafaring in the Indian Ocean in Ancient and Early Medieval Times*, even long before Islam, Arab seafarers and traders were familiar with the Indian Ocean (Princeton, NJ: Princeton University Press, 1995).

26. He was known as al-Turjuman, Arabic and Persian for "translator." Ibn Khordadbeh mentions that his mastery of many languages was the primary reason he was chosen by al-Wathiq for this mission of discovery (*Kitab al-Masalik wa-l-Mamalik*, 163).

27. The literal translation of the Arabic name is the one possessing two horns. The historical identity of *dhu al-qarnayn* has generated a heated debate among Muslim and non-Muslim scholars alike, some of whom identify him as Alexander the Great. Owing to the many differences between the Quranic character (who is described as a pure monotheist and a faithful follower of God) and the historical Alexander the Great, many Muslim scholars refuse this identification.

28. See Gabriel Ferrand's *Voyage du marchand arabe Sulayman en Inde et Chine, rédigé en 851 suivi de remarques par Abu Zayd Hasan (vers 916)* (Paris: Classiques de l'Orient, 1922).

29. In addition to the accounts of al-Masʿudi, al-Biruni, Abu Dulaf, and Ibn Battuta, other major accounts include those of al-Yaʿqubi (d. 880), Ibn al-Faqih (d. 902), al-Maqdisi (d. 980), al-Gardizi (d. 1060), al-Marwazi (d. 1125), al-Idrissi (d. 1165), al-Gharnati (d. 1170), al-Hamawi (d. 1229), and al-Qazwini (d. 1283). Gabriel Ferrand counted approximately 39 medieval Muslim reports of India and China, most of which are in Arabic (33), 5 in Persian, and 1 in Turkish.

30. A growing number of mostly Western scholars have maintained that the source of the account is anonymous. This argument has been rejected by a majority of scholars, especially those from the Middle East and India, who cite that medieval Muslim historians regarded al-Tajir not only as the person who recorded the account but as its uncontested author.

31. See R. C. Zaehner's classic study *Hindu and Muslim Mysticism* (London: Athlone Press, 1960).

32. In Islamic law, although *al-haydh* (menstruation) is seen as a time of ritual impurity during which women, like men after sexual intercourse, are prohibited from staying in mosques and exempted from some obligatory *ʿibadat* (acts of worship)—such as *salat* (prayer) and *sawm* (fasting)—they are not considered, as many think, *najis* (religiously impure) and thus "untouchable" as in Judaism's ritual of *niddah* (Hebrew for separation). In fact, although being *junub* (ritually impure) during menstruation, Muslim women are permitted to engage in their regular lives, such as cooking, touching food and clothes, and so forth. In addition, they stay in their homes and sleep in their regular beds with their husbands. As for marital sex, physical intimacy is allowed, and the couple has a normal sexual life with the exception of *ilaj* (full penetration of the penis into the vagina).

33. Divorce has been recently introduced into Hindu law, as Ahmad states (77).

34. I am indebted to S. Maqbul Ahmad for this reference.

35. There is a rich body of medieval Arabic literature that deals with Arab Muslim views and perceptions of *al-Sud* (blacks) that is yet to be explored

and investigated. In addition to the brief, but succinct, reference to this rich corpus by Aziz al-Azmeh in *Al-' Arab wa-l-Barabira* (London: Dar al-Rayes, 1991), the most comprehensive study, in my view, came to light quite recently with the publication of Nadir Khadhim's book *Tamthilat al-Akhar: Surat al-Sud fi-l-Mutakhayyal al-'Arabi al-Wasit* (Beirut: Al-Mu'assasa al-'Arabiyya li-l-Dirasat wa-l Nashr, 2007). For a Western study, see G. Rotter's PhD dissertation, *Die Stellung des Negers in der islamisch-arabischen Gesellschaft bis zum XVI: Jahrhundert* (Bonn: Rheinische Friedrich-Wilhelms-Universitat, 1976), and David M. Goldenberg's *The Curse of Ham: Race and Slavery in Early Judaism, Christianity, and Islam* (Princeton, NJ: Princeton University Press, 2003).

36. As Pratt puts it, It is "the space of colonial encounters, the space in which peoples geographically and historically separated come into contact" (6).

2 European Barbarity and Civilization in Some Medieval Arabic Geographical Sources: Al-Mas'udi and al-Bakri as Two Case Studies

1. Some scholars coined the phrase "sacred geography," which principally focused on the determination of the correct orientation toward the sanctuary of the Ka'ba in Mecca, the proper time judged by Islamic law as indispensable for the performance of the mandatory daily *salat* (prayer), the mapping of the routes for the hajj, and so on. For more on this topic, see David A. King, *World-Maps for Finding the Direction and Distance to Mecca: Innovation and Tradition in Islamic Science* (Leiden: Brill, 1999).

2. See Gerald R. Tibbetts, "The Balkhi School of Geographers," in *The History of Cartography: Cartography in the Traditional Islamic and South Asian Societies*, vol. 1, ed. J. B. Harley and David Woodward (Chicago: University of Chicago Press, 1992), 108–136.

3. It is to be noted here that the earth is predominately depicted as a sphere and, suggestively, it is always described as resembling *al-mihha fi-jawf al-baydha*, that is, the yoke in the white of the egg (al-Kilani, *Surat Uruba Inda al-'Arab fi-l-'Asr al-Wasit*, 44).

4. It seems clear, therefore, that classical Greek Ptolemaic ideas in the first instance came to dominate much of the medieval Arab-Islamic *taqsim al-ardh* (division of the world) and *tasnif al-umam* (classification of nations), along with some minor Persian and Hindu influences. Briefly speaking, as shown by Nazmi, some classical Muslim geographers "from the eastern caliphate" (*The Muslim Geographical Image of the World*, 115) were influenced by the Persian *kishwar* system dividing the world "into seven circles of equal size" (143). Few others, however, opted for the Indian system of dividing the world "into three squares (instead of circles) which lead out three by three" and corresponded to different nations and countries (145). For more on non-Greek influences on medieval Islamic views of the world, see Adam J. Silverstein, "The Medieval Islamic Worldview:

Arabic Geography in Its Historical Context," in *Geography, Ethnography, and Perceptions of the World from Antiquity to the Renaissance*, ed. K. Raaflaub and R. Talbert (Oxford: Blackwell Publishers, 2009), 273–290.

5. Some scholars have suggested that the quadripartite division should be attributed to ancient Persian or Mesopotamian precedents. Citing D. M. Dunlop, Nazmi has forcefully argued that "the four-fold division is clearly a division into continents (Europe, Libya, Ethiopia and Scythia), and the source is Greek" (*The Muslim Geographical Image of the World*, 141).

6. For Miquel, perhaps because of ancient influences, even North Africa with the exception of Egypt was included in Europe. However, the lands of the Khazars and other lands around the Volga were considered part of Asia (257).

7. As noted by Nazmi, al-Khwarizmi "was not content with merely translating Ptolemy" but rearranged it "with the addition of other contemporary information and the knowledge acquired by the Arabs" (*Commercial Relations*, 17).

8. For a modern Arabic edition of the translation, see *Tarikh al-ʿAlam: Al-Tarjama al-ʿArabiyya al-Qadima*, ed. Abdurrahmane al-Badawi (Beirut: Al-Muʾassasa al-ʿArabiyya li-l-Dirassat wa-l-Nashr, 1982).

9. Author of *Tabaqat al-Attibbaʾ w-al-Hukamaʾ* (Generations of Physicians and Wise Men) and *Tafsir Asmaiʾ al-Adwiya al-Mufrada min Kitab Dyusquridus* (Explanation of the Names of Medicine Based on the Book of *Dioscorides*).

10. For more on the translation of Orosius into Arabic, see Ann Christys's chapter "The Arabic Translation of Orosius" in her own book *Christians in Al-Andalus, 711–1000* (Richmond, UK: Curzon Press, 2002), 134–157.

11. The original Greek title is *Emegal Mathematike*.

12. Although strongly acknowledging the Greek and Roman influences, Middle Eastern scholars such as Nazmi and al-Kilani tend to equally underline the importance of the direct information gathered by ninth-century captives and merchants such as Muslim al-Jarmi and Harun ibn Yahya, whose remarkable account of Rome will be discussed later.

13. As mentioned by several medieval chronicles such as al-Idrissi and al-Himyari, a group of adventurous young cousins are reported to have sailed from Lisbon into the Atlantic Ocean. They were called *al-fitya al-mugharrarin*, which could be translated as "the young men who were deceived," but in the context of their presumed journey, some scholars tend to translate the term as "those who were driven to take a dangerous adventure." There are also reports of an older adventure seemingly undertaken by a sailor by the name of Khashkhash ibn Saʿid of Cordoba, more commonly known as Khashkhash al-Bahri, that is, the sailor. As mentioned by al-Masʿudi based on Andalusian sources, Khashkhash is said to have crossed the Atlantic Ocean around 889 before embarking on what is described as *ardh majhula*, an unknown land from which he sailed back home with valuable and exotic goods (Nazmi, *The Muslim Geographical*

Image of the World, 209–211). For more on this, see in particular Abbas Hamdani, "An Islamic Background to the Voyages of Discovery," in *The Legacy of Muslim Spain*, ed. Salma Jayyusi and Manuela Marín (Leiden: Brill, 1994), 273–306.

14. As mentioned in several sections of his works, the seven climes fall under planetary influences of al-*nujum al-sab'a* (the Seven Stars). In other words, he believed that the first climate was under the influence of Saturn, the second under Jupiter, the third under Mars, the fourth under the sun, the fifth under Venus, the sixth under Mercury, and the seventh under the moon.

15. From the Greek *klimata*.

16. As shown by Tarif Khalidi, this region was also called *iqlim babil* (the region of Babylon) and was described as enjoying "the most moderate of climates, the purest water and air, the most fertile land. In consequence, it is the historical home of the most virtuous, the wisest and the most temperate of men" (*Islamic Historiography: The Histories of al-Mas'udi*, 72).

17. Scholars believe that the Arabic phrase *surrat al-ardh* is adopted from the Greek geo-cosmographical notion of the *omphalos* of the earth. It is interesting that Jews, Christians, and Muslims alike, as noted by Adam J. Silverstein, "adopted the notion and adapted it to their religious worldview" ("The Medieval Islamic Worldview: Arabic Geography in Its Historical Context," 280). Of course, in the case of al-Mas'udi and most Iraqi scholars, the notion was adapted rather to their nationalistic worldview!

18. This highly political cosmo-geographical view was not popular among non-Abbasid scholars, many of whom found no reason to favor Baghdad over Mecca. In fact, it was common to find Mecca-centered *mappae mundi*, especially among the cosmo-geographers of the Balkhi school.

19. The same is true of John Wolff, *Religion in History: Conflict, Conversion and Coexistence* (Manchester: Manchester University Press, 2004), 57.

20. By al-Mas'udi's own account, the sections on non-Muslim nations and civilizations in his two works are only brief summaries of more detailed descriptions he wrote in his older, unfortunately nonextant magnum opus, *Akhabr al-Zaman* (News of the Time).

21. This is true also of his less common fourfold division of the world and his references to *al-rub' al-shamali*, which means the northern quadrant (Europe).

22. In light of this passage, it is unlikely that Sa'id al-Andalusi of Toledo (d. 1070) based his *Kitab Tabaqat al-Umam* (The Book of the Categories of Nations) on al-Mas'udi's *Al-Tanbih*, as a number of scholars have asserted. Centuries before Ernest Renan's controversial Sorbonne lecture *L'Islam et la Science*, in which he argued that Muslims are incapable of producing science, Sa'id al-Andalusi had already taken the opposite controversial view. His main thesis was that nations of the world are to be divided into two classes in accordance with their interest in and production of al-'*ilm* (science). Although he casts the ancient Greeks among

the first group, not interested in science, he paradoxically includes all remaining European nations, among them the Franks and the Slavs, within the second category. For an English translation of this interesting book, see *Science in the Medieval World: Book of the Categories of Nations*, ed. Semaan I. Salem and Alok Kumar (Austin: University of Texas Press, 1996).

23. In addition to Ptolemy Marinus, al-Mas'udi also cites Hippocrates, Herodotus, Hermes, Pliny, and Gales.

24. For Greco-Roman views of the north, see Irmeli Valtonen's informative chapter "The North in Ancient and Early Medieval Geography," in *The North in the "Old English Orosius": A Geographical Narrative in Context* (Helsinki: Societe Neophilologique, 2008), 42–83.

25. It is to be noted here that, mainly in the Andalusian context, the word *saqlab* was also used to designate "the foreign elements of European races that composed the backbone of the Muslim army in Spain for a certain period" (Nazmi, *Commercial Relations*, 77).

26. In apparent conformity to the orthodox Muslim position concerning what is known in Muslim law as Judeo–Christian narratives.

27. There is heated debate among scholars regarding the king's historical identity and the location of his kingdom. See Ahmad Nazmi, "The King of Ad-Dīr in Al-Mas'udi's *Murug ad-dahab*," *Studia Arabistyczne i Islamistyczne* 2 (1994): 5–11.

28. See, for example, Pierre Riché, *The Carolingians: A Family Who Forged Europe* (Philadelphia: University of Pennsylvania Press, 1993).

29. One can cite Tawfiq al-Hakim's *'Usfur min al-Sharq* (Bird from the East) and Suhayl Idriss's *Al-Hayy al-Latini* (The Latin Quarter). For a comprehensive study of these two novels and others, see Rasheed el-Enany's *Arab Representations of the Occident: East-West Encounters in Arabic Fiction* (London: Routledge, 2006).

30. See Nazik Saba Yared's *Arab Travellers and Western Civilization* (London: Saqi Books, 1996).

31. I am indebted to Roxanne L. Euben for this quoted passage (*Journeys to the Other Shore*, 101).

32. In addition to the rebellion of the Indians known as the uprising of the Zutt (820–835) and the Qaramatian movement (Abdullah, *A Short History of Iraq*, 22–23), there was mainly *thawrat al-zinj*, that is the rebellion of African slaves (868–883), which the young al-Mas'udi must have witnessed or at least heard about. This uprising started in the salt marshes in the southern city of Basra mostly by a group of angry African slaves under the leadership of 'Ali ibn Muhammad. After numerous confrontations in Basra and other southern towns, the angry protesters attacked Baghdad and were close to taking over the caliphal seat. This situation changed dramatically, however, when the caliph al-Muwaffaq and his loyal forces succeeded in killing 'Ali bin Muhammad and crushing the rebels in 883 (23).

33. It must be said here that namely in *Al-Tanbih*, al-Mas'udi devoted several lengthy sections to the history of *al-rum*, both Romans and Byzantines, the full exploration of which goes beyond the scope of this section. But as we shall see in the following chapters especially with al-Bakri and mainly Harun ibn Yaya, on numerous occasions, al-Mas'udi speaks with awe of the majesty that *rumiyya* or *ruma* (Rome) had, particularly before the decision of Constantine the Great to move his imperial seat to its eastern archrival (Constantinople). Briefly stated, he focuses rather on Rome as the unmatched capital of the *nasara* (Christians), and he stresses the fact that the Rome of his time owes much of its fame to the fact that it is the seat of *al-baba* (the pope), perhaps more widely known in early medieval Arabic sources as *sahib rumiyya*, the Master of Rome.

34. Although in some editions it is quite confusingly referred to as *yast*.

35. The invasion of Sicily started in 827 AD, but the conquest of the island was not completed before 878.

36. Al-Mas'udi is among the earliest Muslim authors to refer "in passing," to use Shboul's phrase, to medieval Britain. While speaking about the Atlantic Ocean, he briefly states that to the north of this large ocean lie a number of *juzur* (islands) that make up *britaniya* (Shboul, *Al-Mas'udi and His World*, 193).

37. It is to be noted here that after the end of their dynasty in Damascus at the hands of the Abbasids in 750, the Umayyad and their supporters were the targets of cruel persecutions. Abdurrahmane I, one of the surviving Umayyad princes, succeeded in escaping to al-Andalus, where he established a new dynasty in the name of the Umayyad. In 756, Abdurrahmane I declared himself the emir of Cordoba and ruled it until his death in 788. The Umayyad caliphate of Cordoba, known also as the emirate of Cordoba, came to an end in 1031 after nearly three centuries of power and prosperity considered by many as the golden age of Muslim Spain.

38. See N. Levtzion and J. F. Hopkins, *Corpus of Early Arabic Sources for West African History* (Cambridge: Cambridge University Press, 1981), and N. Levtzion and Jay Spaulding, *Medieval West Africa: Views from Arab Scholars and Merchants* (Princeton, NJ: Markus Wiener, 2003).

39. Translated in French as *Description de l'Afrique Septentrionale* by the French Arabist De Slane in 1857.

40. As explained by Charles Ebel, the Spanish scholar A. Garcia Belido once argued in his classic *La Peninsula Iberica* (1953) that the word *Hispania* could be of a Phoenician origin since, according to him, it may be derived from a Phoenician root (*Transalpine Gaul*, 48). Belido's view is strongly echoed by Crow, who asserts that "when the Carthaginians came around 300 BC, they called the country Hispania (from *sphan*, rabbit)" (*Spain: The Root and the Flower*, 7).

41. See, for example, Sir William Smith's magisterial *A New Classical Dictionary of Greek and Roman Biography, Mythology* (New York: Harper and Brothers, 1860), 376; Adrian Room's *Placenames of the World* (Jefferson, NC: McFarland, 2005), 172; Gary W. McDonogh's *Iberian*

Worlds (London: Routledge, 2009), 84; and Carl Waldman and Catherine Mason's *Encyclopedia of European Peoples, Vol. 1* (New York: Infobase Publishing, 2006), 400.

42. Like most medieval Andalusian geographers, al-Bakri mentions that al-Andalus *muthallath al-shakl* is designed in the form of a triangle (65). He also devotes numerous passages to describing and cataloging what he calls the renowned Elvira, Nevada, Pyrenees, Almaden, and Alpes mountains of al-Andalus (84–85).

43. Currently known as St. Nazarius's Basilica.

44. Of course, this is prior to the expulsion of all Jews from Catalonia in 1391.

45. Victor II was the pope from 1055 to 1057.

46. This particular statement is somewhat unconvincing, to say the least. Through his anecdote regarding Barcelona, al-Bakri is definitely exposing the corruption of the priests, rather than highlighting their triumph.

47. In reference to Aden, the coast city in modern Yemen.

48. In some Maghribi communities of Andalusian descent, there is a dominant feeling of Andalusian superiority to this day in regard to their co-citizens and coreligionists of Eastern Arab and Berber descent. Although not as strong as it once was, this mentality is still manifested in the refusal of intermarriages with indigenous Maghribi men and women with whom they have been living since their expulsion from Spain in the early fifteenth century.

49. Other names include Ibn Shuhayd (d. 1043), namely in some sections of his intriguing treatise on poetic genius, *Risalat al-Tawābi‘ wal-Zawābi‘* ("The Treatise of Familiar Spirits and Demons"); Ibn al-Khaqan (d. 1134) in his *Mathmah al-Anfus wa Masrah at Ta'annus fi Mulah Ahl al-Andalus* ("The Aspiration of the Souls and the Theater of Congeniality in the Anecdotes of the People of al-Andalus"); Sa‘id al-Andalusi, who incorporated a separate chapter on the virtues of al-Andalus in his previously mentioned *Tabaqat al-Umam*; and the noted physician and historian Ibn al-Khatib (d. 1375), who composed a epistle in which he argued for the superiority of al-Andalus over North Africa.

50. Translated by Roberto Marín-Guzmán based on Joaquín Vallvé's excellent Spanish rendition of the Arabic in his *La División Territorial de la España Musulmana* (Madrid: Consejo Superior de Investigaciones Científicas, 1986), 169.

51. Religiously speaking, there is near unanimity that no other scholar from the Muslim West had articulated this anti-Mashriqi rhetoric as radically as did Ibn Jubayr, namely when he said, "Let it be absolutely certain and beyond doubt established that there is no Islam save in the Maghrib lands. There they follow the clear path that has no separation and the like, such as there are in these eastern lands of sects and heretical groups and schisms, save those of them whom Great and Glorious God has preserved from this" (*The Travels of Ibn Jubayr*, 73).

52. Ibn Bassam's promotion of an independent Andalusian canon perhaps parallels American and Canadian moves earlier in their respective

histories to set themselves apart from their cultural and literary tradi-
tions of England. See Sarah M. Corse, *Nationalism and Literature: The
Politics of Culture in Canada and the United States* (Cambridge: Cambridge
University Press, 1997).

53. This is in addition to his incorporation of Ibrahim ibn Ya'qub's reports on
the Galicians.

54. There is no question that Orosius must be the basic source of al-Bakri,
especially given that Orosius was a native of Galicia, possibly Braga.

55. These same Galicians would engage in a long struggle for revenge upon
Muslims. It was primarily the Galicians who would reconquer many
northwestern territories and regain most of modern Portugal by 1200.

56. See the previously discussed account of al-Mas'udi.

57. Although originally a literary movement, this phenomenon exemplifies in
essence the sociocultural and political tensions between Persians, the orig-
inators of the movement, and Arabs. Initially the movement was known as
Ahl al-Taswiya, that is, "The People of Equality," some Persian authors and
scholars began it to ascertain the Islamically approved equality between
all Muslims, Arabs and non-Arabs alike. During the Abbasid dynasty,
which witnessed a surge in the power and influence of the Persians at
the expense of the Arabs, it became an overtly anti-Arab campaign.
"In more daring formulations," Persian authors and scholars, to quote Ignác
Goldziher, "attempted even to assert Arab inferiority in face of Persian
superiority" (*Muslim Studies*, 173). Various texts were written to stress the
alleged supremacy of the Persians, to glorify their pre-Islamic heritage of
Persia, and eventually to deride the Arabs and devalue their achievements.
These Shu'bi scholars, to quote Mohsen Zakeri's *Sasanid Soldiers in Early
Muslim Society: The Origins of 'Ayyaran and Futuwwa* (1995), "pointed with
pride to the magnificence of Iran at the time when the Arabs were no
more than Bedouins" (249). Later, Shu'ubism incorporated a whole range
of tensions between Arabs and Muslims of non-Arabs descent, gradually spreading to the Muslim West, that is, North Africa and al-Andalus.
Indeed, in the Andalusian context, the focus of this section, it manifested
itself in the tensions between Andalusians of Arab origins and those with
mainly Berber and European background. Significantly enough, it was
an Andalusian Muslim of European origins, Ibn Gharsiyya al-Bashqunsi
(the Basque), more commonly known as Ibn Garcia (d. 1084), who
authored the best-known Shu'bi work originating from Andalusia. This
book, or rather epistle, led to several responses from Arab scholars who
did their best to refute Ibn Garcia. See in particular James T. Monroe's
The Shu'ubiyya in al-Andalus: The Risala of Ibn Garcia and Five Refutations
(Berkeley: University of California Press, 1970), and Göran Larsson's
*Ibn Garcia's Shu'ubiyya Letter: Ethnic and Theological Tensions in Medieval
al-Andalus* (Leiden: Brill, 2003).

58. See my article "King Arthur in the Lands of the Saracens," *Nebula: Journal
of Multidisciplinary Scholarship* 4 (2007): 131–144.

59. After the conquest of Sicily by the Arabs in 827, a number of Muslim soldiers attacked Rome. After this assault, Pope Leo IV ordered the construction of the famous "Leonine" walls, named in reference to the high and robust nature of these protective walls that surrounded the Vatican; today only remains are still visible.

60. In the interest of space, I have chosen not to discuss al-Bakri's accounts of several European islands, namely, Cyprus, Malta, Crete, and Sicily. Regarding the last, al-Bakri wrote a very long and detailed section about the Muslim conquest of Sicily and its Reconquista.

3 Writing the North: Europe and Europeans in Medieval Arabic Travel Literature

1. Herbert Bloch, for example, in his article "The New Fascination with Ancient Rome," argues that Benedict was chosen by Guido of Citta di Castello, the Cardinal priest of San Marco, to write a detailed account of the route of the royal processions. After finishing this project, known as the *Ordo Romanus* and later incorporated in the *Liber Politicus*, Benedict was inspired to write the *Mirabilia Urbis Romæ* around 1143. Perhaps it is interesting to remember that Ibn Khordadbeh was himself commissioned to write *Kitab al-Masalik wa-l-Mamalik*, which included the section on Rome.

2. See Francis Morgan Nichols and Eileen Gardiner, eds., *The Marvels of Rome: Mirabilia Urbis Romae*, (New York: Ithaca Press, 1986).

3. As demonstrated by Dale Kinney in "Fact and Fiction in the *Mirabilia Urbis Romae*," the numbers mentioned by Benedict in *Mirabilia Urbis Romæ*, albeit less exaggerated, are no less dazzling (235).

4. Whereas De Goeje had in mind Ostia Tiberis, André Miquel spoke of Fitulatus.

5. Indeed, Ibn al-Faqih (d. 902) speaks of a Rome that has one hundred thousand markets, six hundred thousand public baths, twenty-four thousand churches, one hundred thousand bells, and so forth.

6. In his very brief reference to Harun ibn Yahya and without any single explanation or reference, Newman opted to suggest that Harun ibn Yahya's account of Rome is "merely a variation of Constantinople" (201).

7. Not familiar with his father's name (i.e., Ali), some western Arabists have postulated that Harun ibn Yahya may have been a Christian Arab. That is why, according to them, he was, first of all, easily freed by his Byzantine captors and, second of all, able to travel voluntarily as far as Rome. Certainly, these scholars have come to their erroneous conclusions based on the essentialist view that medieval and early modern Muslims, contrary to Europeans, were never curious to know about non-Muslim cultures that flourished outside *dar al-islam* in general and those of Europeans in particular.

8. Harun ibn Yahya was also mentioned by Arturo Graf in his classic *Roma nella memoria e nelle immaginazioni del Medio Evo*, published in Turin in 1882.

9. For an English translation of Yahya's description of Constantinople, see, for example, A. Vasiliev, "Harun ibn Yahya and his Description of Constantinople," *Seminarum Kondakovum* 5 (1932): 149–163. For a more recent summary and discussion, see Nadia Maria el-Cheikh's third chapter, "Islam on the Defensive: Constantinople: The City of Marvels," in her *Byzantium Viewed by the Arabs* (Cambridge, MA: Harvard University Press, 2004), 142–150.

10. In 846 it is reported that a Muslim fleet arrived at the mouth of the Tiber and reached Rome. Some Western sources report that Muslim soldiers sacked the basilica of St. Peter and fled with the gold and silver it contained. Some historians have asserted that after this assault, Pope Leo IV ordered the construction of the famous Leonine walls to surround the Vatican.

11. As we saw earlier with al-Tajir, al-Mas'udi, and al-Bakri and soon with Ibn Fadlan and others.

12. It is said that Benjamin of Tudela left his hometown, Tudela, in northern Spain in 1159 to travel for 14 years. His accounts of Rome, Constantinople, Jerusalem, and Baghdad are of valuable importance. For more on this traveler, see Uri Shulevitz, *The Travels of Benjamin of Tudela: Through Three Continents in the Twelfth Century* (New York: Farrar, Straus, and Giroux, 2005).

13. It must be borne in mind that the word *fitna* (plural *fitan*) is highly polyvalent. It is most commonly used in the context of gender relations, to designate sexual temptation that could lead to unlawful affairs between unmarried men and women or even men and men. In the sociopolitical context, however, it refers to sociopolitical unrest with violent rebellions against lawful rulers, which would be the most extreme manifestation. In its pure religious context, the word *fitan* describes the trials and afflictions that a Muslim faithful must face and overcome to preserve one's faith.

14. In classical Muslim jurisprudence, shaving the beard for a man is not only interpreted as *taghyir li-khalq Allah* (changing God's creation), *tashabbuh bi-l-nisa'* (imitating women), *tashabbuh bi-l-Majus* (imitating Zoroastrians), and *naqdh li-l- muru'a* (opposing sociocultural decorum). It can also be seen as proof of a Muslim's disinterest in *ittiba'* (imitation) and *hubb* (love) of the Prophet. One should mention that shaving the beard was equally unacceptable to non-Muslim Arabs.

15. See J. W. Wright and Everett K. Rowson, eds., *Homoeroticism in Classical Arabic Literature* (New York: Columbia University Press, 1997).

16. By most accounts, one may understand why Rome is more important than Constantinople in the medieval Arabic-Islamic *imaginaire*, contrary to Nadia Maria el-Cheikh's assertion in *Byzantium Viewed by the*

Arabs. In short, in Muslim apocalyptic literature, the Muslim conquest of Constantinople is seen as one of the minor signs of the end of the world.

17. See Barbara Freyer Stowasser, "The End is Near: Minor and Major Signs of the Hour in Islamic Texts and Contexts," in *Apocalypse and Violence*, ed. A. Amanat and J. Collins (New Haven, CT: Yale University Press, 2004), 45–67.

18. Although a comprehensive analysis of medieval Western views of Islam and Muslims is beyond the scope of the present chapter, it should be noted that since the appearance of the pioneering work of Norman Daniel in *Islam and the West: The Making of an Image* (1960) and Richard Southern's *Western Views of Islam in the Middle Ages* (1962), numerous scholars from different backgrounds and interests have convincingly argued that medieval Europe was in many ways haunted by the specter of the Saracens (Muslims). For more on this subject, see John V. Tolan's *Saracens: Islam in the Medieval European Imagination* (New York: Columbia University Press, 2002) and Suzanne Conklin Akbari's *Idols in the East: European Representations of Islam and the Orient, 1100–1450* (Ithaca, NY: Cornell University Press, 2009).

19. For more details on the discovery, history, and Western interest in the manuscript, see James E. McKeithen's introduction in "The *Risala* of Ibn Fadlan: An Annotated Translation with Introduction" (unpublished diss., Indiana University, 1979).

20. The original title of the book is *Kitab Ibn Fadlan Ibn Rashid Ibn Hammad Mawla Muhammad Ibn Sulayman Rasul al-Muqtadir ila Malik al-Saqaliba.*

21. As historians of religions mention, phallus worship (phallism) is an ancient rite that was practiced (mainly) in ancient India, Egypt, and Greece. It is still practiced by a number of Hindu sects among other modern pagan cults. See, for example, Hodder W. Westropp et al., *Ancient Symbol Worship: Influence of the Phallic Idea in the Religions of Antiquity* (New Delhi: Kumar Bros., 1970).

22. See Norman Calder, "Friday Prayer and the Juristic Theory of Government: Sarakhsi, Shirazi, Mawardi," *Bulletin of the School of Oriental and African Studies* 49 (1986): 35–47.

23. There are a number of hadith on this subject, for example the hadith reported by al Bukhari: "Your slaves are your brothers and Allah has put them under your command. So whoever has a brother under his command should feed him of what he eats and dress him of what he wears. Do not ask them [slaves] to do things beyond their capacity [power] and if you do so, then help them" (Al Bukhari, *Summarized Sahih Al Bukhari*, 67).

24. Known in academic circles as the Normanist (Pro-Viking)/Anti-Normanist (Pro-Slav) debate. As demonstrated by Montgomery, "The Rus have now been the subject of heated debate for more than one and a half centuries, though in later years the balance has swung in favour of the Normanists" ("Ibn Fadlan and the Rusiyyah," 1).

25. "We were with the Messenger of Allah when he asked, 'Tell me about a tree that resembles the believer, the leaves of which do not fall in the summer nor the winter, and it yields its fruit at all times by the leave of its Lord.' I thought of the date palm tree, but felt shy to answer when I saw that Abu Bakr and 'Umar did not speak. And when they did not give an answer, the Messenger of Allah said, 'It is the date palm tree'" (Bukhari, 2001).

26. See I. Farooqi, *Plants of the Quran* (Lucknow, India: Sidrah Publishers, 2003).

27. "The wicked among the people in the sight of God on the Day of Judgement is the man who goes to his wife and she comes to him, and then he divulges her secret" (Ibn al-Hajjaj, *Sahih Muslim*, 369).

28. According to James E. Montgomery, the Vikings were particularly known for their "lack of proper burial for slaves and social inferiors" ("Ibn Fadlan and the Rusiyyah," 11).

29. From the city of Jaen in modern-day Andalucia, Spain.

30. His summary of the history of al-Andalus is contained in a long (epic) poem of remarkable poetic genius.

31. As noted by Pons-Sanz, the sacking of Seville by the Vikings was also recorded by non-Muslim Spanish chroniclers. "The Chronicon Rotensis, one of the earliest chronicles of the kingdom of Asturias (c.883) (Ruiz de la Peña 1985, 38.41)," she tells us, "explains that in the year 844 *nordomanorum gens antea nobis incognita, gens pagana et nimis crudelissima, nabali [sic] exercitu nostris peruenerunt in partibus*" ("Whom Did Al-Ghazal Meet?" 5).

32. It is to be noted that some Arabists have expressed their skepticism in regard to the historical reality of al-Ghazal's journey. This skepticism was triggered and advocated by the prominent French Arabist Lévi-Provençal, who argued in *L'Espagne musulmane au Xieme Siècle, institutions et vie sociale* (1932) that al-Ghazal took part only in an embassy to Constantinople speculating that his presumed journey to the land of the *Majus* (Vikings) was nothing but "une contamination postérieure du voyage officiel d' al-Ghazal à Constantinople" (253). Quite recently, Sara M. Pons-Sanz has inclined toward Levi-Provençal's position. As I explained elsewhere, and briefly stated, if many erudite Arabists such as Fabricius (d. 1902), Jacob (d. 1937), Kratschkovsky (d. 1951), and Vasiliev (d. 1953) disregarded Lévi-Provençal's theory as utterly "hypercritical" (66–67), Pons-Sanz's is equally so, if not more. Indeed, with all due respect, it is my conviction that the six "new" arguments she proposed to support Lévi-Provençal's views are not convincing in themselves and are not even as challenging as Lévi-Provençal's. Be that as it may, one can be fully confident that al-Ghazal's embassy to the Vikings was not a literary fabrication of the thirteenth-century chronicler and poet Ibn Dihya, "even if it is accepted that there is confusion or exaggeration in some aspects of Ibn Dihya's account, which need not necessarily be so" (al-Hajji, *Andalusian Diplomatic Relations with Western Europe during the Umayyad Period*, 201).

Ibn Dihya would have certainly gained more literary credit had he claimed the account—and especially the exquisite poems it contained—rather than attributing it to al-Ghazal. In passing, it may be noted that much of this skepticism is related to a Eurocentric mentality that is related to the views discussed in the introduction. For my detailed response to Pons-Sanz's theory, see "The Moor's First Sight: An Arab Poet in a Ninth-Century Viking Court," in *Journeys to the West: The Occident as Other in Narratives of Travel*, ed. Anne R. Richards and Iraj Omidvar (Syracuse, NY: Syracuse University Press, forthcoming 2012).

33. *Algarve* is a distortion of the Arabic word *al-gharb*, that is to say, "the West."

34. The Arabs especially during the pre-Islamic era were not at ease with sailing in the sea. That is why, especially in Pre-Islamic poetry, the sea was not widely referred to and the few poets who alluded to it employed it as a metaphor of fear, uncertainty, separation, and sorrow. Despite the numerous Quranic injunctions to take to the sea, in several aspects, the pre-Islamic fear of the sea did not vanish in classical Arabic literature. Perhaps the most suggestive example of this leitmotif is the following lines by the Arab-Sicilian poet Abu al-ʿArab (d. 1113):

    To the Rum, the sea does belong!
    In it, ships sail only riskily.
    As for the land, it is in Arabian hand! (Abbas,
        Al-ʿArab fi Siqiliyya, 314; translation mine)

35. Some scholars have argued that Daniel Defoe modeled *Robinson Crusoe* (1719) on *Hayy ibn Yaqdan* by the twelfth-century Andalusian writer Ibn Tufayl. Set on an isolated island in the Indian Ocean, the story narrates the material survival and spiritual quest of the solitary protagonist Hayy (Alive). These scholars have postulated that Defoe might have been familiar with Ibn Tufayl's story of survival, citing the fact that before Defoe wrote his novel, *Hayy ibn Yaqdan* was popular in England especially after the appearance of three translations into English: 1674 by G. Keith, 1686 by G. Ashwell, and 1708 by Simon Ockley. For more on this issue, see Samar Attar, *The Vital Roots of European Enlightenment: Ibn Tufayl's Influence on Modern Western Thought* (Lanham, MD: Lexington Books, 2007), G. A. Russell's *The Arabic Interest of the Natural Philosophers in Seventeenth-Century England* (Leiden: Brill, 1994), and in particular Nawal Muhammad Hassan, *Hayy bin Yaqzan and Robinson Crusoe: A Study of an Early Arabic Impact on English Literature* (Baghdad: al Rashid House, 1980).

36. Since (as mentioned earlier) incestuous marriages were akin to that of the Zoroastrians, some may wonder whether al-Ghazal, or perhaps his editor, is trying to relate *al-majus* (Vikings) to the Zoroastrians.

37. As mentioned earlier, other scholars have suggested that al-Ghazal met King Turgeis in Ireland. A few opted even for Norway and Iceland.

38. According to Pons-Sanz, "The identification of the destination of the embassy with Denmark has also been suggested by Vasiliev (1946, 44–45) and Wikander (1978, 15–17), according to whom the embassy could also

have been sent to Norway, Jesch (1991, 93), Kendrick (1968, 202) and Smyth (1977, 162–63)" (6).

39. Most pertinent is the current debate in some parts of Canada concerning *L'accommodement raisonnable*, which concerns the rights, mainly religious, of minorities in relation to the dominant culture and how far this culture can concede in order to accommodate or not those rights.

40. Names of the most-famous female lovers in Arabic culture and literature. Their lovers, 'Antara, Kuthayyir, and Qays, were all poets of great stature and tragic character *à la* Othello.

41. This is the anecdote as translated by Philip K. Hitti:

I once opened a bath in al-Ma'arrah in order to earn my living. To this bath there came a Frankish knight. The Franks disapprove of girding a cover around one's waist while in the bath. So this Frank stretched out his arm and pulled off my cover from my waist and threw it away. He looked and saw that I had recently shaved off my pubes. So he shouted, "Salim!" As I drew near him he stretched his hand over my pubes and said, "Salim, good! By the truth of my religion, do the same for me." Saying this, he lay on his back and I found that in that place the hair was like his beard. So I shaved it off. Then he passed his hand over the place and, finding it smooth, he said, "Salim, by the truth of my religion, do the same to madame" (which in their language means the lady), referring to his wife. He then said to a servant of his, "Tell madame to come here." Accordingly the servant went and brought her and made her enter the bath. She also lay on her back. The knight repeated, "Do what thou has done to me." So I shaved all that hair while her husband was sitting looking at me. At last he thanked me and handed me the pay for my service. (165–166)

42. Contrary to some prevailing Western prejudices, "honor killing" is a cultural phenomenon that has been on the rise in many Middle Eastern countries. Some of these killings are common mainly in rural and tribal regions with both Muslim and Christian populations. This is despite the fact that Muslim jurisprudents have always condemned honor killing as un-Islamic.

43. Here I am referring to, and using creatively, Daniel J. Vitkus's article "Early Modern Orientalism," in *Western Views of Islam in Medieval and Early Modern Europe*, ed. David R. Blanks and Michael Frassetto (New York: St. Martins, 1999). Vitkus differentiates between the "learned" and the "popular" accounts of Islam. Referring to the works of Norman Daniel and Montgomery Watt, Vitkus contends that since the Middle Ages, Islam has been the target of two different, but ideologically complementary, patterns of Orientalism: "popular" and "learned." The first is largely found in the romances that recount the heroic deeds of Christian knights and crusaders. The second is contained in the extensive study of Islam done by many Western theologians and writers, who, despite their "learning," have established "an entire tradition of polemical misrepresentation" that distorted Islam and depicted it "as heresy or fraud, and Muhammad as an impostor" (208).

44. That is, from the town of Tortosa in Catalonia (Cataluña) near present-day Barcelona, Spain.

45. Some excerpts were also incorporated by later geographers such as al-Qazwini, Ibn Dihya, Ibn Saiʿd al-Gharnati, and al-Dimashqi.

46. Based on the fragments of al-ʿUdri's version of Ibn Yaʿqub's account, some scholars argued that he met Pope John XII.

47. He is said to have met the German emperor Otto I in the town of Magdeburg. Some scholars have argued that Ibn Yaʿqub's visit to Otto I could be related to the latter's embassy to Cordova in 953.

48. It is to be noted that alternative itineraries have been suggested.

49. See André Miquel, "L'Europe occidentale dans la relation arabe d'Ibrahim b. Yaʿqub (Xe siècle)," *Annales: Economies, sociétés, civilisations* 21 (1966): 1048–1064.

50. Other scholars such as Lutz Richter-Bernburg have cited "Muslim rather than Jewish sensibilities" reflected in his account ("Ibrāhīm ibn Yaʿqūb," 402).

51. Some scholars such as Lewis have suggested that Ibn Yaʿqub was the original source of the interesting passage on medieval Irish whaling as reported mainly by Persian al-Qazwini (d. 1203) and quoted frequently in later medieval Muslim books of wonders. In short, the passage recounts how the Irish whalers would clap their hands and shout in order to attract younger whales away from their bigger mothers before jumping on their backs and hammering in their harpoons. This would lead to the agitation and anger of the mothers, but since they cannot withstand its strong smell, the whalers would use garlic to drive them away (Lewis, *The Muslim Discovery*, 147). For more on this account, see, for example, D. M. Dunlop, "The British Isles According to Medieval Arabic Authors," *Islamic Quarterly* 4 (1957): 11–28; and D. James, "Two Medieval Arabic Accounts of Ireland," *Journal of the Royal Society of Antiquaries of Ireland* 108 (1978): 5–9. As for an English translation of the passage based on al-Qazwini's report, see Lewis, *The Muslim Discovery of Europe*, 146–147.

52. As with Ibn Fadlan, and given the outstanding quality and availability of Rapoport's translation, I have opted to use his rather than mine.

53. This theory was most firmly espoused by German philosophers such as Johann Gottlieb Fichte and Wilhelm von Humboldt.

54. "Narrated by Jabir: My father died and left seven or nine girls and I married a matron. Allah's Apostle said to me, 'O Jabir! Have you married?' I said, 'Yes.' He said, 'A virgin or a matron?' I replied, 'A matron.' He said, 'Why not a virgin, so that you might play with her and she with you, and you might amuse her and she amuse you.' I said, 'Abdullah (my father) died and left girls, and I dislike to marry a girl like them, so I married a lady (matron) so that she may look after them.' On that he said, 'May Allah bless you,' or 'That is good'" (Al-Bukhari, *Summarized Sahih Al Bukhari*, 470).

55. See Emilia Horvathova, *Cigani na Slovensku* (Bratislava, Slovakia: Vytadel stvo Slovenskej Akademie Vied, 1964), and Eva Davidova, "The Gypsies in Czechoslovakia: Main Characteristics and Brief Historical

Development," trans. D. E. Guy, *Journal of the Gypsy Lore Society* 69 (July–October 1970): 84–97.

56. It should be stated that through the course of the centuries, its locations have changed dramatically, reflecting perhaps the constant change in interest in different unknown and distant lands (al-Azmeh, "Mortal Enemies, Invisible Neighbors," 202). Always citing Ibn Yaʿqub, al-Idrisi (d. 1150) located the Amazons on an island in the Atlantic. Al-Qazwini (d. 1203) claimed in *Athar al-Bilad* that the Amazons lived in the Mediterranean Sea, but in his book on marvels entitled *ʿAjaʾib al-Makhluqat*, he had them living on an island in China (al-Hajji, *Andalusian Diplomatic Relations*, 170).

57. This is in addition to the *mirabilia* of the miraculous olive tree that celebrates Christmas mentioned by the pope during his presumed meeting with Ibn Yaʿqub.

58. Some suggest the Persian word *hamazan*, that is to say warrior, as the origin of the Greek word.

59. In light of what was said earlier regarding the familiarity of Andalusian chroniclers with Orosius and in the absence of any research in this regard, one can surmise that the name Orisius is a more likely direct source of al-Bakri. This makes sense if we remember that Orisius is always cited among the later Roman chroniclers who spoke of the Amazons as a historical fact based on the accounts of previous Roman historians, such as Pliny and Justin.

60. "The islands called fortunate by the Greeks, which means in their language 'the happy one,' are situated near Tanga [Morocco]. They are called this because their trees and shrubs produce all sorts of delicious fruits having been planted or cultivated, and their ground bears corn instead of grass and different sorts of aromatic plants instead of thorns" (Nazmi, *The Muslim Geographical Image*, 257).

61. Literally, "A Succinct Account Regarding Some Marvels of the West." Jean-Charles Ducène translated it as "Exposition claire sur les merveilles de l'Occident." Aside from early interest in his text by several leading Arabists such as Krachkovsky, Fraehen, and Jacob, *Al-Mutrib* has never competed with other occidental *rahhala* such as those of Ibn Jubayr and Ibn Battuta. Nevertheless, as early as 1925, the French Arabist Gabriel Ferrand edited and published the first modern Arabic edition. In 1953, the Spanish Arabist Cesar E. Dubler published an edition in Spanish translation of the Eurasian account under the title *Abu Ḥamid el granadino y su relación de Viaje por tierras euroasiáticas.* Then in 2003, the most complete and comprehensive Arabic edition was published by Qasim Wahb in the United Arab Emirates under the title *Rihlat al-Gharnati.* Recently, Jean-Charles Ducène produced the first full French translation of the *rihla: De Grenade à Bagdad: la relation de voyage d'Abû Hâmid al-Gharnâti* (2006).

62. Most of these studies have been done by a plethora of noted Russian and Czech scholars, namely O. G. Bolshakov and A. L. Mongayt in Russian and I. Hrbek in Czech.

63. As demonstrated by several scholars such as Dubler, al-Hajji, and Hmeida, al-Gharnati most likely meant the Siberian tribes of the Ogor, the Woguls, and the Yorak, who lived north of the Volga River.

64. See also J. Dresbeck LeRoy, "The Ski: Its History and Historiography," *Technology and Culture* 8, no. 4 (1967): 467–479.

65. I am using the modern words *Ukraine* and *Ukrainians* while acknowledging that some would debate the accuracy of this usage since they may posit there was no such country or people in the twelfth century.

66. See Russell Zguta, "The Ordeal by Water (Swimming of Witches) in the East Slavic World," *Slavic Review* 36 (1977): 220–230.

67. Some exceptions exist, namely Wolfgang Behringer, who has, albeit briefly, referred to al-Gharnati's testimony in his exploration of periodic witch hunts in medieval Russia. See Wolfgang Behringer, *Witches and Witch-Hunts: A Global History* (Cambridge, UK: Polity Press, 2004), 56.

68. As he mentioned in his account, he reached Hungary in 545 AH (1150 AD).

69. In reference to Alexander Pope's famous line "For fools rush in where angels fear to tread" in "An Essay on Criticism," (1711), which almost 200 years later inspired the title of E. M. Forster's novel *Where Angels Fear to Tread* (1905).

70. For a classic study of Arabic-Islamic naming of medieval Hungarians (Magyars), see T. Lewicki, "Madjar, Madjaristan," *Encyclopaedia of Islam*, vol. 2 (Leiden: Brill, 1984), 1010–1022.

71. As mentioned earlier, the word *saqlab* (plural *saqaliba* or *saqalib*) in the Andalusian context "denoted in general white slaves of European origins, who served in the Muslim army and at the court of Qurtuba (Cordova)" (Nazmi, *Commercial Relations*, 77). As Nazmi explained, Andalusian Arabs adopted "the lexical form of the world 'sclavi' from the Latin world" to refer "to the foreign elements of European races that composed the backbone of the Muslim army in Spain for a certain period" (77).

72. It must be borne in mind that scholars have argued that the political relations of Hungary and Byzantium were complex and multifaceted. For more on this, see, for example, Paul Stephenson, *Byzantium's Balkan Frontier: A Political Study of the Northern Balkans, 900–1204* (Cambridge: Cambridge University Press, 2000).

4 Poetry, Frontiers, and Alterity: Views and Perceptions of *al-Rum* (Byzantines) and *al-Ifranja* (Franks)

1. This antagonism culminated in the long Byzantine-Sassanid wars (602–628).

2. The opening verses of the chapter "*Al-Rum*" are worth mentioning here: "*Alif, Lam, Mim.* The Byzantines (Romans) have been defeated in the nearer land, and they, after their defeat, will be victorious within ten years, Allah's is the command in the former case and in the latter and

on that day believers will rejoice" (1–4). In this context, although most exegetes of the Quran read and interpreted the verses as aforementioned, some medieval Muslim scholars had another interpretation according to a variance in the *qira'* (reading) of the key words of those verses: *ghulibat al-rum* or *ghalabat al-rum*. The first would mean that the Byzantines have been defeated and after their defeat they will be victorious. The second would mean that the Byzantines have defeated the Persians and after their victory they will be defeated—by Muslims. For a comprehensive account of this controversy, see Nadia Maria el-Cheikh's "Surat Al-Rum: A Study of the Exegetical Literature," *Journal of the American Oriental Society* 118 (1998): 356–364.

3. The renowned Arabist and Byzantanist Vassilios Christides in "Byzantium and the Arabs: Some Thoughts on the Spirit of Reconciliation and Cooperation" (1996) even spoke of "a modus vivendi" and "a constant undercurrent of communication between the two superpowers of the time" (131–142). Quite recently in "Periplus of the Arab-Byzantine Cultural Relations," Christides has reiterated his view, arguing forcibly that one should not speak of a monolithic Arab attitude toward the Byzantines and vice versa. According to Christides, especially after the tenth century A.D., a spirit of reconciliation appeared between Arabs and Byzantines. This spirit, he goes on to explain, was intensified with the Crusades. Nowhere is this more evident than in a plethora of Arabic epic romances such as 'Umar al-Nu'man and that of 'Antar, whereby one even comes across a fictitious alliance between Byzantines and Arabs against the Crusaders.

4. For two different views on this issue, see G. E. von Grunebaum's "Byzantine Iconoclasm and the Influence of the Islamic Environment," *History of Religions* 1 (1962): 1–10, and Leslie William Barnard's *The Graeco-Roman and Oriental Background of the Iconoclastic* (Leiden: Brill, 1974).

5. Arabs also showed a high interest in Byzantine maritime technology in spite of the latter's great effort to hide their military technology. Nowhere is this better illustrated than in the translation and the ensuing extensive paraphrasing by Arab authors of the work of Leo VI "Naumachica," part of the *Taktika*. This translation has been preserved by mainly by the fourteenth-century Arab scholar Ibn al-Manqali. For more on this subject, see Vassilios Christides, "Ibn al-Manqalī (Manglī) and Leo VI: New Evidence on Arabo-Byzantine Ship Construction and Naval Warfare," *Byzantinoslavica* 56 (1995): 83–96, and Taxiarchis Kolias, "The Taktika of Leo VI the Wise and the Arabs," *Graeco-Arabica* 3 (1984): 129–135.

6. Perhaps it is worth noting that efficiency of Byzantine engineering is better demonstrated in the practical trade work *Kitab al–Tabassur bi-l Tijara*, attributed to al-Jahiz.

7. Among these towns, Tarsus gained legendary status. For more details, see from the same author "The Naming of the Frontier: 'Awasim, Thughur, and the Arab Geographers," *Bulletin of the School of Oriental and African*

Studies 57 (1994): 17–24, and "Some Observations Concerning the Early Development of Jihad on the Arab-Byzantine Frontier," *Studia Islamica* 7 (1992): 5–31.

8. The opening hemistich of this *qasida* (i.e., *al-sayfu asdaqu anba'an min al-kutubi* [the sword is truer in telling than books]) has become among the most quoted verses of Arabic poetry. On this poem, see M. M. Badawi's "The Function of Rhetoric in Medieval Arabic Poetry: Abu Tammam's Ode on Amorium," *Journal of Arabic Literature* 9 (1978): 43–56.

9. One can cite the Fatimids in North Africa and Egypt and the Buwayhids in Iraq.

10. Qudama was the author of a foundational book on criticism of poetry titled *Kitab Naqd al-Shi'r* (Book of Poetic Criticism). For a comprehensive study of this Abbasid scholar, see Paul L. Heck's *The Construction of Knowledge in Islamic Civilization: Qudama b. Ja'far and His Kitab al-Kharaj wa Sina'at al-Kitaba* (Leiden: Brill, 2002).

11. As we will see in the following section, the Crusaders were also sometimes described as *'uluj*.

12. M. Canard once translated them as "Les Greques." See M. Canard, "Abu Firas," in *Byzance et les Arabes*, ed. A. A. Vasiliev (Brussels: Fondation Byzantine, 1950), 349–370.

13. The word *tawaghit* (singular *taghut*) is the most common word that medieval Muslim writers used to refer to the Byzantine emperors. In essence, it is a Quranic word that designates all types of idols worshipped other than or in addition to Allah (God). Thus, it is synonymous either with *kufr* (infidelity) or *shirk* (associationism/polytheism). However, in the context of medieval literature and contemporary jihadist rhetoric, it denotes more than its original theological meaning. Today it is commonly translated as "tyrant."

14. See S. Bonebakker, "Ibn al-Mu'tazz and Kitáb al-Badi," in *'Abbasid Belles-Lettres*, vol. 1, ed. J. Ashtiany et al., 388–409 (Cambridge: Cambridge University Press, 1990).

15. As mentioned earlier, this refers to the legal privilege given by medieval Shari'a law to a concubine-slave who bore a child (son or daughter) to her master. With the status of *um-walad*, it becomes illegal for her master to sell her or give her away. Upon her master's death, she would be freed.

16. As M. Canard once phrased it, Abu Firas belonged to "une des rares de L'ancienne aristocratie arabe syro-mésopotamienne qui ait joué un rôle politique au xe siècle" ("Abu Firas," 350).

17. This is true for his best-known love poem, "Araka 'asiyya al-dam'i," brought to unprecedented fame by the Arab singer Um Kulthum.

18. See Ioannis Caminiatae, *De expugnatione Thessalonicae*, ed. G. Böhlig (Berlin: de Gruyter, 1973), and for an English edition, *John Kaminiates: The Capture of Thessaloniki*, ed. D. Frendo and Athanasios Fotiou (Perth: Bizantina Australiensia 12, 2000).

19. All poems in this section are my personal translation. See the appendix for the Arabic originals.

20. For an excellent study, see Jaroslav Stetkevych's *The Zephyrs of Najd: The Poetics of Nostalgia in the Classical Arabic Nasib* (Chicago: University of Chicago Press, 1993).

21. For more details on the meaning of *tadhmin* and its place in classical Arabic literature, see Adrian Gully's "Tadhmin, 'Implication of Meaning,' in Medieval Arabic," *Journal of the American Oriental Society* 117 (1997): 466–480.

22. This refers to the presumed reply of Harun al-Rashid to the letter sent by the Byzantine emperor Nicephorus I (d. 803) in which he condemns the truce signed by his predecessor Irene with the Abbasid caliph and he declares not only his refusal to pay a tribute to the caliph but also his readiness to settle the matter with the sword. The insulting reply of al-Rashid starts as follows: "From Harun al-Rashid, Commander of the Faithful to Nicephorus *kalb al-rum*, the dog of the Romans." For more on this letter, see Hugh Kennedy's "Byzantine-Arab Diplomacy in the Near East from the Islamic Conquests to the Mid-Eleventh Century," in *Byzantine Diplomacy*, ed. J. Shepard and S. Franklin (Aldershot, UK: Variorum, 1992), 133–143.

23. Interestingly enough, scholar Gustave E. von Grunebaum did not refer to Ibn Hazm's poem. Indeed, while introducing the Byzantine polemical poem and the Muslim response(s), he did not allude even in passing to Ibn Hazm. There is no question, however, that by translating the two poems into German, Grunebaum's effort is foundational, to say the least. See Gustave E. von Grunebaum, "Eine Poetische Polemik Zwischen Byzanz und Bagdad im X. Jahrhundert," in *Islam and Medieval Hellenism: Social and Cultural Perspectives*, ed. Dunning S. Wilson (London: Variorum Reprints, 1976), 43–64.

24. Although quite slowly, news of the "cursed poem" spread west of Baghdad until it reached the Iberian Peninsula decades after it was first heard of in the Abbasid court. The Andalusian historian Ibn Khayr al-Ishbili was the first in the Muslim west to refer to the poem in *Al-Fihrist* (al-Munajjid, *Qasidat 'Imbratur al-Rum*, 38). Ibn Kathir mentions that two Andalusian scholars responded to Nicephorus. The first is Ibn Hazm and the second is Ibn Zarwal. Of the two, al-Munajjid remarks, only the response of Ibn Hazm survived. Ibn Hazm was at the court of al-Mu'tad Billah al-Umawi, the last of the Umayyad emirs of Muslim Spain, when the poem was mentioned. Ibn Hazm, as reported by Ibn Kathir and al-Subki, was so enraged by its mockery of Islam and its Prophet that he improvised a response to it. Ibn Hazm was particularly known for his improvised poetry, and the Andalusian historian al-Humeidi used to say that no one could improvise poetry with the ease and prowess of Ibn Hazm (38).

25. Like that of Nicephorus, al-Qaffal's response is thematically well structured. In the introductory lines, he responds to Nicephorus's claims of purity and reprimands him for bragging about a number of great deeds, many of which, according to al-Qaffal, he did not do. The real

victories of Nicephorus were, in the view of al-Qaffal, the result of Nicephorus's deceit and treachery. Al-Qaffal then reminds Nicephorus of the power of Muslims throughout the centuries by cataloging the victories of Muslims against the Byzantines. In this part, al-Qaffal has also highlighted the fact it was the Prophet who ordered Muslims to treat the Christians well. Otherwise, they would have exterminated them. After that, he refutes the claim that the Byzantines have captured thousands of Muslim women, reminds Nicephorus of the humane treatment of captives by Muslims, and rebukes him for his treatment of Muslim prisoners of war. He then mocks Nicephorus's statement that Muslims were humiliated by the Byzantines because of the injustices of their rulers and judges. If so, al-Qaffal adduces, then that is a compelling sign of the truth of Islam. The last part is a polemical response to the Trinitarian doctrine of Christianity and an attempt by the poet to refute Christianity and prove the truthfulness of the message of Muhammad.

26. For an exhaustive non-Muslim study of Muslim *tahara*, see Ze'ev Maghen's "Strangers and Brothers: The Ritual Status of Unbelievers in Islamic Jurisprudence," *Medieval Encounters* 12 (2006): 173–223.

27. See also Christine Hayes, *Gentile Impurities and Jewish Identities: Intermarriage and Conversion from the Bible to the Talmud* (Oxford: Oxford University Press, 2002).

28. Although in many lines Ibn Hazm echoes al-Qaffal, his response is still original. He starts his poem by linking the victories of the Byzantines to the weakness of al-Mutee, whose reign was characterized by divisions among Muslims. He then proceeds to catalog the victories of Muslims in different lands and mentions the power of Muslims throughout the centuries. After that he pledges that Muslims will conquer Constantinople, China, and all India since, as he mentions, it is the promise of God and the prophecy of Muhammad. Then he embarks on a polemical refutation of the Trinity, the Bible, and the Christian doctrine of the crucifixion of Jesus. He then compares the Trinity to the pure monotheistic belief of Islam. The last part is rather a eulogy of Muhammad. He catalogs his victories and mentions his miracles.

29. It is interesting to note here that after the outburst of the Mongols and their invasions of many Muslim and European countries in the thirteenth century, both Muslims and Europeans would consider them the ultimate "Scourge of God," ascribing to them all possible topoi of Otherness. For example, they were depicted in Muslim and Western sources alike as unimaginably cruel, bloodthirsty, bestial, and God's just punishment for their respective sins.

30. The reader is referred to the anthologies of *hamasa* collected by Abu Tammam and al-Buhturi. *Hamasa*, in Reynold A. Nicholson's words, "denotes the virtues most highly prized by the Arabs—bravery in battle, patience in misfortune, persistence in revenge, protection of the weak and defiance of the strong" (*A Literary History of the Arabs*, 79).

31. As shown by Hillenbrand and other scholars, the Arabic *al-hurub al-salibiyya*, which is a close equivalent to the English word *Crusades*, and *al-salibiyyun* (Crusaders) are modern expressions that came into common usage in the nineteenth century (*The Crusades*, 31). "Interestingly enough," Hillenbrand explains, "the etymology of both terms, Crusaders from the Latin crux (cross) and *salibiyyun* (from the Arabic *salib*, or cross), stresses the centrality of the symbolism of the cross underlying the European military campaigns which came to be known as the Crusades (in modern Arabic called 'the Crusading wars' (*al-hurub al-salibiyya*)" (31). It is noteworthy, however, that some scholars still prefer the English phrase "holy war" to describe the Crusades, and they suggest that the Arabic word *al-salibiyyun* is better translated as "those bearing a cross," highlighting the latter's derogative nuances.

32. It is to be noted that this view is not shared by some of the most prominent Western scholars of the Crusades, such as Jean Richard, Hans Eberhard Mayer, and Jonathan Riley-Smith.

33. For an excellent study of the accounts of the massacre at Jerusalem, see Benjamin Z. Kedar, "The Jerusalem Massacre of July in the Western Historiography of the Crusades," *Crusades* 3 (2004): 15–76.

34. A niche in a mosque that indicates the *qibla* (the orientation of Mecca).

35. As explained by Sivan, jihad "n'est plus présenté seulement sous son aspect de *farida* (précepte) mais encore sous celui de *fadila* (mérite, vertu)" (62).

36. See Daniella Talmon-Heller's "Muslim Martyrdom and Quest for Martyrdom in the Crusading Period," *Al-Masaq: Islam and the Medieval Mediterranean* 14 (2002): 131–139.

37. Here I use the word *discourse* with the very "comparable vagueness" highlighted by Suzanne Conklin Akbari in the introduction to her article "Orientation and Nation in Chaucer's *Canterbury Tales*" (102).

38. His full name is Muhammad ibn Nasr ibn Saghir. He was born in Acre but grew in Caesarea, hence his alias Ibn al-Qaysarani (the son of the Caesareanian). After the Frankish occupation of the city in 1101, he left it to Aleppo and later to Damascus, where he died (Kilani, *Al-Hurub al-Salibiyya*, 357–360).

39. In reference to Ibn 'Arabi's often quoted poem, which R. A. Nicholson in *Mystics of Islam* translated as follows: "My heart has become capable of every form / It is a pasture for gazelles and a convent for Christian monks / And a temple for idols, and the pilgrim's Ka'ba / And the tables of the Torah and the book of the Koran" (67).

Conclusion

1. In many ways, the reality has proved otherwise especially since the eruption in the ninth century of the previously mentioned *al-shu'ubiyya* (ethnic tensions), which among other things rekindled the animosity between Arabs and Persians.

2. See, for example, "O Mankind, We created you from a single (pair) of a male and a female and made you into nations and tribes, that you may know each other. Verily the most honored of you in the sight of God is he who is the most righteous of you" (Quran 49:13).

3. See Ernest Renan, *Qu'est-ce qu'une nation?* (Paris: Mille Et Une Nuits, 1997).

4. "Allah forbiddeth you not those who warred not against you on account of religion and drove you not out from your homes, that ye should show them kindness and deal justly with them. Lo! Allah loveth the just dealers. Allah forbiddeth you only those who warred against you on account of religion and have driven you out from your homes and helped to drive you out, that ye make friends of them. Whosoever maketh friends of them (All) such are wrong doers." (Quran, Al-Mumtahina, 8–9).

5. This is in addition to other concepts, such as *dar al-silm* (abode of peace), *dar al-sulh* (abode of truce), *dar al-hudna* (abode of calm), and *dar al-da'wa* (abode of call).

6. Even before the early modern period, as recently shown by Nabil Matar in his introduction to *Europe through Arab Eyes: 1578–1727* (2008).

7. In an obvious reference to the previously mentioned visit of al-Tahtawi to Paris (1826–1831) and his travel account *Takhlis al-Ibriz fi Talkhis Bariz*.

8. The full cover title is *Ibn Fadlan's Journey to Russia: A Tenth-Century Traveler from Baghdad to the Volga River*.

9. See M. Berge, *Pour un humanisme vécu: Abu Hayyan al-Tawhidi* (Damascus: Institut Français de Damas, 1979).

BIBLIOGRAPHY

Primary Sources

Al-Bakri. *Jughrafiyat al-Andalus wa Uruba min-Kitab al-Masalik wa-l-Mamalik.* Edited by A. al-Hajji. Beirut: Dar al-Irshad, 1978.

Al-Biruni, Abu Raihan. *Tahdid Nihayat al-Amakin.* Unpublished manuscript. Istanbul: Al-Fath Mosque.

———. *Tahqiq ma li-l-Hind min Maqula Maqbula fi-l-'Aql aw Marthula.* Da'irat al-Ma'arif al-Uṯmaniyya, 1958.

Al-Gharnati, Abu Hamid. *Tuhfat al-Albab wa Nukhbat al-I'jab.* Beirut: Dar al-Jabal, 1979.

Al-Hamdani, Abu Firas. *Diwan al-Amir Abu Firas al-Hamdani.* Edited by Muhammad Al-Tunji. Damascus: al-Mustashariyya, 1987.

———. *Diwan Abu Firas al-Hamdani.* Edited by Abbas Abdulsatir. Beirut: Dar al-Kutub al-'Ilmiyya, 1983.

Al-Isfahani, fImad al-Din. *Al-Fath al-Qussi.* Cairo: al-Dar al-Qawmiyya, 1965.

Al-Jahiz. *Rasa'il al-Jahiz.* Beirut: Maktabat al-Hilal, 1987.

Al-Mas'udi. *Al-Tanbih wa-l-Ishraf.* Edited by Abdullah Sawi. Baghdad: Maktabat al-Muthni, 1967.

———. *Muruj al-Dhahab wa Ma'adin al-Jawhar,* vol. 2. Edited by Charles Pellat. Beirut: Lebanese University Press, 1966.

Al-Munajjid, Salahuddine, ed. *Qasidat 'Imbratur al-Rum Naqfur Fuqas fi-Hija' al-Islam wa-l-Rad 'Alaih.* Beirut: Dar al-Kitab al-Jadid, 1982.

Al-Sarisi, Abdurrahmane. *Nusus min-Adab 'Asr al-Hurub al-Salibiyya.* Jeddah, Saudi Arabia: Dar al-Manara, 1985.

Al-Tawhidi. *Al-Imta' wa-l-Mu'anasa.* Beirut: al-Maktaba al-'Asriyya, 1963.

———. *Al-Mu'rib 'an Ba'd 'Aja'ib al-Maghrib.* Beirut: Dar al-Kutub al-'Ilmiyya, 1999.

Ibn al-Athir. *Al-Kamil fi-l-Tarikh.* Beirut: Dar al Kitab al-Arabi, 1997.

Ibn al-Faqih. *Mukhtasar Kitab al-Buldan.* Beirut: Dar Sadir, 1960.

Ibn Jubayr. *The Travels of Ibn Jubayr.* Translated by R. J. C. Broadhurst. London: J. Cape, 1952.

Ibn Khaldun. *Al-Muqaddima.* Beirut: Dar al-Qalam, 1978.

Ibn al-Qaysarani. *Shi'r Ibn al-Qaysarani.* Edited by Adil Jabir. Amman: Al-Wikala al-'Arabiyya li-l-Tawzi', 1991.

Ibn Dihya. *Al-Mutrib fi Ash'ar Ahl al-Maghrib.* Edited by Ibrahim al-Ibyari. Cairo: Al-Maktba al-'Amiriyya, 1954.

Ibn Fadlan, Ahmad. *Risalat Ibn Fadlan*. Beirut: al-Sharika al-ʿAlamiyya
li-l-Kitab, 1994.

———. *Risalat Ibn Fadlan*. Edited by Sami al-Dahhan. Damascus: al-Majmaʿ
al-ʿIlmi al-ʿArabi, 1959.

Ibn Kathir. *Al-Bidaya wa-l-Nihaya*. Beirut: Maktabat al-Maʿarif, 1982.

Ibn Khordadbeh. *Kitab al-Masalik wa-l-Mamalik*. Baghdad: Maktabat al-Mathna,
1954.

Ibn Rusta. *Kitab Al-Aʿlaq al-Nafisa*. Leiden: Brill, 1893.

Kilani, Muhammad Sayyid. *Al-Hurub al-Salibiyya wa Atharuha fi-l-Adab al-ʿArabi
fi-Misr wa-l-Sham*. Cairo: Dar al-Firjani, 1989.

Secondary Sources

Abbas, Ihsan. *Al-ʿArab fi Siqiliyya*. Beirut: Dar al-Thaqafa, 1975.

Abdullah, Thabit. "Arab Views of Northern Europeans in Medieval History and
Geography." In *Images of the Other: Europe and the Muslim World before 1700*,
edited by D. R. Blanks, 73–80. Cairo: American University Press, 1996.

———. *A Short History of Iraq: From 636 to the Present*. New York: Pearson-
Longman, 2003.

Abdulmahdi, Abduljalil. *Bayt al-Maqdis fi Adab al-Hurub al-Salibiyya*. Amman:
Dar al-Bashir, 1989.

Abu-Haidar, J. A. *Hispano-Arabic Literature and the Early Provençal Lyrics*.
Richmond, UK: Curzon, 2001.

Abu Dawud. *Sunan Abu Dawud*. Translated by Ahmad Hasan. Lahore:
Sh. M. Ashraf, 1984.

Adang, Camilla. *Muslim Writers on Judaism and the Hebrew Bible: From Ibn Rabban
to Ibn Hazm*. Leiden: Brill, 1996.

Affayya, M. N. *Al-Gharb al-Mutakhayyal*. Casablanca: Toubkal, 1997.

Agius, D. A., ed. *Across the Mediterranean Frontiers: Trade, Politics and Religion,
650–1450*. Leeds: University of Leeds, 1996.

Ahmad, Nafis. *Muslim Contribution to Geography*. Lahore: Sh. Muhammad Ashraf,
1972.

Ahmad, S. Maqbul. "Al-Masʿudi's Contributions to Medieval Arab Geography."
Islamic Culture 27 (1953): 61–77.

———. *Arabic Classical Accounts of India and China*. Shimla, India: Indian Institute
of Advanced Study, 1989.

———. *A History of Arab-Islamic Geography*. Mafraq, Jordan: Al al-Bayt University,
1995.

Akbari, Suzanne Conklin. "From Due East to True North: Orientalism and
Orientation." In *The Postcolonial Middle Ages*, edited by Jeffrey Jerome Cohen,
19–34. New York: Palgrave Macmillan, 2000.

———. "Imagining Islam: The Role of Images in Medieval Depictions of
Muslim." *Scripta Mediterranea* 19–20 (1998–1999): 9–27.

———. "Orientation and Nation in Chaucer's *Canterbury Tales*." In *Chaucer's
Cultural Geography*, edited by Kathryn Lynch, 102–134. New York: Routledge,
2002.

Al-Adawi, Ibrahim. *Al-Sifarat al-Islamiyya ila Uruba fi-l-'Usur al-Wusta*. Cairo: Dar al-Ma'arif, 1957.

Alam, Shahid. "Articulating Group Differences: A Variety of Autocentrisms." *Science and Society* 67 (2003): 205–217.

Alavi, S. M. *Arab Geography in the Ninth and Tenth Centuries*. Aligarh, India: Aligarh Muslim University, 1965.

Al-Azmeh, Aziz. *Al-'Arab wa-l-Barabira*. London: Dar al-Rayes, 1991.

———. "Barbarians in Arab Eyes." *Past and Present* 134 (1994): 3–18.

———. "Mortal Enemies, Invisible Neighbors: Northerners in Andalusian Eyes." In *The Legacy of Muslim Spain*, edited by Salma Khadra Jayyusi, 259–272. Leiden: Brill, 1994.

Albrecht, Rosenthal. "The Isle of the Amazons: A Marvel of Travelers." *Journal of the Warburg Institute* 3 (1938): 257–259.

Al-Bukhari, Muhammad. *Summarized Sahih Al Bukhari*. Translated by Muhammad Muhsin Khan. Riyadh: Darussalam, 1996.

Al-Ghazal, S. K. "The Influence of Islamic Philosophy and Ethics on the Development of Medicine in the Islamic Civilisation." *FSTC* 4 (2007): 1–12.

Al-Hakim. *Al-Mustadrak 'Ala al-Sahihayn*. Beirut: Dar al-Kutub al-'Ilmiyya, 1990.

Al-Hajji, Abdurrahmane. "Al-Turtushi, the Andalusian Traveler and the Meeting with Pope John." *Islamic Quarterly* 11 (1967): 129–136.

———. *Andalusian Diplomatic Relations with Western Europe during the Umayyad Period*. Beirut: Dar al-Irshad, 1970.

Al-Jubouri, I. M. N. *History of Islamic Philosophy: With View of Greek Philosophy and Early History of Islam*. Hertford, UK: Authors Online, 2004.

Al-Kilani, Shamsuddine. *Surat Uruba Inda al-'Arab fi-l-'Asr al-Wasit*. Damascus: Ministry of Culture, 2004.

Allen, E. John B. *The Culture and Sport of Skiing: From Antiquity to World War II*. Amherst: University of Massachusetts Press, 2007.

Allen, W. E. D. *The Poet and the Spae-Wife: An Attempt to Reconstruct Al-Ghazal's Embassy to the Vikings*. Dublin: Allen Figgis and Co., 1960.

Al-Musawi, Muhsin Jassim. *Arabic Poetry: Trajectories of Modernity and Tradition*. London: Routledge, 2006.

Anzaldúa, Gloria. *Borderlands/La Frontera: The New Mestiza*. San Francisco: Aunt Lute, 1987.

Ataman, Kemal. "Re-reading al-Biruni's India: A Case for Intercultural Understanding." *Islam and Christian Muslim Relations* 16 (2005): 141–154.

———. *Understanding Other Religions: Al-Biruni's and Gadamer's "Fusion of Horizons."* Washington, DC: Council for Research in Values and Philosophy, 2008.

Attar, Samar. "Conflicting Accounts on the Fear of Strangers: Muslim and Arab Perceptions of Europeans in Medieval Geographical Literature." *Arab Studies Quarterly* 27 (2005): 17–29.

Aurell, Martin. *Les Noces du Comte: Mariage et pouvoir en Catalogne (785–1213)*. Paris, Publications de la Sorbonne, 1995.

Aydin, Mehmet. "Turkish Contributions to Philosophical Culture." *Er* 4 (1986): 59–85.

Barker, John W., and Christopher Kleinhenz. "Benevento." In *Medieval Italy: An Encyclopedia*, vol. 1, edited by Christopher Kleinhenz, 107. London: Routledge, 2004.

Beardsell, Peter R. *Europe and Latin America: Returning the Gaze*. Manchester: Manchester University Press, 2000.

Beeston, A. F. L. "Idrissi's Account of the British Isles." *Bulletin of the School of Oriental and African Studies* 13 (1950): 265–280.

———. *Selections from the Poetry of Bashshār*. Cambridge: Cambridge University Press, 1977.

Bello, Iysa A. *The Medieval Islamic Controversy between Philosophy and Orthodoxy: Ijmāʿ and Taʾwīl in the Conflict between al-Ghazālī and Ibn Rushd*. Leiden: Brill, 1989.

Benjamin, Sandra. *The World of Benjamin of Tudela: A Medieval Mediterranean Travelogue*. Madison, NJ: Fairleigh Dickinson University Press, 1995.

Bennison, Amira K. "The Peoples of the North in the Eyes of the Muslims of Umayyad al-Andalus (711–1031)." *Journal of Global History* 2 (2007): 157–174.

Berend, Nora. *At the Gate of Christendom: Jews, Muslims and "Pagans" in Medieval Hungary, c. 1000–c. 1300*. Cambridge: Cambridge University Press, 2005.

———. "Hungary in the Eleventh and Twelfth Century." In *The New Cambridge Medieval History*, edited by Rosamond McKitterick and Christopher Allmand, 304–314. Cambridge: Cambridge University Press, 2005.

Bhabha, Homi K., ed. *Nation and Narration*. London: Routledge, 1990.

Binkley, Peter, ed. *Pre-Modern Encyclopedic Texts*. Leiden: Brill, 1997.

Bloch, Herbert. "The New Fascination with Ancient Rome." In *Renaissance and Renewal*, edited by Robert L. Benson, 615–636. Cambridge, MA: Harvard University Press, 1982.

Block, Josine. *The Early Amazons: Modern and Ancient Perspectives on a Persistent Myth*. Leiden: Brill, 1995.

Boas, Adrian J. *Jerusalem in the Time of the Crusades: Society, Landscape, and Art in the Holy City under Frankish Rule*. London: Routledge, 2001.

Bohnstedt, John W. *The Infidel Scourge of God: The Turkish Menace as Seen by German Pamphleteers of the Reformation Era*. Philadelphia: American Philosophical Society, 1968.

Bonner, Michael. *Arab-Byzantine Relations in Early Islamic Times*. Burlington, VT: Ashgate Publishing, 2004.

———. *Aristocratic Violence and Holy War: Studies on the Jihad and the Arab-Byzantine Frontier*. New Haven, CT: American Oriental Society Monograph Series, 1996.

Bosworth, C. E. "The City of Tarsus and the Arab-Byzantine Frontiers in Early and Middle Abbasid Times." *Oriens* 33 (1992): 268–286.

Boxhall, Peter. "Arabian Seafarers in the Indian Ocean." *Asian Affairs* 20 (1989): 287–295.

Brauer, Ralph W. *Boundaries and Frontiers in Medieval Muslim Geography*. Philadelphia: American Philosophical Society, 1995.

Bromberger, Christian. "Hair: From the West to the Middle East through the Mediterranean." *Journal of American Folklore* 121 (2008): 379–399.

Burns, William E. *Witch Hunts in Europe and America: An Encyclopedia*. Westport, CT: Greenwood, 2003.

Burton, Jonathan. *Traffic and Turning: Islam and English Drama, 1579–1624*. Newark: University of Delaware Press, 2005.

Burton, Sir Richard F., trans. *Arabian Nights*. Vol. 9. New York: Cosimo Classics, 2008.

Buruma, Ian, and Avishai Margalit. *Occidentalism: The West in the Eyes of Its Enemies*. New York: Penguin, 2004.

Cardini, Franco. *Europa e Islam: Storia di un Malinteso*. Roma-Bari: Gius. Laterza and Figli, 1999.

———. *Europe and Islam*. Translated by Caroline Beamish. Oxford and Malden: Blackwell, 2001.

Carey, Elizabeth. *The Tragedy of Mariam, the Fair Queen of Jewry*. Peterborough, ON: Broadview, 2000.

Clements, Jonathan. *Marco Polo*. Dulles, VA: Haus Publishing, 2007.

Charvát, Petr, and Jiří Prosecký, eds. *Ibrahim ibn Ya'qub at-Turtushi: Christianity, Islam and Judaism Meet in East-Central Europe, c. 800–1300 A.D.* Prague: Oriental Institute, 1996.

Christides, Vassilios. "Byzantium and the Arabs: Some Thoughts on the Spirit of Reconciliation and Cooperation." In *Byzanz und seine Nachbarn*, edited by A. Hohlweg, 131–142. Munich, Südosteuropa-Gesellschaft, 1996.

———. "Periplus of the Arab-Byzantine Cultural Relations." In *Cultural Relations between Byzantium and the Arabs*, edited by Y. Y. al-Hijji and V. Christides, 29–52. Athens: Institute for Graeco-Oriental and African Studies, 2007.

Constable, Olivia Remie. *Trade and Traders in Muslim Spain: The Commercial Realignment of the Iberian Peninsula, 900–1500*. Cambridge: Cambridge University Press, 1994.

Cordery, Leona F. "The Saracens in Middle English Literature: A Definition." *Al-Masaq: Islam and the Medieval Mediterranean* 14 (2002): 87–99.

Crow, John Armstrong. *Spain: The Root and the Flower: An Interpretation of Spain and the Spanish*. Berkeley and Los Angeles: University of California Press, 2005.

Dajani-Shakeel, Hadia. "Natives and Franks in Palestine: Perceptions and Interactions." In *Conversion and Continuity: Indigenous Christian Communities in Islamic Lands Eighth to Eighteenth Century*, edited by Michael Gerves and Ramzi Jibran Bikhazi, 161–184. Toronto: University of Toronto Press, 1990.

———. "A Reassessment of Some Medieval and Modern Perceptions of the Counter-Crusade." In *The Jihad and Its Times*, edited by Hadia Dajani-Shakeel, 41–70. Ann Arbor: University of Michigan Press, 1992.

Dalrymple, William. "The Truth about Muslims." Review of *In the Lands of the Christians*, by Nabil Matar. *The New York Review of Books*, November 17, 2004: 1–12.

Daniel, Norman. *Islam and the West: The Making of an Image*. Edinburgh: Edinburgh University Press, 1960.

Daston, Lorraine, and Katherine Park. *Wonders and the Orders of Things, 1150–1750*. New York: Zone Books, 1998.

Dietrich, A. "Al-Ghazal." In *Reallexikon der germanischen Altertumskunde*, edited by Johannes Hoops, 65–66. Berlin: Walter de Gruyter, 2004.

D'souza, Dinesh. *The End of Racism: Principles for a Multiracial Society*. New York: Free Press, 1995.

Dubler, Cesar E. *Abu Hamid el granadino y su relación de Viaje por tierras euroasiáticas*. Madrid: Imprenta y Editorial Maestre, 1953.

Ducène, Jean-Claude, ed. *De Grenade à Bagdad: la relation de voyage d'Abû Hâmid al-Gharnâti*. Paris: L'Harmattan, 2006.

———. Une deuxième version de la relation d'Harun ibn Yahya sur Constantinople." *Der Islam* 82 (2005): 241.

Du Mesnil, Emmanuelle Tixier. "Panorama de la Géographie Arabe médiévale." In *Géographes et voyageurs au Moyen Age*, edited by Henri Bresc and Emmanuelle Tixier du Mesnil, 15–17. Paris: Presses universitaires de Paris, 2010.

Dunlop, D. M. "The British Isles According to Medieval Arabic Authors." *Islamic Quarterly* 4 (1957): 11–28.

Duroselle, Jean-Baptiste. *Europe: A History of Its Peoples*. London: Viking, 1990.

Ebel, Charles. *Transalpine Gaul: The Emergence of a Roman Province*. Leiden: Brill, 1976.

El-Cheikh, Nadia Maria. "Byzantium through the Islamic Prism from the Twelfth to the Thirteenth Century." In *The Crusades from the Perspective of Byzantium and the Muslim World*, edited by Angeliki E. Laiou and Roy Parviz Mottahedeh, 53–70. Washington, DC: Dumbarton Oaks, 2001.

———. *Byzantium Viewed by the Arabs*. Cambridge, MA: Harvard University Press, 2004.

———. "Describing the Other to Get at the Self: Byzantine Women in Arabic Sources (8th–11th Centuries)." *Journal of the Economic and Social History of the Orient* 40 (1997): 239–250.

El-Manssouri, F. "Abu-Hamid: The Twelfth Century Granadan Traveler." *International Journal of the Islamic and Arabic Studies* 5 (1988): 43–58.

El-Tayib, A. "Abu Firas al-Hamdani." In *'Abbasid Belles Lettres*, edited by Julia Ashtiany et al., 315–327. Cambridge: Cambridge University Press, 1990.

Engel, Pál. *The Realm of St Stephen: A History of Medieval Hungary 859–1526*. London: I. B. Taurus, 2001.

Ephrat, Daphna, and M. D. Kabha. "Muslim Reactions to the Frankish Presence in *Bilād al-Shām*: Intensifying Religious Fidelity within the Masses." *Al-Masaq: Islam and the Medieval Mediterranean* 15 (2003): 47–59.

Euben, Roxanne L. "The Comparative Politics of Travel." *Parallax* 9 (2003): 18–28.

———. *Journeys to the Other Shore: Muslim and Western Travelers in Search of Knowledge*. Princeton, NJ: Princeton University Press, 2006.

Evans, Roger Steven. *Sex and Salvation: Virginity as a Soteriological Paradigm in Ancient Christianity*. New York: University Press of America, 2004.

Fahim, H. M. *Adab al-Rahalat*. Kuwait: Ministry of Culture, 1989.

Fakhry, Majid. *A History of Islamic Philosophy*. New York: Columbia University Press, 2004.

———. *Philosophy, Dogma and the Impact of Greek Thought in Islam*. Aldershot, UK: Variorum, 1994.

Fanning, Steven. "Clovis I." In *Medieval France: An Encyclopedia*, edited by William W. Kibler, 239. London: Routledge, 1995.

Farrukh, 'Umar. *Abu Firas, a Knight and Romantic Poet*. Amman: Maktabat Manimanah, 1988.

France, Peter. *The Oxford Guide to Literature in English Translation*. Oxford: Oxford University Press, 2000.

Frye, Richard N. *Ibn Fadlan's Journey to Russia: A Tenth-Century Traveler from Baghdad to the Volga River*. Princeton, NJ: Markus Wiener, 2005.

Gabrieli, Francesco. *Arab Historians of the Crusades*. Translated by E. J. Costello. London: Routledge, 1984.

———. "Rome au IX siècle chez un voyager arabe." *Al Mashriq* 35 (1993): 43–46.

Gabriel, Judith. "Among the Norse Tribes: The Remarkable Account of Ibn Fadlan." *Saudi Aramco* 50 (2000): 36–42.

Gammeltoft, Peder. "Scandinavian Naming-Systems in the Hebrides." In *West over Sea: Studies in Scandinavian Sea-Borne Expansion and Settlement before 1300*, edited by Beverley Ballin Smith et al., 479–496. Leiden: Brill, 2007.

Gellens, Sam. "The Search for Knowledge in Medieval Muslim Societies: A Comparative Approach." In *Muslim Travelers: Pilgrimage, Migration, and the Religious Imagination*, edited by Dale Eickelman and James Piscatori, 50–63. Berkeley: University of California Press, 1990.

Gilliot, Claude. "Bakri, Al-, Geographer." In *Medieval Islamic Civilization: An Encyclopedia*, edited by Josef W. Meri and Jere L. Bacharach, 96–97. London: Routledge, 2006.

Goldschmidt, Arthur. *A Concise History of the Middle East*. Boulder, CO: Westview, 2001.

Goldziher, Ignác. *Muslim Studies*. Edited by Sámuel Miklós Stern. New Brunswick, NJ: Transaction Publishers, 2009.

Goodman, L. E. "The Translation of Greek Materials into Arabic." In *Religion, Learning and Science in the Abbasid Period*, edited by M. J. L. Young et al., 477–494. Cambridge: Cambridge University Press, 1990.

Gowen, Herbert. *An Outline History of China*. Safety Harbor, FL: Simon Publications, 2001.

Grant, David. *History of Natural Philosophy: From the Ancient World to the Nineteenth Century*. Cambridge: Cambridge University Press, 2007.

Greenblatt, Stephen. *Marvelous Possessions: The Wonder of the New World*. Chicago: University of Chicago Press, 1991.

Groff, Peter S., and Oliver Leaman. *Islamic Philosophy A-Z*. Edinburgh: Edinburgh University Press, 2007.

Gutas, Dimitri. *Greek Thought, Arabic Culture: The Graeco-Arabic Translation Movement in Baghdad and Early Abbasid Society*. London: Routledge, 1998.

Hamori, Andras. *The Composition of Mutanabbi's Panegyrics to Sayf al Dawla*. Leiden: Brill, 1992.

Harvey, L. P. "Al-Ghazal." In *Literature of Travel and Exploration: An Encyclopaedia*, edited by J. Speake, 486. London: Routledge, 2003.

Hassan, Zaki Muhammad. *Al-Rahala al-Muslimun fi-l-'Usur al-Wusta*. Beirut: Dar al-Ra'id al-'Arabi, 1981.

Heath, Peter. "Knowledge." In *The Literature of al-Andalus*, edited by Maria Rosa Menocal, Raymond P. Scheindlin, and Michael Sells, 96–125. Cambridge: Cambridge University Press, 2000.

Heinen, Anton M. "Geographical Investigations under the Guidance of Islam." In *Culture and Learning in Islam*, edited by Ekmeleddin İhsanoğlu, 457–510. Beirut: UNESCO, 2003.

Heng, Geraldine. *Empire of Magic: Medieval Romance and the Politics of Cultural Fantasy*. New York: Columbia University Press, 2003.

Higgins, Iain Macleod. *Writing East: The "Travels" of Sir John Mandeville*. Philadelphia: University of Pennsylvania Press, 1997.

Hillenbrand, Carole. *The Crusades: Islamic Perspectives*. London: Routledge, 2000.

Hitti, Philip K., ed. *An Arab-Syrian Gentleman and Warrior in the Period of the Crusades: Memoirs of Usamah ibn-Munqidh*. New York: Columbia University Press, 2000.

Hmeida, Abdurrahmane. *A'lam al-Jughrafiyyin al-'Arab*. Damascus: Dar al-Fikr, 1988.

Homerin, Emil. *'Umar Ibn Al-Faridh: Sufi Verse, Saintly Life*. New York: Paulist Press, 2001.

Hopkins, J. F. P. "Geographical and Navigational Literature." In *Religion, Learning and Science in the Abbasid Period*, edited by M. J. L. Young et al., 301–327. Cambridge: Cambridge University Press, 1990.

Hunwick, John O. "A Region of the Mind: Medieval Arab Views of African Geography and Ethnography and Their Legacy." *Sudanic Africa* 16 (2005): 103–136.

Hussein, Mahmud. *Adab al-Rihla Inda al-'Arab*. Beirut: Dar al-Andalus, 1983.

Ibn al-Hajjaj, Muslim. *Sahih Muslim*. Translated by Nasiruddin al-Khattab. Riyadh: Darussalam, 2007.

Ibrahim, Abdullah. *Al-Markaziyya al-Islamiyya: Al-Akhar fi al-Adab al-'Arabi al-Wasit*. Beirut: Dar al-Baida, 2001.

Ibrahim, Mahmud. *Songs of an Arab Prince: Verses from the Poetry of Abu Firas al-Hamdani*. Baghdad: Ministry of Culture and National Heritage, 1988.

Israel, Raphael. "Medieval Muslim Travelers to China." *Journal of Muslim Minority Affairs* 20 (2000): 314–321.

'Izzidin, M. "Harun b. Yahya." In *Encyclopaedia of Islam*, edited by H. A. R. Gibbs et al., 232. Leiden. Brill, 1960.

Jackson, Richard. *Writing the War on Terrorism: Language, Politics and Counter-Terrorism*. Manchester: Manchester University Press, 2005.

Jesch, Judith. *Women in the Viking Age*. Woodbridge, UK: Boydell Press, 1991.

Jones, Gwyn. *A History of the Vikings*. Oxford: Oxford University Press, 2001.

Jukka, Jouhki. "Imagining the Other: Orientalism and Occidentalism in Tamil-European Relations in South India." Diss., University of Jyväskylä, 2005.

Kabbani, Rana. *Europe's Myths of Orient: Divide and Rule.* London: Macmillan, 1986.

Karamustafa, Ahmet T. "Introduction to Islamic Maps." In *The History of Cartography: Cartography in the traditional Islamic and South Asian Worlds,* vol. 2, edited by J. B. Harley and David Woodward, 108–136. Chicago: University of Chicago Press, 1992.

Kassis, Hanna. "The Depiction of Europe in Medieval Arabic Sources." In *From Arabye to Engelond,* edited by A. E. Christa Canitz and Gernot R. Wieland, 9–23. Ottawa: University of Ottawa Press, 1999.

Kazimi, M. R. "Mas'udi and Cultural Geography." *Journal of the Pakistani Historical Society* 46 (1998): 75–79.

Khair, Tabish, et al. *Other Routes: 1500 Years of African and Asian Travel Writing.* Oxford: Signal Books, 2005.

Khalidi, Tarif. *Arabic Historical Thought in the Classical Period.* Cambridge: Cambridge University Press, 1994.

———. *Islamic Historiography: The Histories of al-Mas'udi.* Albany: State University of New York Press, 1975.

———. "Islamic Views of the West in the Middle Ages." *Studies in Interreligious Dialogue* 5 (1995): 31–42.

Khan, M. Muhsin, trans. *Sahih al-Bukhari.* Riyadh: Darussalam, 2004.

Khan, M. S. "Al-Biruni, the Pioneer Indologist." *Islamic Culture* 76 (2002): 33–67.

Khattab, 'Alya. *Das Bild der Franken in der arabischen Literatur des Mittelalters: Ein Beitrag zum Dialog über die Kreuzzüge.* Göppingen, Germany: Kümmerle, 1989.

Kinney, Dale. "Fact and Fiction in the Mirabilia Urbis Romae." In *Roma Felix: Formation and Reflections of Medieval Rome,* edited by Éamonn Ó Carragáin and Carol L. Neuman de Vegvar, 235–252. Burlington, VT: Ashgate, 2007.

Kinoshita, Sharon. "Discrepant Medievalisms: Deprovincializing the Middle Ages." In *Worldings: World Literature, Field Imaginaries, Future Practices: Doing Cultural Studies in the Era of Globalization,* edited by Rob Wilson and Chris Connery, 75–89. Santa Cruz, CA: New Pacific Press, 2006.

———. *Medieval Boundaries: Rethinking Difference in Old French Literature.* Philadelphia: University of Pennsylvania Press, 2006.

Kropacek, Lubos. "In Memory of I. Hrbek." In *Ibrahim ibn Ya'qub at-Turtushi: Christianity, Islam and Judaism Meet in East-Central Europe, c. 800–1300 A.D.,* edited by Petr Charvát and Jiří Prosecký, 52–64. Prague: Oriental Institute, 1996.

Kratschkovsky. *Tarikh al-Adab al-Jughrafi al-'Arabi.* Translated by S. O. Hashim. Cairo: Arab League, 1963.

Kurz, Isolde. *Vom Umgang Mit Dem Anderen: Die Orientalismus-Debatte zwischen Alteritätsdiskurs und interlektueller Kommunikation.* Wurzburg, Germany: Ergon, 2000.

Labib, al-Tahir, ed. *Surat al-Akhar: Al-'Arabi Nadhir wa Mandhur Ilayh.* Cairo: Markaz Dirasaat al-Wihda al-'Arabiyya, 1999.

Lasater, Alice E. *Spain to England: A Comparative Study of Arabic, European, and English Literature of the Middle Ages.* Jackson: University of Mississippi Press, 1974.

Le Bon, G. *La Civilisation des Arabs*. Syracuse, NY: IMAG, 1884.

Le Goff, Jacques. "The Medieval West and the Indian Ocean: An Oneiric Horizon." In *Facing Each Other: The World's Perception of Europe and Europe's Perception of the World*, edited by Anthony Padgen, 1–20. Burlington, VT: Variorum, 2000.

Lenker, Michael Karl. "The Importance of the Rihla for the Islamization of Spain." Diss., University of Pennsylvania, 1982.

Lévi-Provençal, E. "Abu Hamid al-Gharnati." In *Encyclopaedia of Islam*, edited by H. A. R. Gibbs et al., vol. Q, 125–126. Leiden: Brill, 1960.

———. "Un echange d'ambassades entre Cordoue et Byzance au IX siecle." *Byzantion* 12 (1937): 1–24.

Levtzion, N., and J. F. Hopkins. *Corpus of Early Arabic Sources for West African History*. Cambridge: Cambridge University Press, 1981.

Levtzion, N., and Jay Spaulding. *Medieval West Africa: Views from Arab Scholars and Merchants*. Princeton, NJ: Markus Wiener, 2003.

Levy, M. "Ibrahim ibn Ya'qub." In *Encyclopaedia of Islamic Science and Scientists*, edited by Zaki Kirmani and N. K. Singh, 468–469. New Delhi: Global Vision Publishing House, 2005.

Lewicki, T. "Madjar, Madjaristan." In *Encyclopaedia of Islam*, edited by H. A. R. Gibbs et al., vol. 2, 1010–1022. Leiden: Brill, 1984.

Lewis, Bernard. *From Babel to Dragomans: Interpreting the Middle East*. Oxford: Oxford University Press, 2004.

———. *Islam and the West*. New York: Oxford University Press, 1993.

———. *A Middle East Mosaic: Fragments of Life, Letters, and History*. New York: Random House, 2000.

———. *The Muslim Discovery of Europe*. New York: Norton, 1982.

———. "The Use by Muslim Historians of Non-Muslim Sources." In *Historians of the Middle East*, edited by P. M. Holt and Bernard Lewis, 180–191. London and New York: Oxford University Press, 1962.

Lunde, Paul, and Caroline Stone, trans. *The Meadows of Gold: The Abbasids*. London: Kegan Paul International, 1989.

Lukowski, Jerzy, and Hubert Zawadzki. *An Outline of the History of Poland*. Warsaw: Interpress, 1986.

Maalouf, Amin. *The Crusades through Arab Eyes*. New York: Schocken Books, 1985.

Macfie, A. L. *Orientalism*. Edinburgh: Pearson Education, 2002.

Mackintosh-Smith, Tim. *The Travels of Ibn Battutah*. London: Macmillan, 2002.

Madden, Thomas F. *The New Concise History of the Crusades*. Oxford: Rowman and Littlefield, 2005.

Malallah, Mohsin. *Adab al-Rahalat 'Inda al-'Arab*. Baghdad: al-Irshad, 1978.

Marín-Guzmán, Roberto. "Some Reflections on the Institutions of Muslim Spain: Unity in Politics and Administration (711–929)." *American Journal of Islamic Social Sciences* 21 (2004): 26–56.

Marlowe, Christopher. *Tamburlaine the Great*. Toronto: Dover Publications, 2002.

Matar, Nabil. "Arab Views of Europeans 1578–1727: The Western Mediterranean." In *Re-orienting the Renaissance: Cultural Exchanges with the East*, edited by Gerald MacLean, 126–148. New York: Palgrave Macmillan, 2005.

———. *Europe through Arab Eyes: 1578–1727.* New York: Columbia University Press, 2008.

———. *In the Lands of the Christians: Arabic Travel Writing in the Seventeenth Century.* New York: Routledge, 2003.

———. *Turks, Moors, and Englishmen in the Age of Discovery.* New York: Columbia University Press, 1999.

McKeithen, James E. "The *Risala* of Ibn Fadlan: An Annotated Translation and Introduction." Diss., Indiana University, 1979.

Melman, Billie. *Women's Orients: English Women and the Middle East, 1718–1918.* Ann Arbor: University of Michigan Press, 1992.

Meisami, Julie Scott, and Paul Starkey, eds. *Encyclopedia of Arabic Literature.* London. Routledge, 1998.

Menocal, Maria Rosa. *The Arabic Role in Medieval Literary History: A Forgotten Heritage.* Philadelphia: University of Pennsylvania Press, 1987.

Metlitzki, Dorothee. *The Matter of Araby in Medieval England.* New Haven, CT: Yale University Press, 1977.

M'Ghirbi, Salah. *Les voyageurs de l'occident musulman du XIIe au XIVe siècles.* Tunis, Tunisia: Faculté des lettres, 1996.

Miedema, Nine. "Mirabilia Urbis Romae." In *Medieval Italy: An Encyclopedia, V1,* edited by Christopher Kleinhenz, 722–723. New York: Routledge, 2004.

Mikkelsen, Egil. "The Vikings and Islam." In *The Viking World,* edited by Stefan Brink and Neil Price, 543–549. London: Routledge, 2008.

Miquel, André. *La géographie humaine du monde musulman jusqu'au milieu du 11e siècle.* Paris: Haye, 1975.

———. "Ibn Ya'qub." In *Encyclopaedia of Islam,* edited by H. A. R. Gibbs et al., 2nd ed., 999. Leiden: Brill, 1960.

———. "Rome chez les géographes arabes." *Comptes-rendus des séances de l'Académie des inscriptions et Belles-Lettres* 119, no. (1975): 281–291.

Mollin, Richard A. *Codes: The Guide to Secrecy from Ancient to Modern Times.* Boca Raton, FL: Chapman and Hall, 2005.

Montgomery, J. E. "Ibn Fadlan." In *Literature of Travel and Exploration: An Encyclopedia,* edited by Jennifer Speake, 579. London: Routledge, 2003.

———. "Ibn Fadlan and the Rusiyyah." *Journal of Arabic and Islamic Studies* 3 (2000): 1–25.

———. "Ibn Rusta's Lack of Eloquence, the Rús and Samanid Cosmography." *Edebiyat* 12 (2001): 73–93.

———. "Spectral Armies, Snakes, and a Giant from Gog and Magog: Ibn Fadlan as Eyewitness among the Volga Bulghars." *Medieval History Journal* 9 (2006): 63–87.

———. "Traveling Autopsies: Ibn Fadlan and the Bulghars." *Middle Eastern Literatures* 7 (2004): 4–32.

Montgomery, Scott L. *Science in Translation: Movements of Knowledge through Cultures and Time.* Chicago: University of Chicago Press, 2000.

Morgan, David. "Persian perceptions of Mongols and Europeans." In *Implicit Understandings: Observing, Reporting, and Reflecting on the Encounters Between Europeans and Other Peoples in the Early Modern Era,* edited by Stuart B. Schwartz, 201–217. Cambridge, UK: Cambridge University Press, 1994.

Munis, Hussein. *Tarikh al-Jughrafiya wa-l-Jughrafiyyin fi-l-Andalus.* Madrid: Institute of Islamic Studies, 1968.

Muwafi, Abdurraziq. *Al-Rihla fi-l-Adab al-'Arabi.* Cairo: Al-Jam'ia al-Misriyya, 1995.

Naggar, Mona. "The Barbarians of the North: Venturing into the Darkness of Europe." *Qantara.de*, January 12, 2005; http://www.qantara.de/webcom /show_article.php/_c-591/_nr-8/_p-1/i.htm

Nasir, Sari J. *The English and the Arabs.* London: Longman, 1979.

Nazmi, Ahmad. *Commercial Relations between Arabs and Slavs (9th–11th Centuries).* Warsaw: Academic Publishing House, 1998.

———. *The Muslim Geographical Image of the World in the Middle Ages.* Warsaw: Academic Publishing House, 2007.

Netton, Ian Richard. "Basic Structures and Signs of Alienation in the Rihla of Ibn Jubayr." In *Golden Roads: Migration, Pilgrimage and Travel in Mediaeval and Modern Islam*, edited by Ian R. Netton, 57–74. Richmond, UK: Curzon Press, 1993.

———. *Seek Knowledge: Thought and Travel in the House of Islam.* Richmond, UK: Curzon Press, 1996.

Newman, D. L. "Arab Travelers to Europe until the End of the 18th Century and Their Accounts: Historical Overviews and Themes." *Chronos* 4 (2001): 7–61.

———. "Italy in Arabic Travel Literature until the End of the 19th Century: Cultural Encounters and Perceptions of the Other." *Equivalences* 29 (2001): 197–234.

Nichols, Francis Morgan, and Eileen Gardiner, eds. *The Marvels of Rome: Mirabilia Urbis Romae.* New York: Ithaca Press, 1986.

Nicholson, Reynold A. *A Literary History of the Arabs.* New York: Cosimo, 2010.

———. *The Mystics of Islam.* Bloomington, IN: World Wisdom, 2002.

Noonan, Thomas. "European Russia: c500–1050." In *The New Cambridge Medieval History*, edited by Timothy Reuter, 487–513. Cambridge: Cambridge University Press, 1995.

Nusrat, Abdurrahmane. *Shi'r al-Sira' ma'a-al-Rum.* Beirut: Maktabat al-Aqsa, 1977.

Oakes, Leigh. *Language and National Identity: Comparing France and Sweden.* Amsterdam: John Benjamins, 2001.

Oxfeldt, Elizabeth. *Nordic Orientalism: Paris and the Cosmopolitan Imagination 1800–1900.* Copenhagen: University of Copenhagen Press, 2005.

Penelas, Mayte. "A Possible Author of the Arabic Translation of Orosius' Historiae." *Al-Masaq: Islam and the Medieval Mediterranean* 13 (2001): 113–135.

Picken, Gavin. "Mu'tazilim." In *Encyclopedia of Islamic Civilization and Religion*, edited by Ian Richard Netton, 472–473. London: Routledge, 2008.

Pinto, Karen. "Cartography." In *Medieval Islamic Civilization: An Encyclopedia*, edited by Josef W. Meri and Jere L. Bacharach, 138–140. London: Routledge, 2006.

Pizzi, Giancarlo. *Al-Mas'udi e I prati d'oro e le miniere di gemme: la enciclopedia di un umanista arabo del decimo secolo.* Milan: Jaca Book, 2001.

Pons-Sanz, Sara M. "Whom Did Al-Ghazal Meet? An Exchange of Embassies between the Arabs from Al-Andalus and the Vikings." *Saga-Book* 38 (2004): 5–28.

Price, Neil. "The Vikings in Spain, North Africa and the Mediterranean." In *The Viking World*, edited by Stefan Brink and Neil Price, 452–469. London: Routledge, 2008.

Pratt, Mary Louise. *Imperial Eyes: Travel Writing and Transculturation*. London: Routledge, 1992.

Rapoport, Semen. "On the Early Slavs: The Narrative of Ibrahim ibn Yakub." *The Slavonic and East European Review* 8 (1929): 331–341.

Raphael, Israeli. "Medieval Muslim Travelers to China." *Journal of Muslim Minority Affairs* 20 (2000): 313–321.

Rastegar, Kamran. "Revisiting Orientalism." *History Today* 58 (2008): 49–51.

Richter-Bernburg, Lutz. "Ibrāhīm ibn Yaʿqūb al-Isrāʾīlī al-Ṭurṭūshī." *The Oxford Companion to World Exploration*, edited by David Buisseret, 402–403. Oxford: Oxford University Press, 2007.

Robinson, Chase F. *Islamic Historiography*. Cambridge: Cambridge University Press, 2003.

Rogerson, Barnaby. *The Prophet Muhammad*. London: Little, Brown, 2003.

Romero, Eduardo Morales. *Historia de los Vikingos En España: Ataques E Incursiones Contra Los Reinos Cristianos Y Musulmanes De Peninsula Iberica En Los Siglos Ix–Xi*. Madrid: Miraguano, 2004.

Rorlich, Z. "The Bulghar State." *Vassil Karloukovski's Page*, February 11, 2008; http://groznijat.tripod.com/fadlan/rorlich2.html.

Róna-Tas, András. *Hungarians and Europe in the Early Middle Ages: An Introduction to Early Hungarian History*. Budapest: Central European University Press, 1999.

Rosenthal, Albrecht. "The Isle of the Amazons: A Marvel of Travellers." *Journal of the Warburg Institute* 1 (1938): 257–259.

Rosenthal, Franz. *Knowledge Triumphant: The Concept of Knowledge in Medieval Islam*. Leiden: Brill, 1970.

Rouse, Carolyn Moxley. *Engaged Surrender: African American Women and Islam*. Berkeley: University of California Press, 2004.

Said, Edward. *Culture and Imperialism*. New York: Alfred A. Knopf, 1993.

———. *Orientalism: Western Conceptions of the Orient*. New York: Pantheon Books, 1978.

Samarrai, Alauddin. "Some Geographical and Political Information on Western Europe in the Medieval Arabic Sources." *Muslim World* 62 (1972): 304–322.

Sardar, Ziaddin. *Orientalism*. Buckingham, UK: Open University Press, 1999.

Sarnecki, W., and D. Nicolle. *Medieval Polish Armies 966–1500*. Westminster, MD: Osprey Publishing, 2008.

Scheppler, Bill. *Al-Biruni: Master Astronomer and Muslim Scholar of the Eleventh Century Persia*. New York: Rosen Publishing Group, 2006.

Semotanová, Eva. "Prague." In *The Encyclopaedia of the Middle Ages*, edited by André Vauchez et al., 1177–1178. London: Routledge, 2001.

Shahid, Irfan. *Byzantium and the Arabs in the Fourth Century*. Washington, DC: Dumbarton Oaks, 2006.

Shboul, Ahmad. *Al-Masʿudi and His World: A Muslim Humanist and His Interest in Non-Muslims*. London: Ithaca Press, 1979.

———. "Byzantium and the Arabs: The Image of the Byzantines as Mirrored in Arabic Literature." In *Arab-Byzantine Relations in Early Islamic Times*, edited by Michael Bonner, 235–262. New York: Ashgate, 2004.

Silverstein, Adam J. "The Medieval Islamic Worldview: Arabic Geography in Its Historical Context." In *Geography and Ethnography: Perceptions of the World in Pre-modern Societies*, edited by Kurt A. Raaflaub and Richard J. A. Talbert, 273–290. Chichester, UK: Wiley-Blackwell, 2010.

Singh, N. K., and A. Samiuddin, eds. *Encyclopaedic Historiography of the Muslim World*. Delhi: Global Vision, 2004.

Sivan, Emmanuel. *L'islam et la croisade: Idéologie et propagande dans les réactions musulmanes aux croisades*. Paris: Adrien-Maisonneuve, 1968.

Smethurst, Paul. "The Journey from Modern to Postmodern in the Travels of Sir John Mandeville and Marco Polo's *Divisament dou Monde*." In *Postmodern Medievalisms*, edited by Richard Utz and Jesse Swane, 159–179. Rochester, NY: Boydell and Brewer, 2005.

———. "Writing the East: Marco Polo and Sir John Mandeville." *English Courses*. Hong Kong University, May 28, 2008; http://www0.hku.hk/english/courses /engl2045/ENGL2045lecturenotes_Week2.pdf.

Spekke, Arnolds. "Arabian Geographers and the Early Baltic People." *Baltic and Scandinavian Countries* 9 (1928): 155–159.

Starkey, Paul. "Al-Biruni." In *Encyclopedia of Islamic Civilization and Religion*, edited by Ian Richard Netton, 102–103. London: Routledge, 2008.

Stern, Sacha. *Jewish Identity in Early Rabbinic Writings*. Leiden: Brill, 1994.

Stetkevych, S. P. *Abū Tammām and the Poetics of the 'Abbāsid Age*. Leiden: E. J. Brill, 1991.

———. *The Poetics of Islamic Legitimacy: Myth, Gender, and Ceremony in the Classical Arabic Ode*. Bloomington: Indiana University Press, 2002.

Stone, Caroline. "Ibn Fadlan and the Midnight Sun." *Saudi Aramco* 30 (1979): 1–3.

———. "A Model for the Historians." *Aramco World* 56 (2005): 18–23.

Strielkowski, Wadim. "Road Calls: Ethnic Origin and Migration: A Case-study of Slovak Roma Asylum Seekers in the Czech Republic," January 25, 2007; http://ies.fsv.cuni.cz/default/file/download/id/4956

Sykes, Percy M. *A History of Persia*. New ed. London: Routledge, 2004.

Talmon-Heller, D. "Muslim Martyrdom and Quest for Martyrdom in the Crusading Period." *Al Masaq: Islam and the Medieval Mediterranean* 14 (2002): 131–139.

Tavakoli-Targhi, Mohamed. *Refashioning Iran: Orientalism, Occidentalism, and Historiography*. New York: Palgrave Macmillan, 2001.

Todorov, Tzvetan. *The Conquest of America*. Translated by Richard Howard. Norman: University of Oklahoma Press, 1984.

Tolan, John Victor. *Saracens: Islam in the Medieval European Imagination*. New York: Columbia University Press, 2002.

Tolmacheva, Marina A. "Geography." In *Medieval Islamic Civilization: An Encyclopedia*, edited by Josef W. Meri and Jere L. Bacharach, 284–488. London: Routledge, 2006.

Valtonen, Irmeli. *The North in the "Old English Orosius": A Geographical Narrative in Context*. Helsinki: Societe Neophilologique, 2008.

Varisco, Daniel Martin. *Reading Orientalism: Said and the Unsaid*. Seattle: University of Washington Press, 2007.

Vinson, Irmin. "Jews, Islam, and Orientalism." *Flawless Logic*, June 15, 2008; http://library.flawlesslogic.com/orientalism.htm

Wahb, Qasim, ed. *Rihlat al-Gharnati*. Abu Dhabi: Dar al-Suwaydi, 2003.

Walzer, R. *Greek into Arabic*. Cambridge, MA: Harvard University Press, 1962.

William of Tyre. *A History of Deeds Done beyond the Sea*. Edited by Emily Atwater Babcock, and August Krey. New York: Columbia University Press, 1943.

Wink, Andre. *Al-Hind, The Making of the Indo-Islamic World: Early Medieval India and the Expansion of Islam, 7th–11th Centuries*. Leiden: Brill, 2002.

Winter, Tim, ed. *The Cambridge Companion to Classical Islamic Theology*. Cambridge: Cambridge University Press, 2008.

Wolfram, Herwig. *The History of the Goths*. Berkeley: University of California Press, 1988.

Wright, Jonathan. *The Ambassadors: From Ancient Greece to Renaissance Europe, the Men Who Introduced the World to Itself*. Boston: Houghton Mifflin, 2006.

Yared, Nazik Saba. *Arab Travelers and Western Civilization*. London: Saqi Books, 1996.

Young, M. J. L. *Religion, Learning and Science in the Abbasid Period*. Cambridge: Cambridge University Press, 1990.

Yusuf Ali, A. *The Noble Quran, a Translation with Arabic Text*. Riyadh: Dar al Salam, 1985.

Zakeri, Mohsen. *Sasanid Soldiers in Early Muslim Society: The Origins of 'Ayyaran and Futuwwa*. Wiesbaden, Germany: Harrassowitz Verlag, 1995.

Zakiev, Mirfatykh. *Tatars: Problems of a History and Language*. Kazan, Russia: n.p., 1995.

Zawati, Hilmi. *Is Jihad a Just War? War, Peace, and Human Rights under Islamic and Public International Law*. Lewiston, NY: Edwin Mellen Press, 2001.

Ziyada, Khalid. *Tatawwur al-Nadhra al-Islamiyya il-a-Uruba*. Beirut: Ma'had al-Inma' al-'Arabi, 1983.

Ziyada, Niqola. *Al Jughrafiya wal Rahalat 'Inda al-'Arab*. Beirut: al-Ahliyya, 1962.

INDEX

Initial articles and name particles in all languages (Al-, El-, La, The) are ignored in alphabetization, e.g., al-Harami is sorted as 'Harami'. Notes are indicated by n following the page number, e.g., 187n30.

CPSIA information can be obtained
at www.ICGtesting.com
Printed in the USA
LVHW020058020920
664773LV00019B/1042